methodology (1968)

1. Hypothesis
     (what if...)
2. Demonstration
     (it could be like this...)
3. Theory
     (therefore it seems that...)

The original location, with its shape and spatial qualities, had become entirely coated by a new vocabulary that was generated by the interference of its source.

3108 = 59,0 (3)
0109 = 50,8 (3)
0209 = 59,4 (1)
0309 = 59,0 (2)
0409 = 58,4 (10)

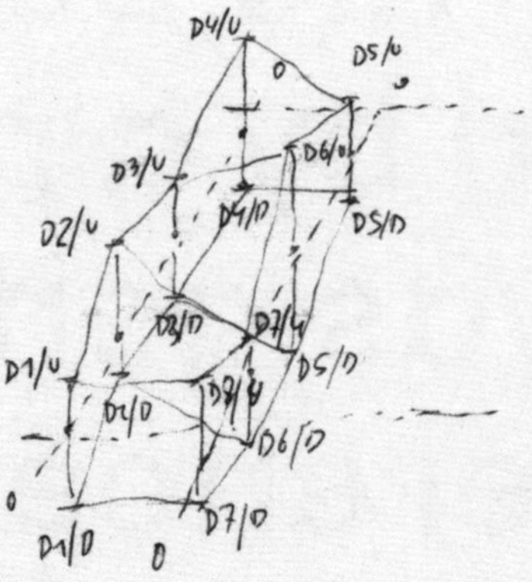

DOWNLOAD DURCHSCHNITT

2107 = 0
2307 = 0
2707 = 649,7 (5)
2507 = 676,1 (7)
2607 = 691,2 (4)   } Row 1

2707 = 673,4 (1)
2807 = 442,5 (3)
2907 = 594,1 (3)
3007 = 538,3 (2)
3107 = 764,4 (1)   } Row 2

0108   768,5   (1)
0208   549,6   (1)
0308   656,5   (4)
0408   ___
0508   685,3   (2)   } Row 3

0608   684,8   (2)
0708   707,1   (1)
0808   663,1   (2)
0908   627,8   (3)
1008   354,6   (2)   } Row 4

1108   656,8   (5)   21
1208   664,9   (1)   22
1308   697,8   (5)   23   } Row 5
1408   613,8   (3)   24
1508   736,2   (1)   25

1608 = 723,7 (3)   26
1708 = 574,4 (3)   27   } Row 6
1808 = 262,9 (1)   28
1908 = 721,2 (3)   29
2008 = 704,0 (2)   30

2108 = 744,0 (2)   31
2208   671,1 (1)   32
2308 = ___   33
2408   709,5 (2)   34
2508   758,0 (7)   35

2608   764,0 (2) (764) 36
2708   740,0 (2) (710) 37
2808   720,8 (1)   38
2908   714,5 (3)   39
3008   719,3 (4)   40

3108   696,5 (3)   41
0109   723,3 (3)   42
0209   677,4 (1)   43
0309   770,9 (2)   44
0409   702,0 (10) 45

4

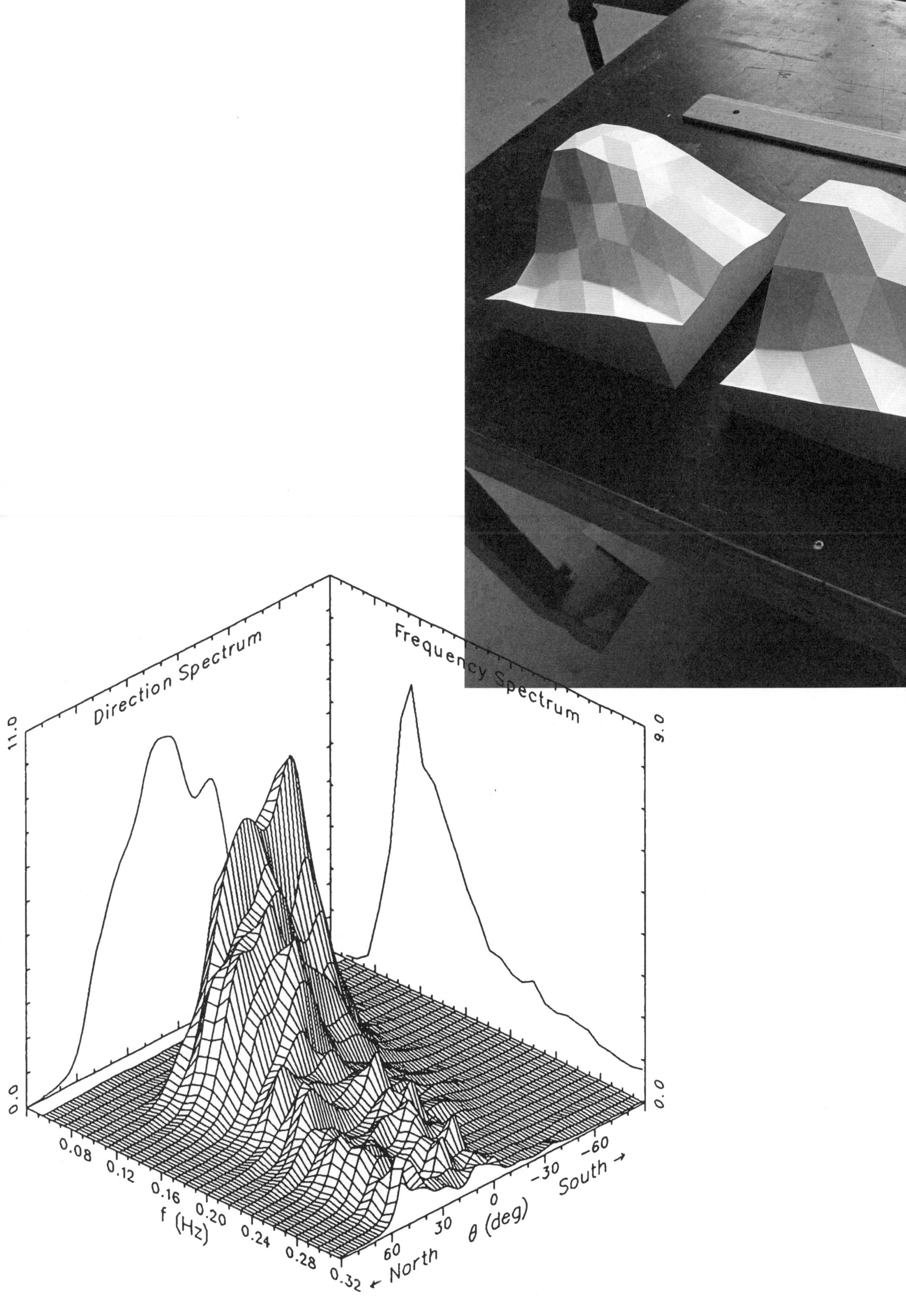

Direction Spectrum
Frequency Spectrum
11.0
9.0
0.0
0.0
f (Hz)
0.08
0.12
0.16
0.20
0.24
0.28
0.32
North
60
30
0
-30
-60
θ (deg)
South

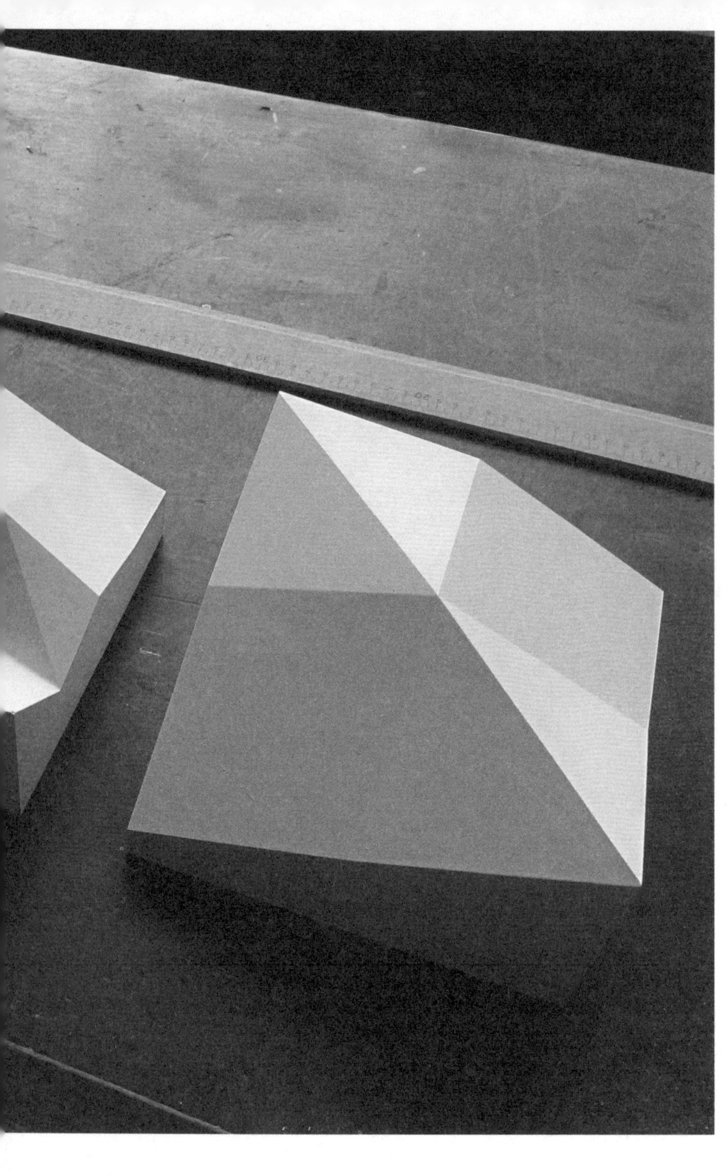

2407M - 11:11 ①/1
PING: 82 ms
DOWNLOAD: 592,5 kB/s
UPLOAD: 59,1 kB/s

2407M - 11:15 1/2
PING: 115 ms
DOWNLOAD: 745,2 kB/s
UPLOAD: 59,2 kB/s

2407M - 14:47 1/3
PING: 136 ms
DOWNLOAD: 637,2 kB/s
UPLOAD: 52,6 kB/s

2407M - 16:20 1/4
PING: 59 ms
DOWNLOAD: 668,1 kB/s
UPLOAD: 52,8 kB/s

2407M - 22:38 1/5
PING: 45 ms
DOWNLOAD: 655,6 kB/s
UPLOAD: 58,8 kB/s

2507
PING:
DOWN
UPLO

2507
PING:
DOWN
UPLO

2507
PING:
DOWN
UPLO

2507
PING
DOWN
UPLO

2507
PING
DOWN
UPLO

— 09:44 (2/1)	2507 M – 17:56 (2/6)	2607 M – 23:27 (3/4)

— 09:44 (2/1)
2 ms
661,8 kB/s
9,1 KB/s

10:26 (2/2)
8 ms
663,8 kB/s
55,0 kB/s

10:30 (2/3)
? ms
620,5 kB/s
53,0 kB/s

10:32 (2/4)
3 ms
818,8 kB/s
4,0 kB/s

13:28 (2/5)
27 ms
705,9 kB/s
59,4 kB/s

2507 M – 17:56 (2/6)
Ping: 132 ms
Download: 650,0 kB/s
Upload: 59,0 kB/s

2507 M – 18:26 (2/7)
Ping: 55 ms²
Download: 614,9 kB/s
Upload: 49,2 kB/s

2607 M – 11:00 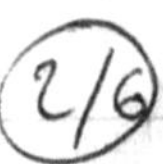 **(3/1)**
Ping: 133 ms
Download: 562,0 kB/s
Upload: 58,9 kB/s

2607 M – 11:35 (3/2)
Ping: 117 ms
Download: 840,9 kB/s
Upload: 58,9 kB/s

2607 M – 19:23 (3/3)
Ping: 113 ms
Download: 816,9 kB/s
Upload: 59,4 kB/s

2607 M – 23:27 (3/4)
Ping 75 ms
Download 579,9 kB/s
Upload 59,2 kB/s
FOW1

2707 M – 21:12 (4/1)
Ping 163 ms
Download 673,4 kB/s
Upload 55,1 kB/s

2807 M – 07:08 (5/1)
Ping 137 ms
Download 426,8 kB/s
Upload 59,2 kB/s

2807 M – 08:55 (5/2)
Ping 182 ms
Download 422,5 kB/s
Upload 59,5 kB/s

2807 M – 18:30 (5/3)
Ping 91 ms
Download 478,1 kB/s
Upload 54,4 kB/s

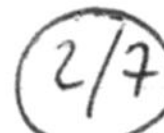
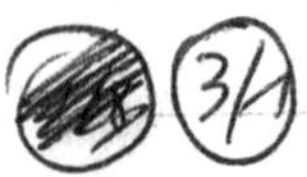
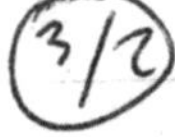

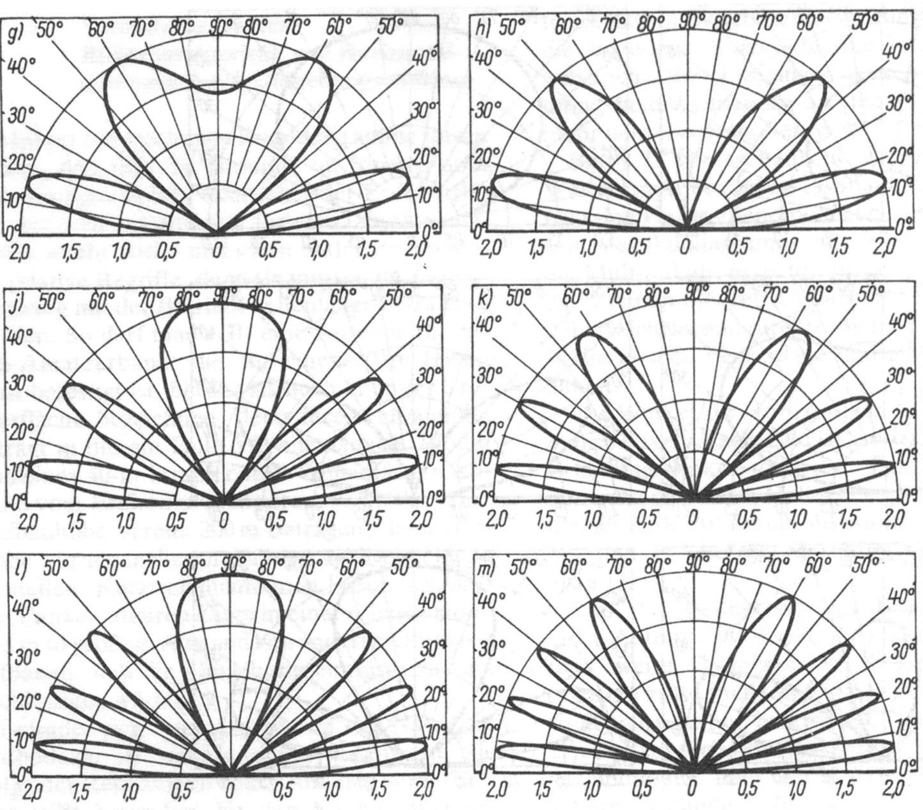

zu Bild 3.12
g – Höhe 7/8 λ, h – Höhe 1 λ, j – Höhe 5/4 λ,
k – Höhe 3/2 λ, l – Höhe 7/4 λ, m – Höhe 2 λ

Strahlung erheblich vergrößert ist, stark unterdrückt. Diese Strahlungskonzentration für niedrige Erhebungswinkel hat für Weitverbindungen besondere Wirkung. Auch vertikal gestockte Antennen mit Horizontalpolarisation folgen der obigen Regel. In diesem Fall ist nur zu beachten, daß als Bezugspunkt für die Aufbauhöhe über der Erdoberfläche der mittlere Abstand der Ebenen über Boden gilt.

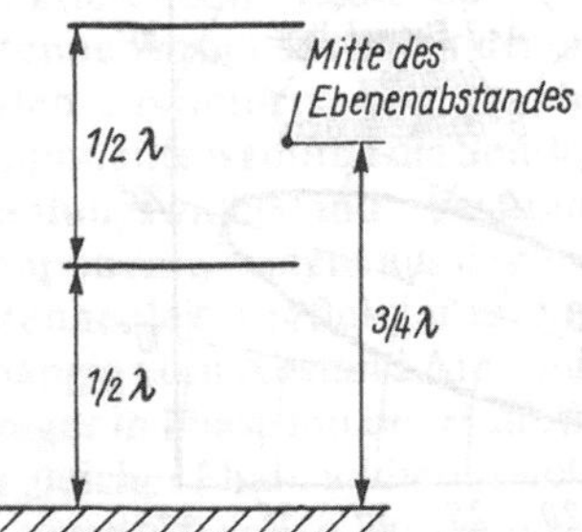

Bild 3.14
Beispiel für die Ermittlung der wirksamen Aufbauhöhe über idealer Erde bei vertikal gestockten Horizontalantennen

Beispiel
Nach Bild 3.14 befindet sich eine einfach gestockte, horizontale Richtantenne mit ihrer unteren Ebene in λ/2 Abstand vom Erdboden. Der Abstand der beiden Etagen beträgt ebenfalls λ/2. Daraus ergibt sich eine wirksame Aufbauhöhe von 3/4 λ.

3.2.2.2. Veränderungen der Richtcharakteristik von Vertikalantennen durch Umgebungseinflüsse

Vertikal polarisierte Antennen werden – mit Ausnahme der sogenannten Ground-Plane (siehe Abschnitt 19.4.1.) – im Kurzwellen-Amateurbetrieb nur selten verwendet. Im 2-m-Amateurband hat die Vertikalpolarisation im Zusammenhang mit dem FM-Relais Bedeutung.

Bei einer vertikal polarisierten Antenne wird bei erhöhter Aufstellung als Folge der Erdbodenreflexionen das Richtdiagramm der E-Ebene verformt, das in diesem Fall das Vertikaldiagramm

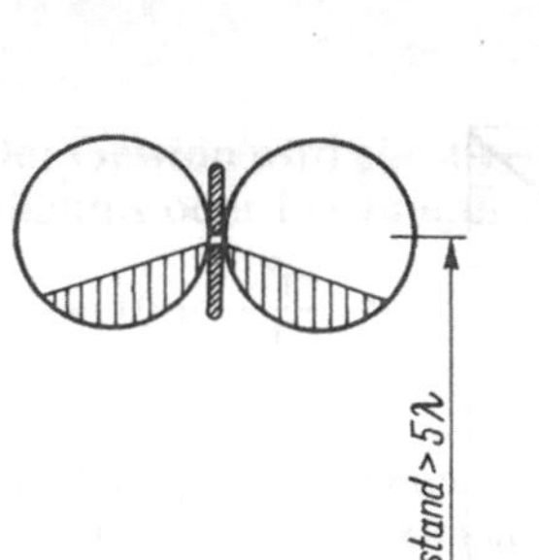

Bild 3.15
Vertikaldiagramm eines vertikalen Halbwellendipols in
sehr großem Abstand vom Erdboden

darstellt (Bild 3.15). Der untere, schraffierte Teil
des Diagramms soll etwa den Winkelbereich
kennzeichnen, dessen Strahlungsanteil bei Erd-
annäherung von der Erdoberfläche wieder nach
oben reflektiert wird. Wie bereits angedeutet
wurde, addieren sich die reflektierten Wellen
vektoriell mit den direkten Wellen in Abhängig-
keit von der auf die *Strahlermitte* bezogenen Aufbauhöhe in λ über der idealen Erde. Bild 3.16
zeigt Beispiele dafür. Der kleinste vertikale Erhebungswinkel beträgt dabei 0°. Das könnte be-
deuten, daß die Hauptstrahlung sehr flach und
annähernd tangential zur Erdoberfläche verlau-
fen würde. Leider ist diese für die Ausbreitung
über die Ionosphäre so günstige Flachstrahlung
nur bedingt wirksam, denn die Strahlungsanteile

mit dem Erhebungswinkel $< 5°$ gehen durch Ab-
sorption an der Erdoberfläche verloren. Die ge-
strichelten Kurven kennzeichnen diese Erdver-
luste.

Der Einfluß des Erdbodens auf die Strahlungs-
eigenschaften von vertikal polarisierten Kurzwel-
lenantennen wird in Abschnitt 19. ausführlicher
besprochen.

3.2.3. Gewinn und Richtfaktor

Wichtige Kenngrößen von Antennen sind *Gewinn* und *Richtfaktor*. Entsprechend dem Rezi-
prozitätsprinzip gelten die folgenden Betrachtun-
gen für den Sendefall und für den Empfangsfall
gleichermaßen.

Der Gewinn G_E einer Empfangsantenne ist das
Verhältnis der verfügbaren Empfangsleistung P_E
einer bezüglich Richtcharakteristik und Polarisa-
tion optimal im ebenen Wellenfeld orientierten
Empfangsantenne zur Empfangsleistung P_K des
Kugelstrahlers im ebenen Wellenfeld.

$$G_E = \frac{P_E}{P_K}. \qquad (3.13.)$$

Aus der Beziehung $P = U^2/R$ geht hervor, daß
man den Gewinn auch als Spannungsverhältnis
angeben kann, sofern der Verbraucherwider-
stand R für beide Strahler gleich ist

$$G_E = \left(\frac{U_E}{U_K} \right)^2. \qquad (3.14.)$$

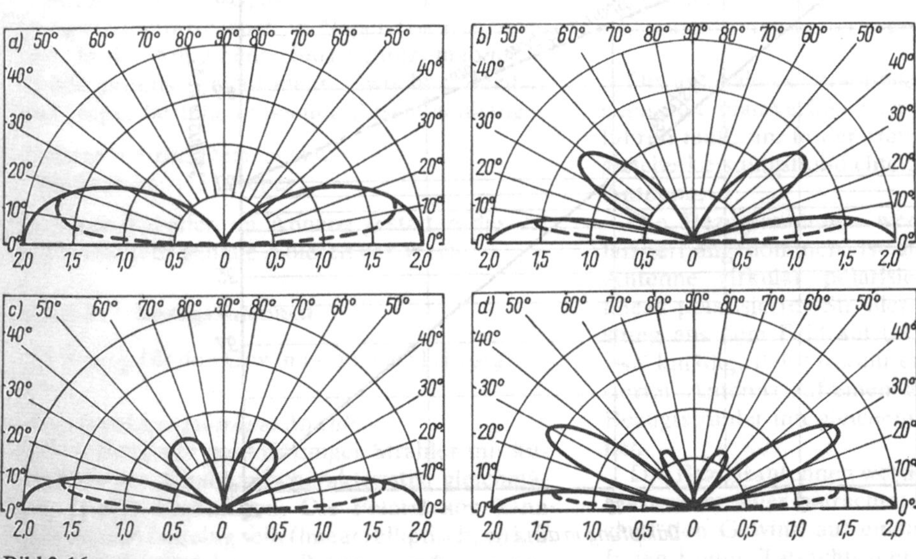

Bild 3.16
Vertikaldiagramme senkrechter Halbwellendipole. Als Aufbauhöhe gilt der Abstand Erde zur geometrischen Mitte
des Dipols; a – Höhe 1/4 λ, b – Höhe 3/4 λ, c – Höhe 1/2 λ, d – Höhe 1 λ

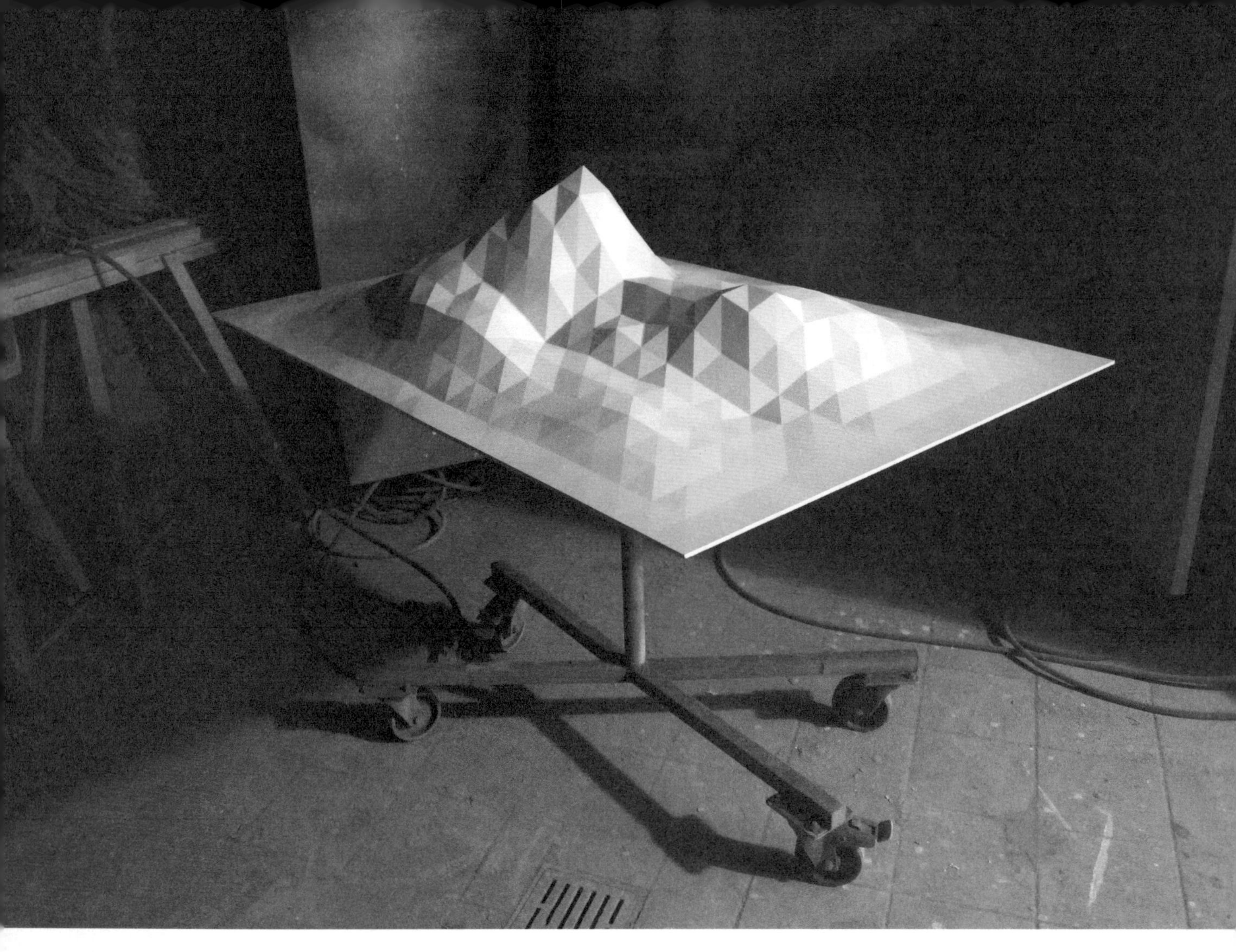

Bleecker Street
Dialogue

A Conversation
with Peter Jellitsch
and Joseph Becker

Austrian artist Peter Jellitsch has found a new approach to representing spatial realities, both seen and unseen. With his recent project, Jellitsch has taken to task the idea of a temporal-spatial condition that permeates all of our urban airspace. *Bleecker Street Documents*, titled for the location of the project, rigorously analyzes and explores the micro-measurements of atmospheric change activated by wireless data networks.

Jellitsch has focused on these subtle changes —invisible to our physical perceptions and yet so implicit in our modes of operation in today's world —as a launching point. Our data-driven and hyper-connected society often negates the spatial implications of Hertzian space.[1] We're usually unaware of, or choose to ignore, the vast amount of information that is broadcast intangibly through our homes, streets, and bodies. We undeniably co-exist with data in a very architectural sense, and the *BSD* project begins as an investigation into the mapping, and mining, of the shifting landscape of the engaged electromagnetic field. Peter's work proposes that our virtual world, and its effects, operates in parallel to our physical world. A straightforward proposition, no doubt, but one that presupposes that each sphere's influence maintains a similar cadre of definitions —we could argue that the notion of the infinite might disrupt any parallel existence of the physical and the virtual. By manifesting the measured virtual into the tangible physical, Peter calls attention to this line —one that is becoming increasingly blurry, and not just optically.

I sat down, virtually, with Peter to discuss *Bleecker Street Documents*.

Hi Peter, where are you right now?

PJ   Hello Joseph, I am momentarily on an A.i.R.-Program at Citè des Arts in Paris where I am working on a new project and prepare an exhibition for La Panaceè in Montpellier (FR) next year.

1   Anthony Dunne, *Hertzian Tales: Electronic Products, Aesthetic Experience, and Critical Design* (MIT Press, 2001).

And I'm in San Francisco. We're compressing the 5,500 physical miles between us into the immediate proximity of the virtual, our information transmitted through thousands of miles of optical cabling and terminating in an electromagnetic cloud on either end. It's precisely this cloud that your project begins to interpret. The *Bleecker Street Documents* are the culmination of hours of constant data mining of the nuances of the performance of this wireless atmospheric space. What led you to this as an approach to represent the virtual?

PJ The intersection of actual space and virtual space serves us a multitude of new technical and narrative possibilities. Fragments of these new capabilities are the foundation of my artistic practice. The primary idea for the project in New York was to experiment with methods that unveil visually hidden conditions. Through devices one has the possibility to literally peel-off and distinguish certain capacities as well as leave others in the dark.

John Cage, commenting on the imperceptible physicality of radio, said that we are "bathed in radio waves."[2] In its poetic essence, Cage paints a clear picture of the immersive spatial quality of electromagnetic transmissions. Other artists have explored this spatiality, but with the *BSD* you are more interested in the climate of the space, rather than its shape?

PJ The work varies between written and unwritten, materiality and immateriality, visibility and concealment, preserving and converting. The original location that the investigation is focused on, with its shape and spatial qualities, had become entirely coated by a new vocabulary that was generated by the interference of its source.

Can you tell me a bit about the intentionality behind the mapping of the data, as opposed to the mapping of the three-dimensional space that Wi-Fi inhabits?

PJ The data was recorded during a residency I had at a collector's apartment in Manhattan.

2   John Cage, Excerpt from *Radio Happenings I–V*, WBAI New York City, 1966.

From the very beginning of the project, my ideas culminated around the representation of this certain space where I lived, through the method of fragmentation. I've used a radio wave measuring device several times a day and translated the numeric result daily on notice paper. This repetitive method of post-scripting is something I found in concrete poetry, that Theo Van Doesburg proclaimed in his *Manifesto of Concrete Art,* where he says: "The language is not the description of a situation anymore, but it is itself the purpose and object of the poem."[3] Transferred to art practice, it would mean that numeric information is already the ultimate language of space.

With your STB project, you focused on the vectors of motion and flow across virtual objects. The EMI project focused on the space-frame response to specific node quantities. Do you see the *BSD* project as a synthesis of some of your earlier work, but calling attention to existing urban conditions?

PJ I have already worked with urban conditions and its connection to the behavior of radio waves before I started with *Bleecker Street Documents* in New York. In my 2010 work *Electronic Topographies*, the historic city center of Vienna was used as a testing laboratory — standing as an exemplarily example of the extremely dense European network coverage. With the *Electronic Topographies* drawing series I have tried to simulate the electromagnetic cones of mobile emitters generated in relationship to the surrounding physical space. What unifies my work is the investigation into how science and media are trying to approach the creation of "reality," through new technological methods of simulation. While these simulations are trying to imitate reality, I am imitating the imitation of reality mostly with my hand — the drawing or more generally the handwork is an essential part of my practice. For me it allows a physical acquisition of invisible digital calculations, and of course includes mistakes

3   Theo Van Doesburg defined Concrete Art in the manifesto titled "The Basis of Concrete Art," published in the only issue of the magazine *Art Concret*, 1930. The manifesto was co-signed by van Doesburg, Otto G. Carlsund, Jean Hélion, and Leon Tutundjian.

and instinctive extensions. Until a work is finished it passes through several stations of analog and digital realms.

You've talked about the evidence of process being very much a part of this project. It's obvious that you approached the *BSD* project both analytically and theoretically. Do you see the presentation of *BSD* as a holistic visualization of your process?

PJ   During the work on *BSD* I took a lot of inspiration browsing through scientific publications in libraries and reading media studies. Even if my work cannot directly be seen as contribution to scientific knowledge production, it is obvious too that I am influenced by representation techniques such as mathematical diagrams and explanatory models. To punctuate the inconsistent character of the connectivity subject, I left the milled model directly on the pallet of the workshop and placed the scaled copy right on the floor. In an arrangement like this, I have the vertical axis with the measured notations on the wall and the horizontal axis with the model on the floor. The framed and scaled copy, leaned on the wall, is in dialogue with both the model and the notations. The contradictory fact: to produce static works on the basis of highly flexible data is the only way for me to come close to its origin. Joseph Kosuth said about *One and Three Chairs*: "I liked that the work itself was something other than simply what you saw."[4]

It seems impossible to escape the contemporary notion of a quantified life. New products, and their corresponding smartphone apps, track our every movement, location, our sleep patterns and our caloric intake, and chart infographics to compel us towards a more efficient, healthy, or safe lifestyle. Artists such as Nicholas Felton focus entirely on their own insipid micro-moments, but taken as a whole paint a beautiful holistic interpretation of their tracked lives. I wonder how the documentation and quantification of this digital engagement perhaps calls attention to our contemporary

4   Joseph Kosuth, *Art as Idea as Idea* in Jeanne Siegel, *Artwords: Discourse on the 60s and the 70s* (Ann Arbor: UMI Research Press, 1985).

moment of digital dependency. Is there a subtext to the *Bleecker Street Documents*?

PJ There is some certainty that the *Bleecker Street Documents*, regardless of the exhibition context, are covered by the same haze that they attempt to make light of, and thus induce a number of questions. Through the components of the work, each in constant dialogue with the next, I invite the viewer to layer their own subtext or personal narrative. We are all engaged through this digital haze, which could be read as an overarching conceptual ribbon, but I don't feel that this realization plays a key role in the interpretations of the work.

Peter, thanks for insights into your work. I think that the immersive, invisible, yet increasingly relative information-space has become a new medium for artists to manipulate, analyze, and represent. As José Luis de Vicente and Honor Harger write in the catalog to their exhibition, *Invisible Fields: Geographies of Radio Waves*, the field, through the lens of artists such as Semiconductor, Claire Boj and Diego Diaz, and Rafael Lozano-Hemmer is exposed, interpreted, and engaged in its many incarnations.[5] Contemporary multi-disciplinary practices are opening the door, and through it we stand to gain some clarity about our invisible extension of the natural world — one that is becoming increasingly ubiquitous and indispensable. The *Bleecker Street Documents* attest to our current condition, simultaneously unveiling an incredible density of information, and our unwavering dedication to its constant flow.

PJ Great to chat, Joseph.

5 Jose Luis de Vincente, et al. *Invisible Fields: Geographies of Radio Waves* (Barcelona: Actar Editorial: Arts Santa Monica, 2011).

Joseph Becker is the Associate Curator of Architecture and Design at the San Francisco Museum of Modern Art. Since 2007, Joseph has contributed to over twenty exhibitions at SFMOMA, including curating *Field Conditions* (2012) and co-curating *Lebbeus Woods, Architect* (2013-14) and SFMOMA's inaugural reopening exhibition, *Typeface to Interface: Graphic Design from the Collection* (2016) with Jennifer Dunlop Fletcher. In addition, he has been responsible for the exhibition design and visual direction of the majority of SFMOMA's A+D exhibitions during his nine-year tenure. He has moderated and served on numerous design panels, been an invited juror at many national architecture programs, led workshops on exhibition and experiential design, and lectured internationally. He received both his Bachelor of Architecture and his Masters of Advanced Architectural Design in Design Theory and Critical Practice from the California College of the Arts.

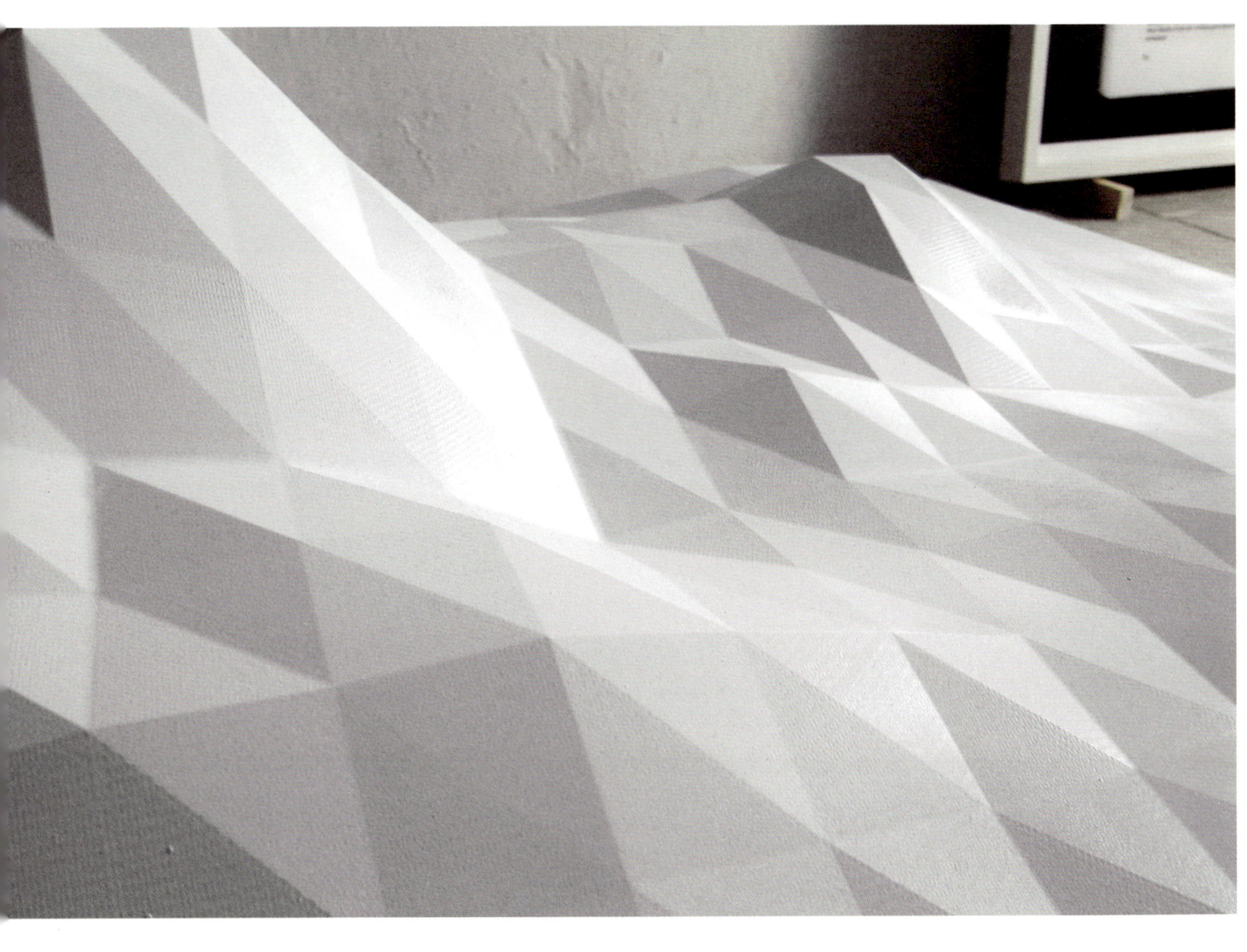

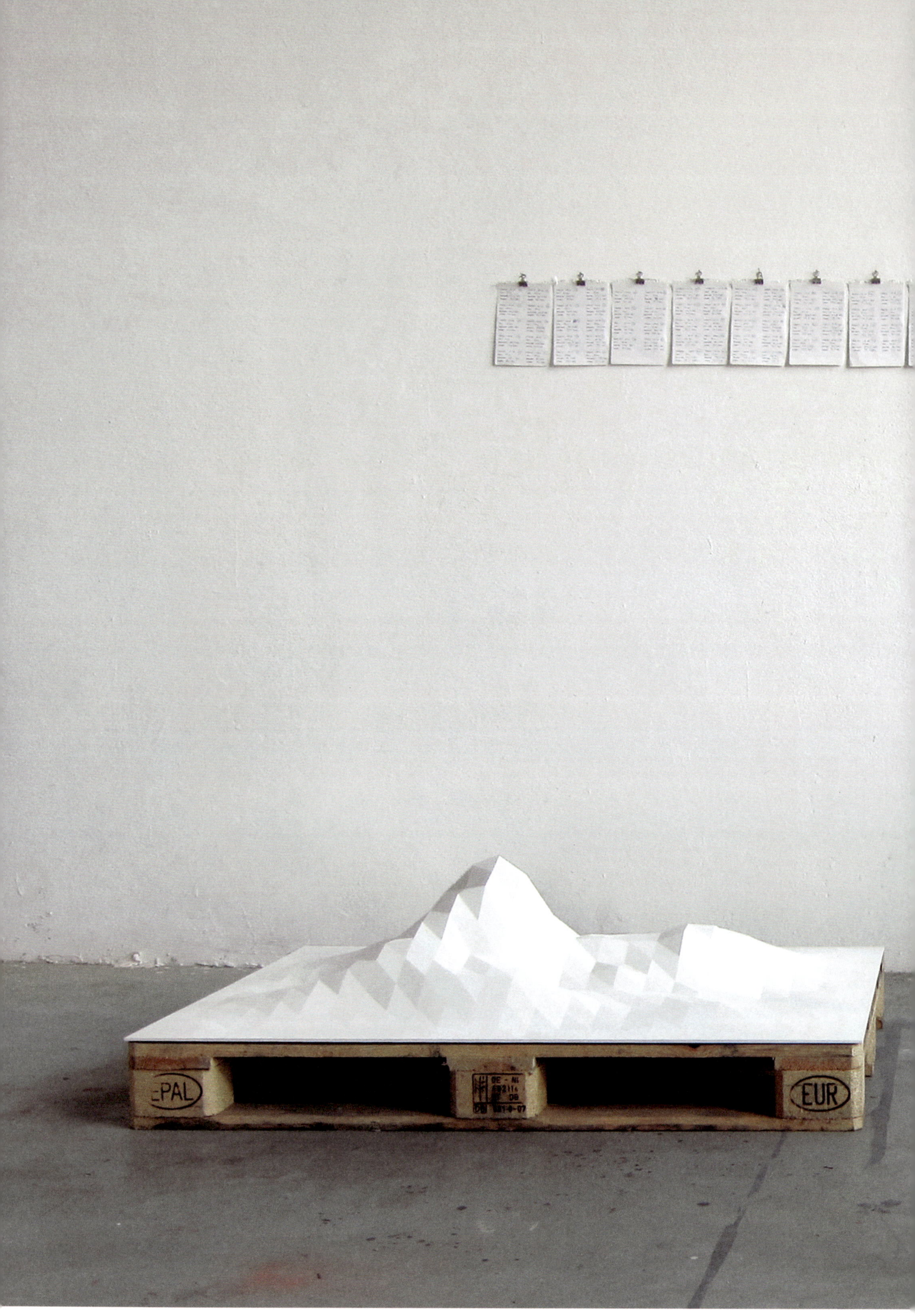

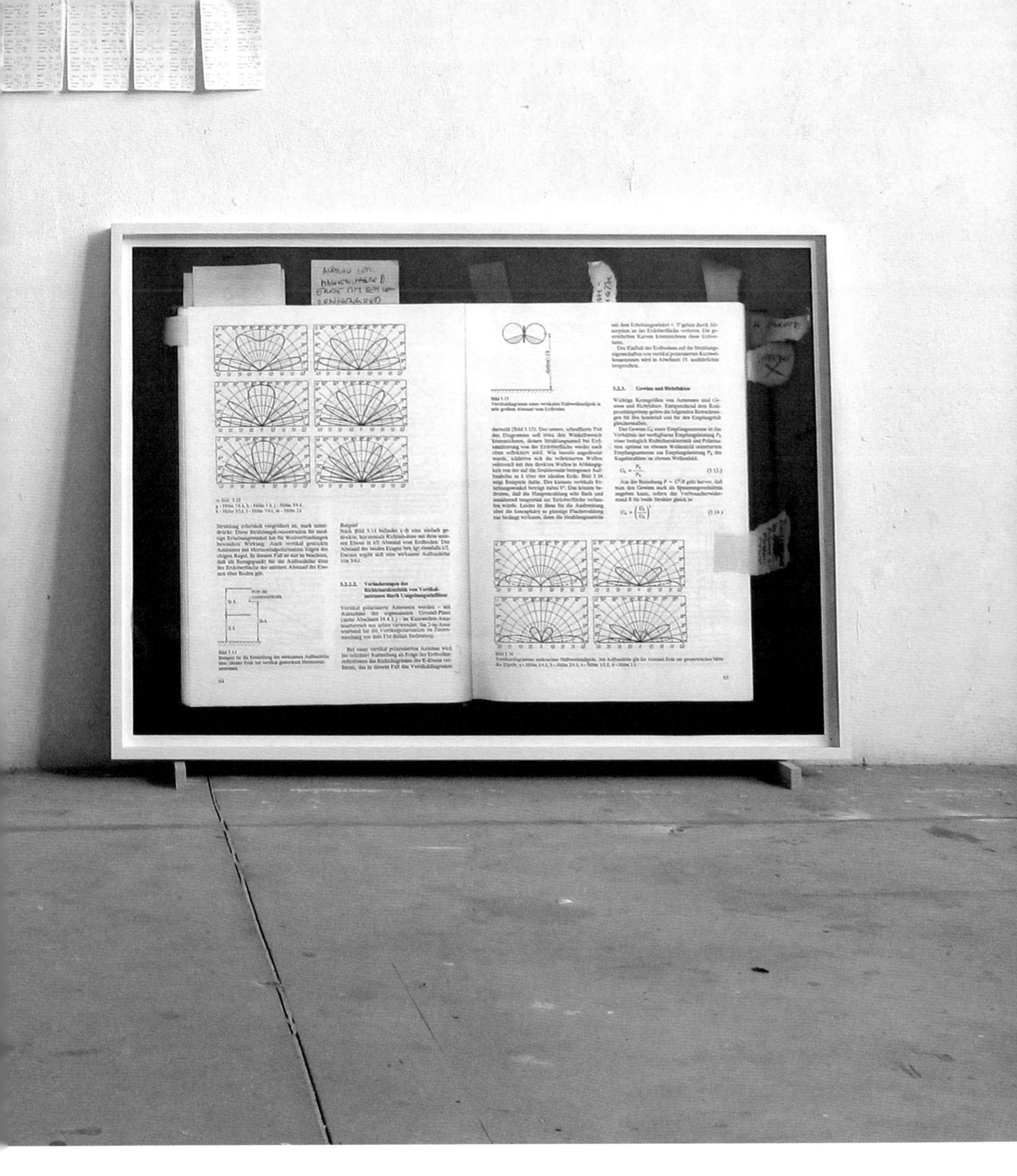

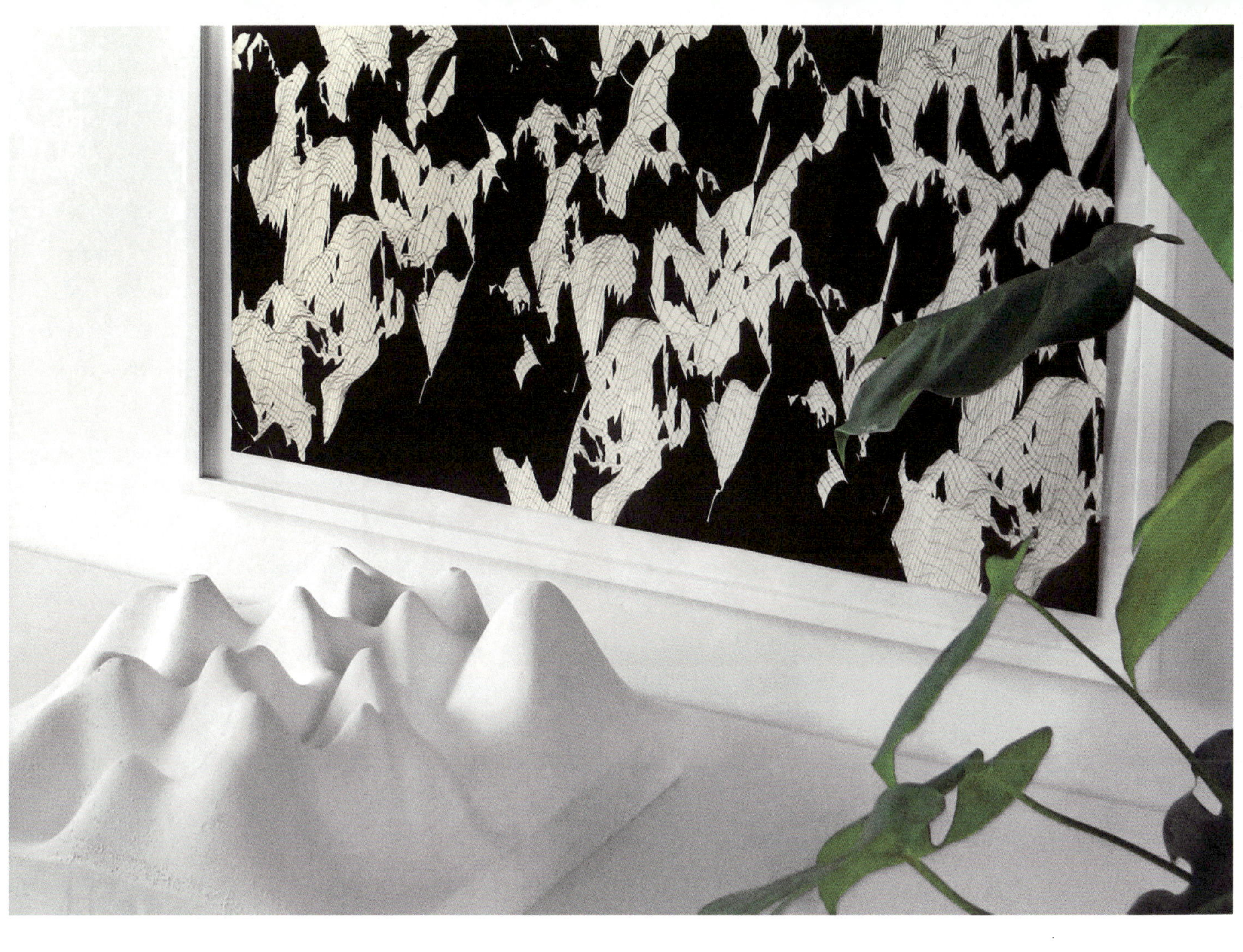

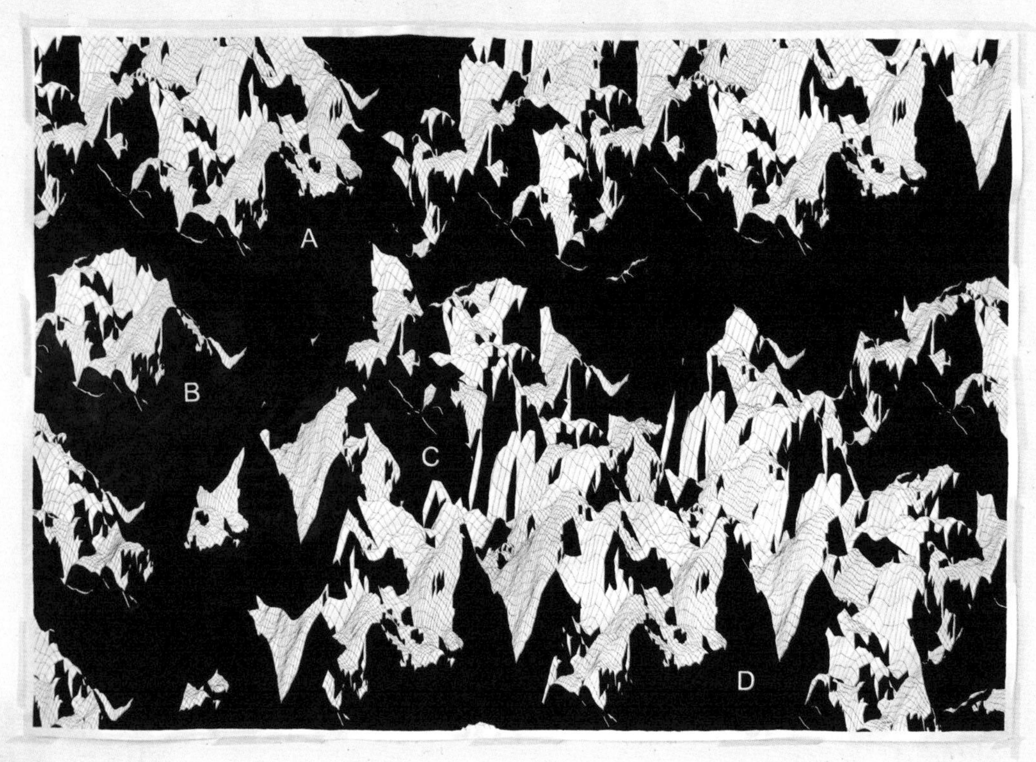

Data Drawing 1, 2013 (above)
Pencil, acrylic, crayon, lacquer on paper
150 × 210 cm

Data Drawing 2, 2013 (right page)
Pencil, acrylic, crayon, lacquer on paper
102 × 72 cm

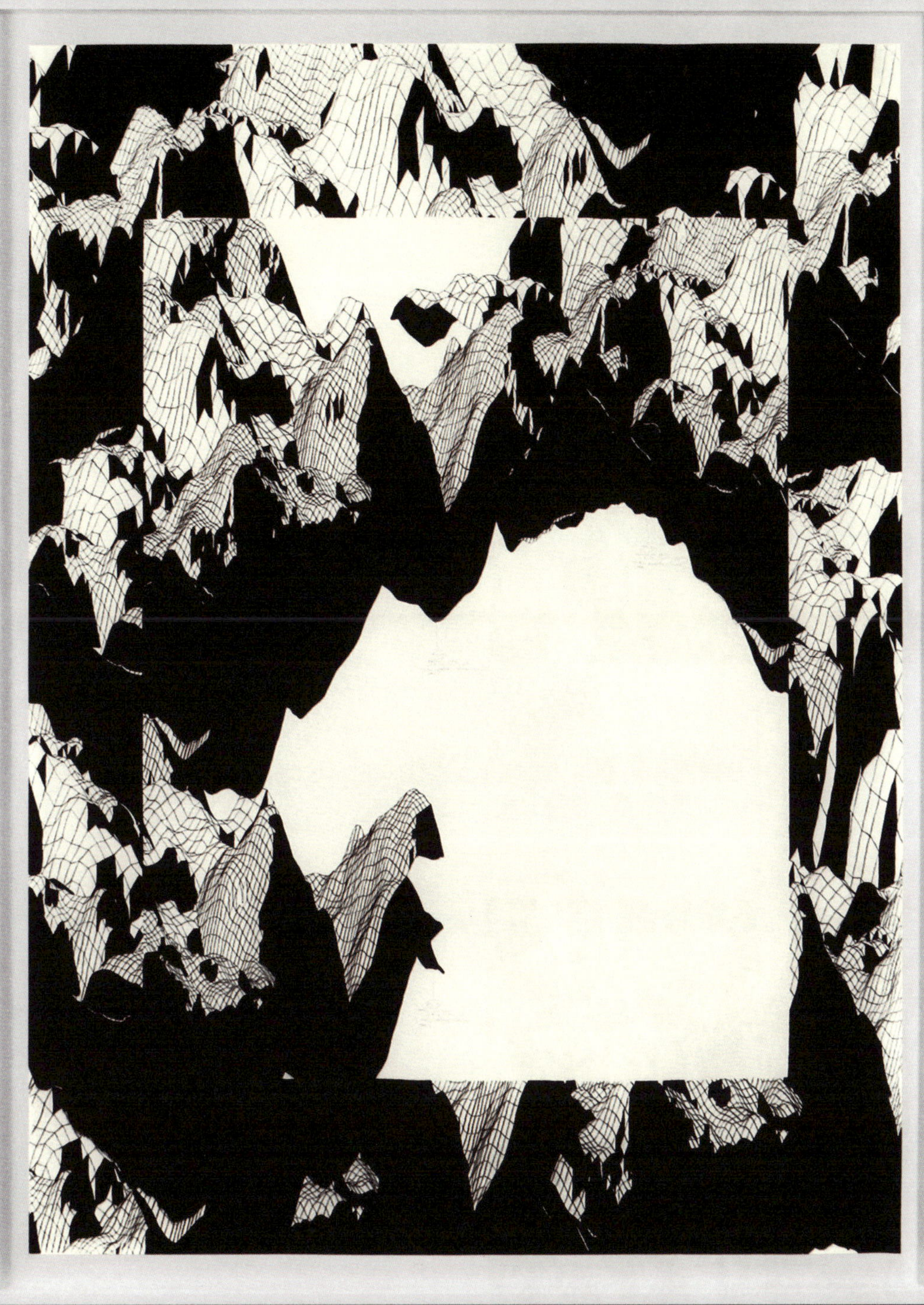

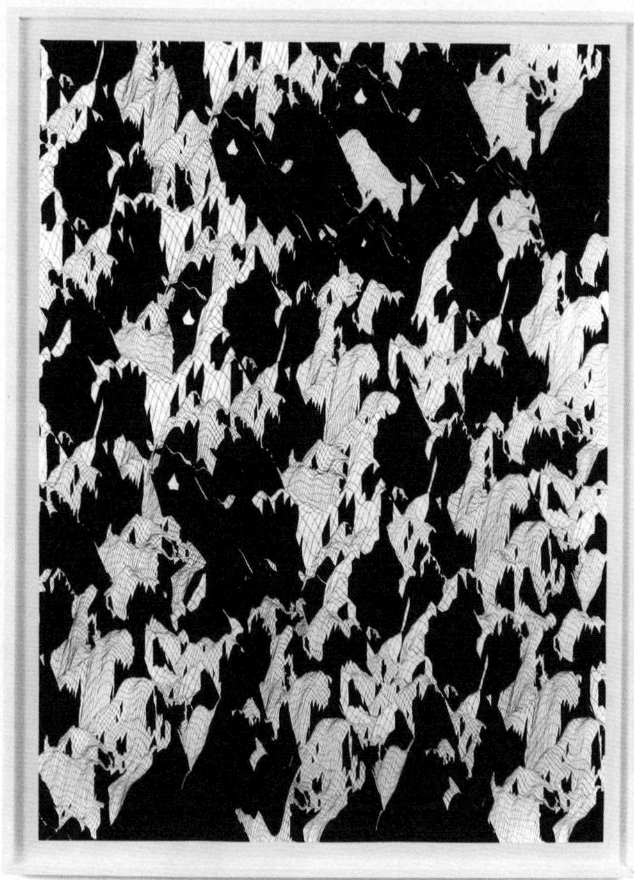

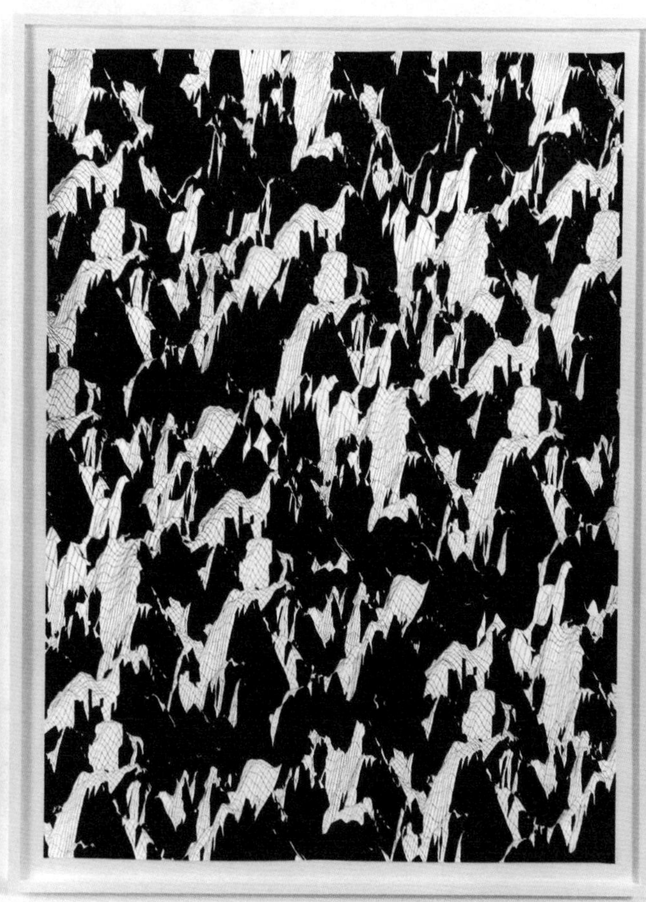

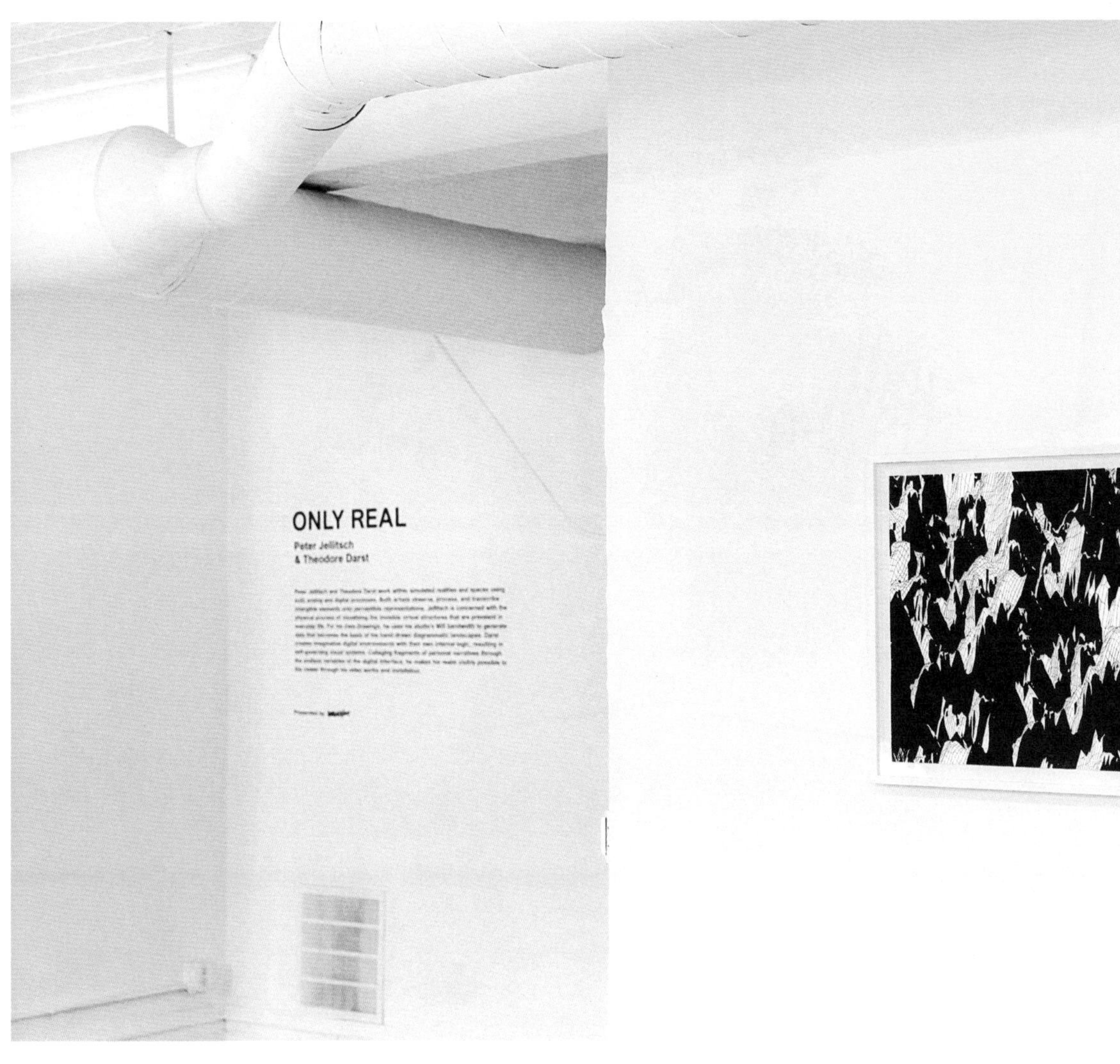

Exhibition
Only Real, 2014
(curated by: Helen Koh)
Peter Jellitsch & Theodore Darst
Public Works
Chicago, US

Data Drawing 3, 2013 (top left page)
Pencil, acrylic, crayon, lacquer on paper
102 × 72 cm

Data Drawing 5, 2013 (bottom left page)
Pencil, acrylic, crayon, lacquer on paper
102 × 72 cm

Data Drawing 4, 2013 (above)
Pencil, acrylic, crayon, lacquer on paper
50 × 70 cm

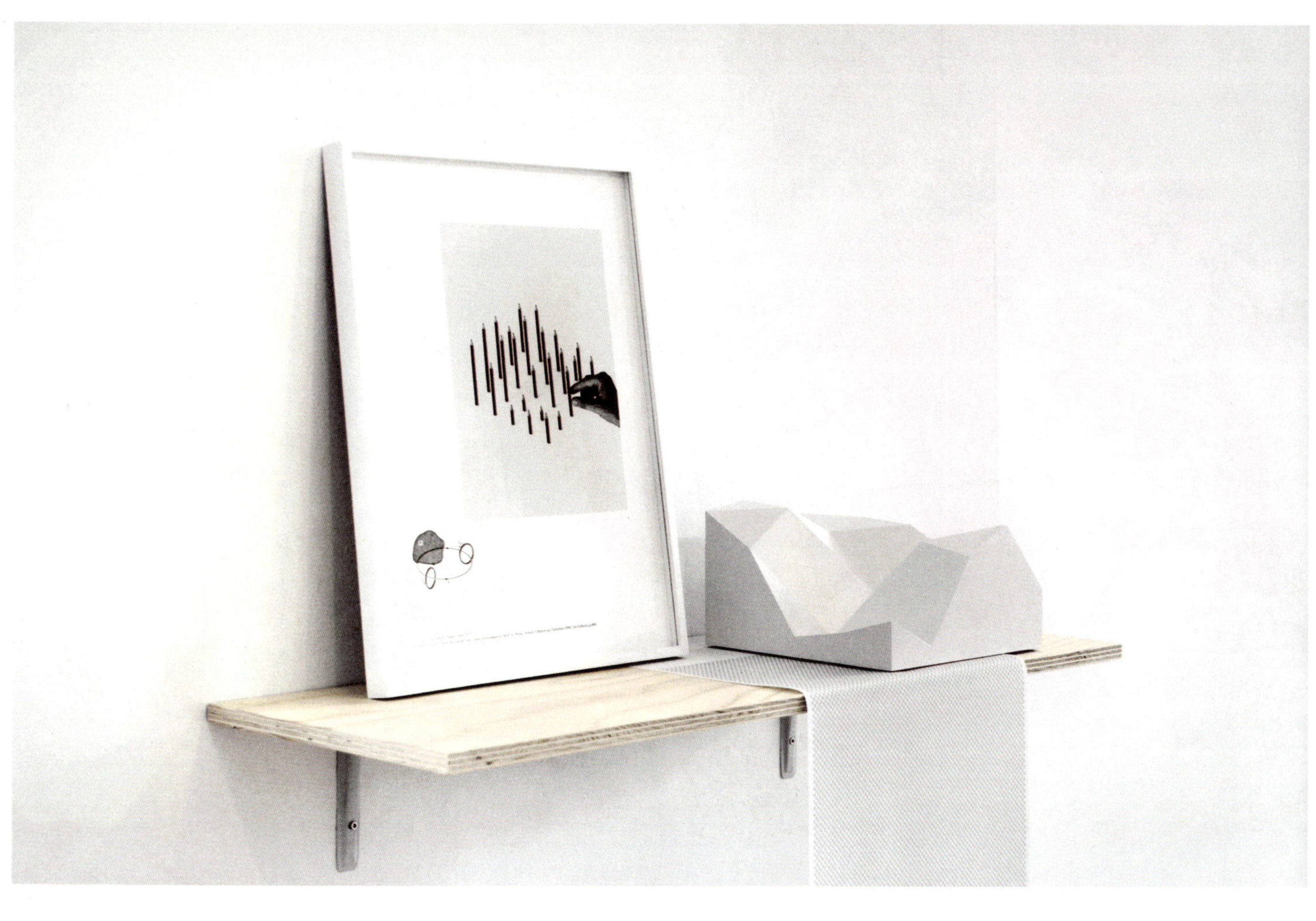

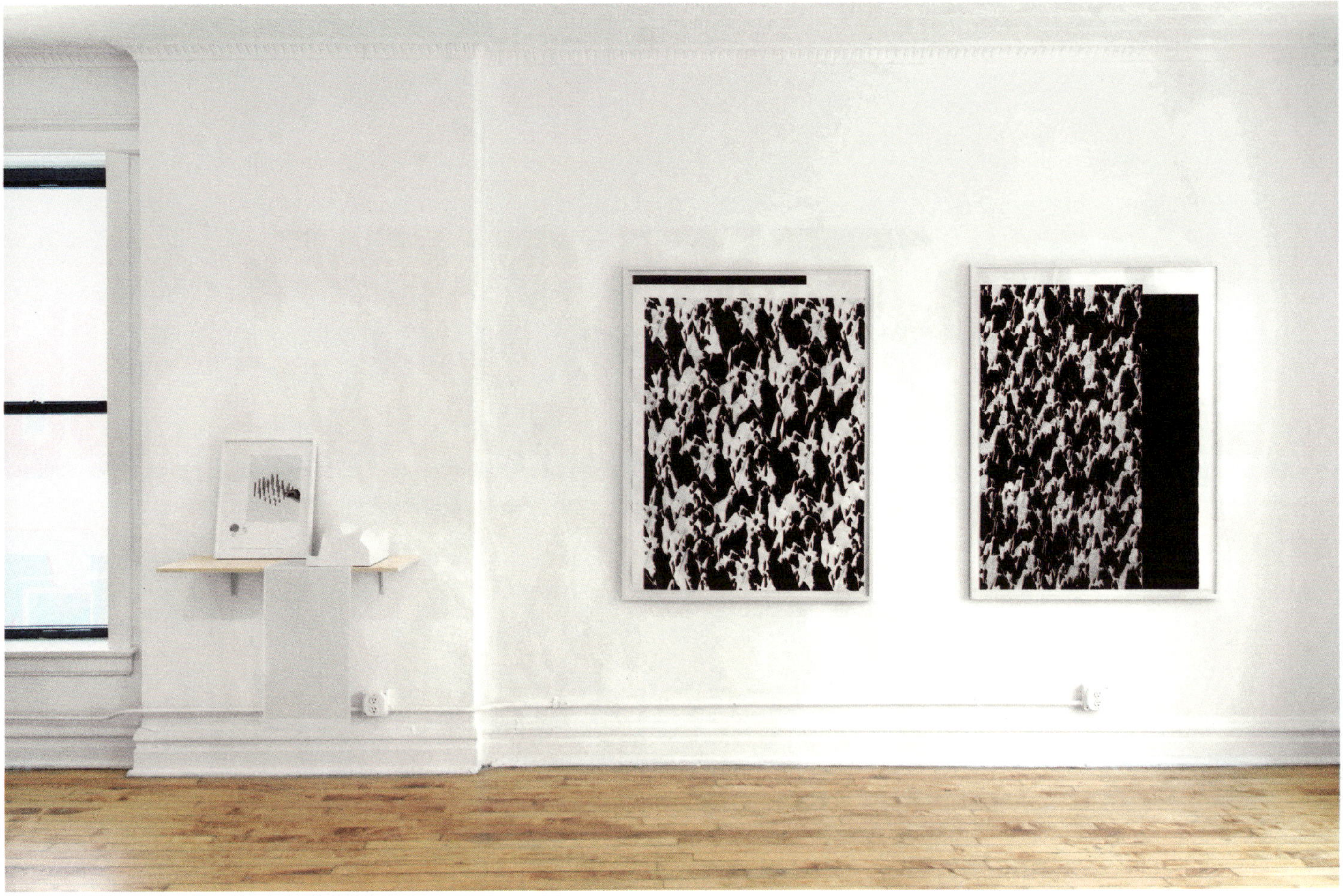

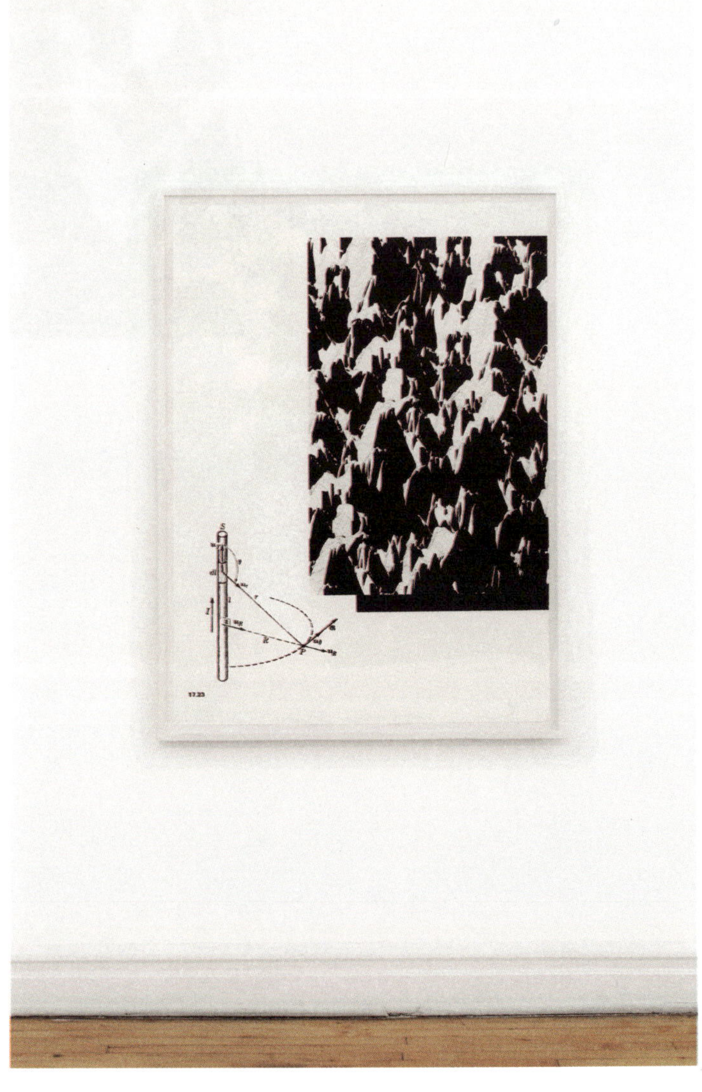

Reference Shelf, 2014 (left page)
Mixed media
95×120×28 cm

Data Drawing 7, 2013 (above left)
Pencil, acrylic, crayon, lacquer on paper
139×101 cm

Data Drawing 8, 2013 (above right)
Pencil, acrylic, crayon, lacquer on paper
139×101 cm

Data Drawing 6, 2013 (right)
Pencil, acrylic, crayon, lacquer on paper
139×101 cm

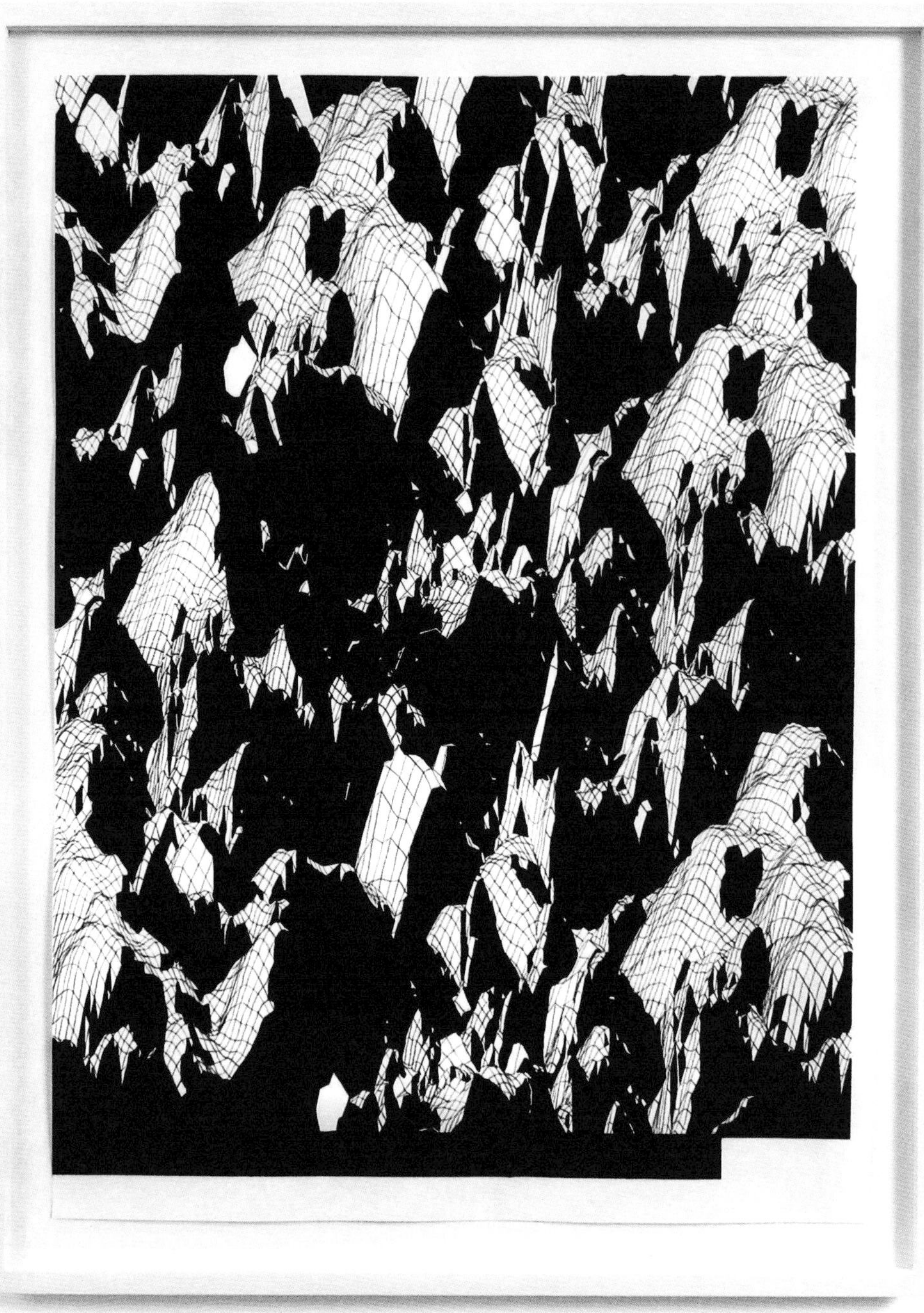

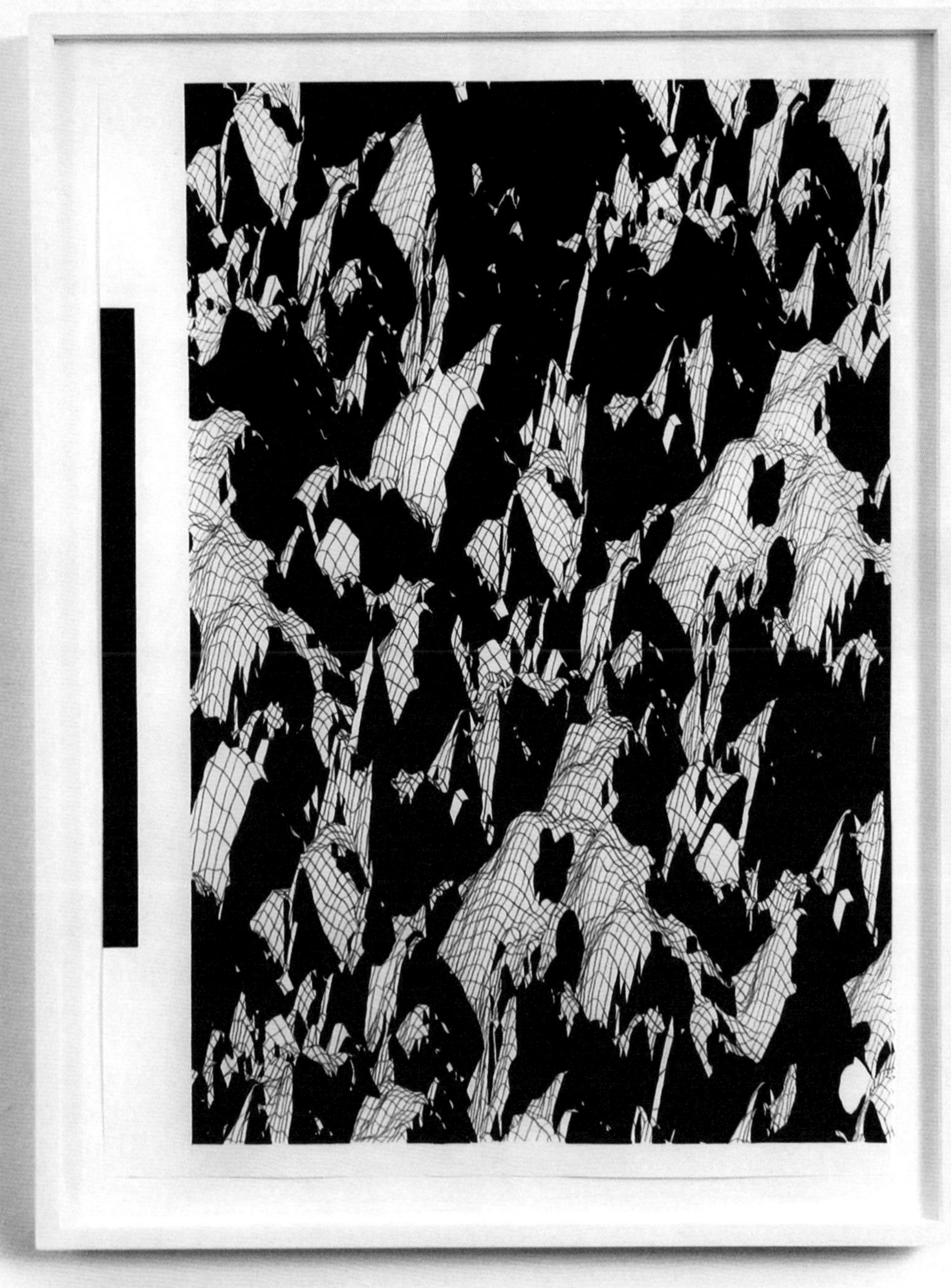

Data Drawing 10, 2014 (left page)
Pencil, acrylic, crayon, lacquer on paper
56×40 cm

Data Drawing 11, 2014 (above)
Pencil, acrylic, crayon, lacquer on paper
56×40 cm

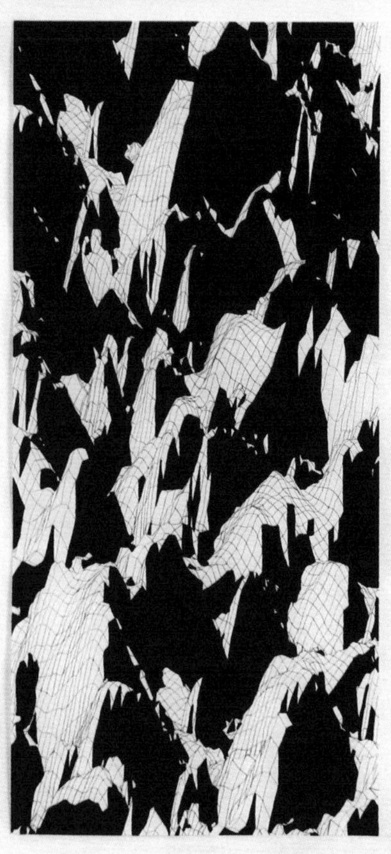

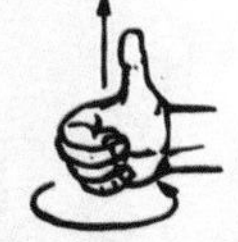

17.22

 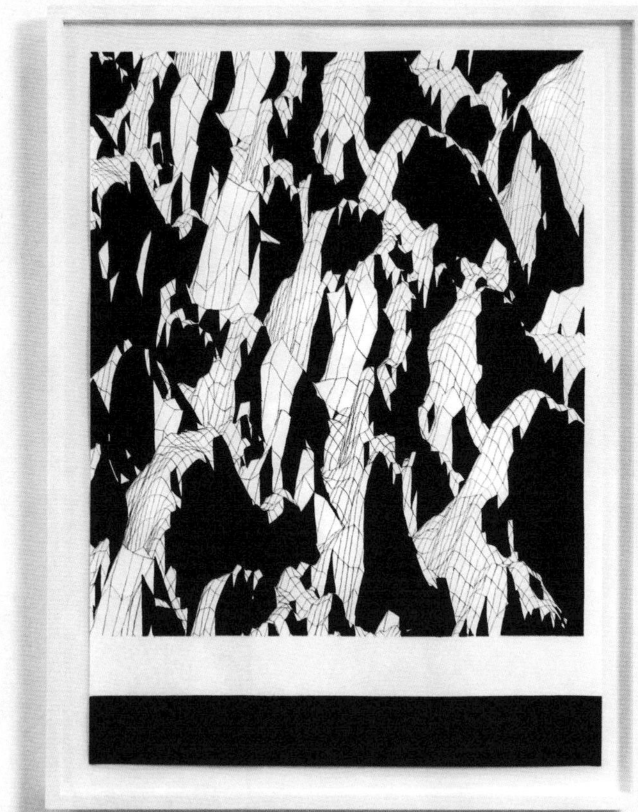

Data Drawing 12, 2014 (left page)
Pencil, acrylic, crayon, lacquer on paper
56×40 cm

Data Drawing 13, 2014 (left)
Pencil, acrylic, crayon, lacquer on paper
56×40 cm

Data Drawing 14, 2014 (right)
Pencil, acrylic, crayon, lacquer on paper
56×40 cm

Data Drawing 15, 2014
Pencil, acrylic, crayon, lacquer on paper
56×40 cm

The cloud for Renaissance painting would entail the same kind of mystery as what lies behind the Cloud© of the digital age.

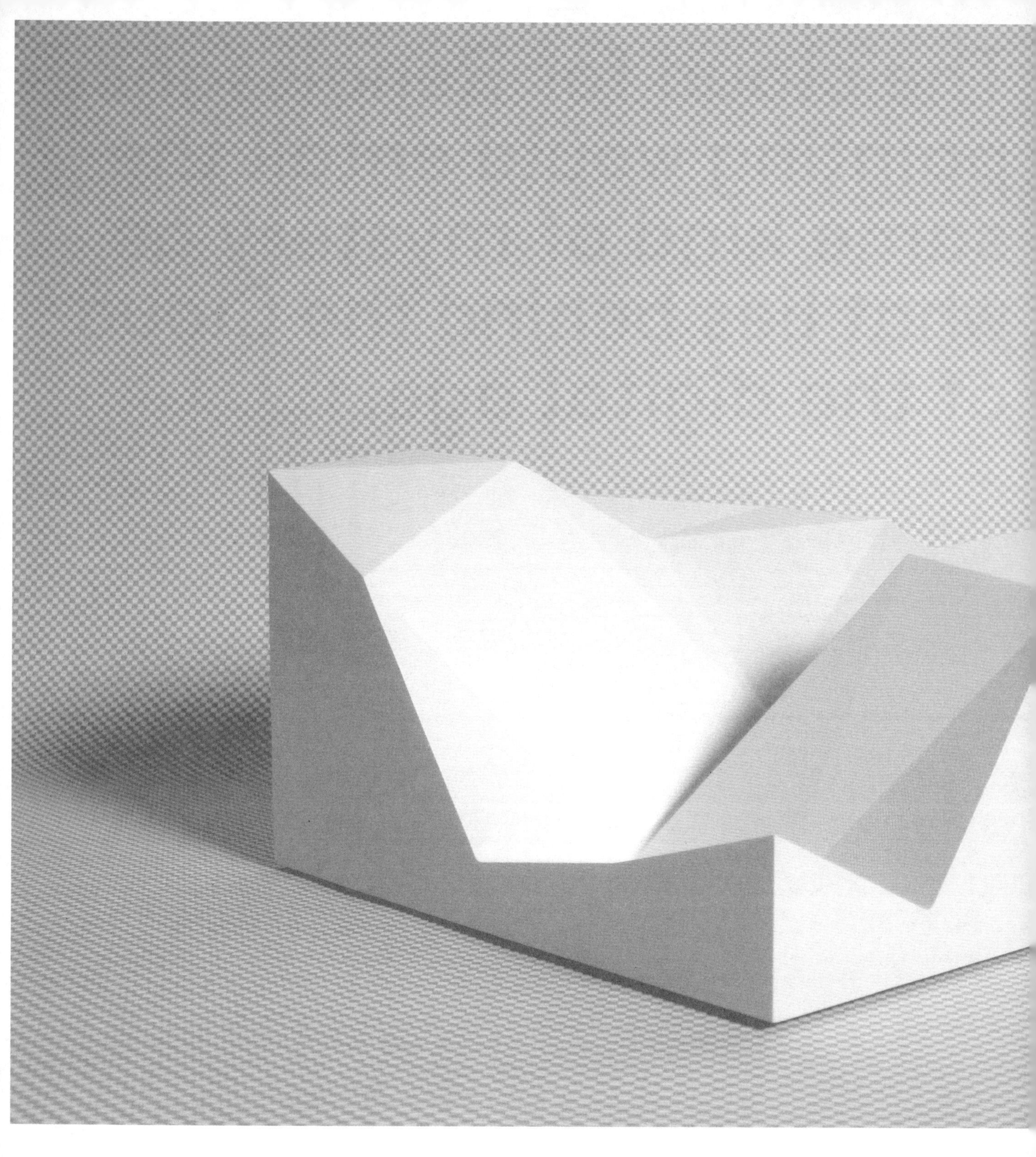

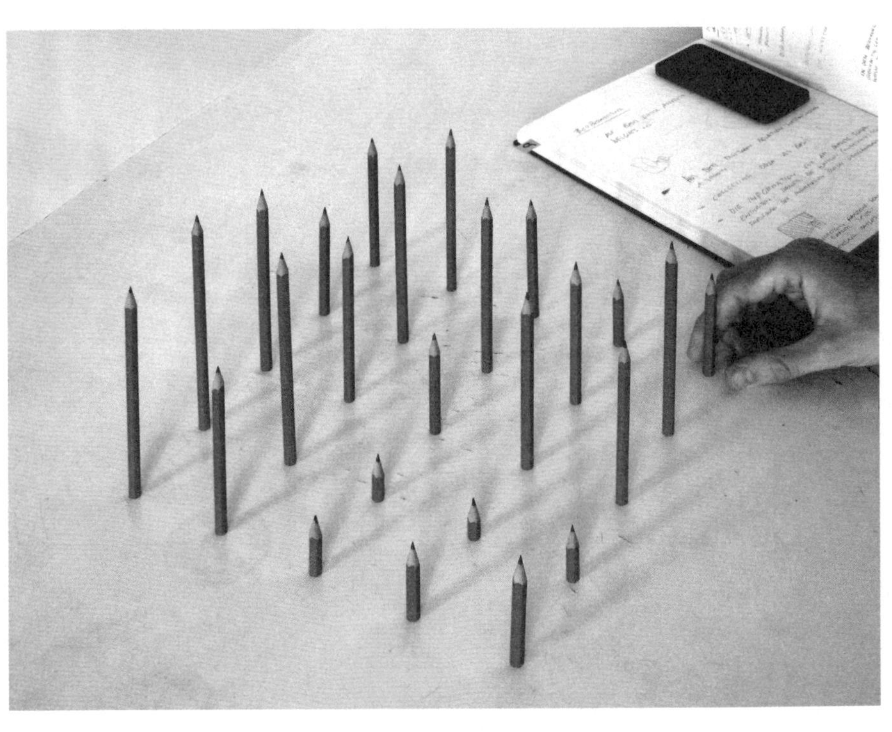

35

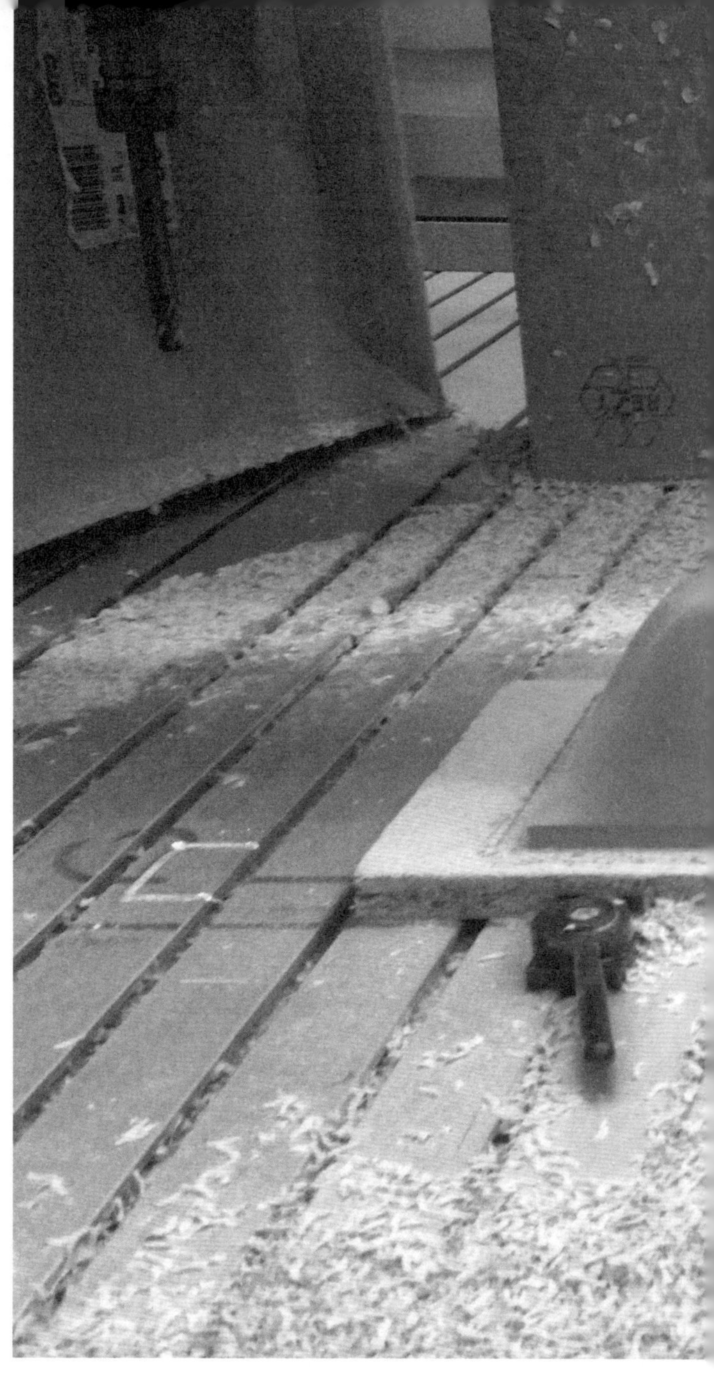

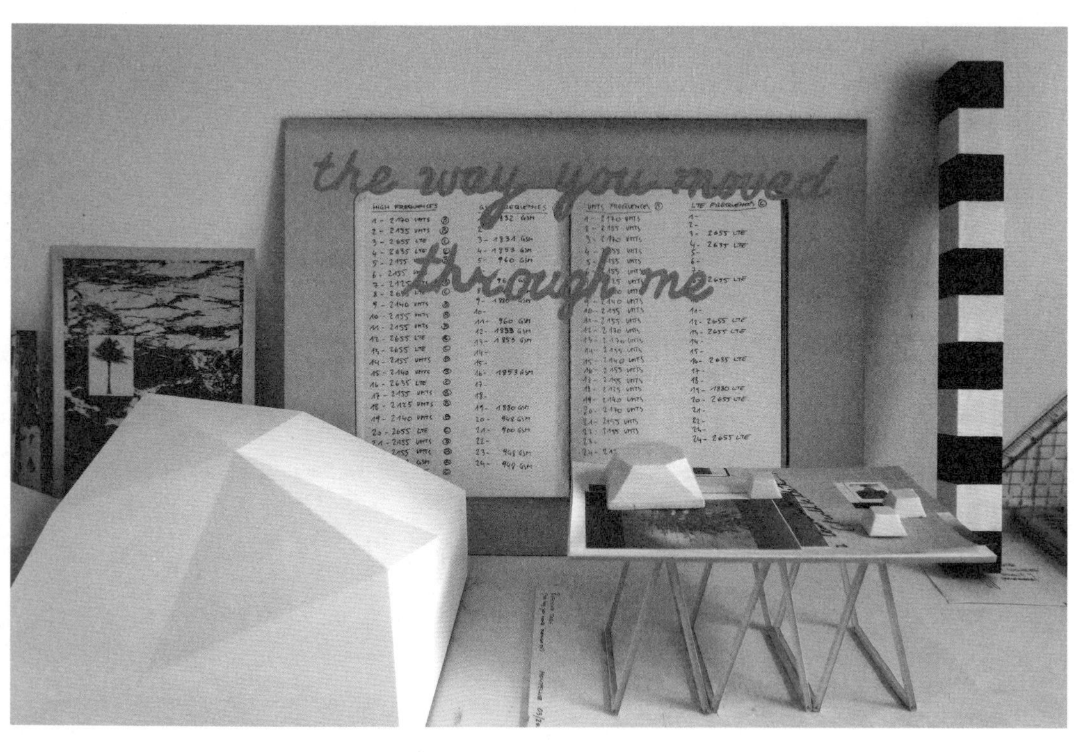
the way you moved
through me

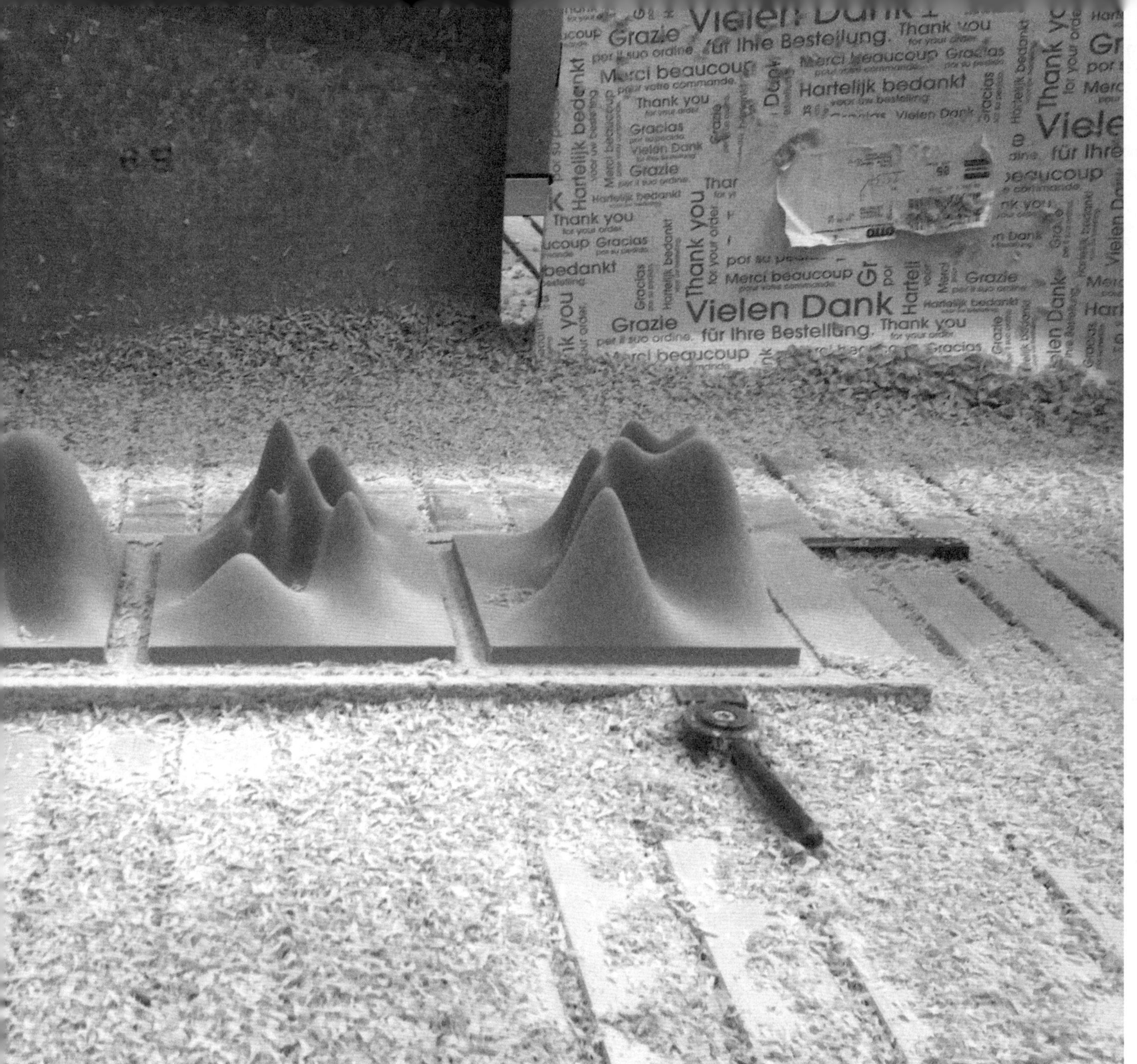

Vielen Dank
für Ihre Bestellung. Thank you
for your order
Grazie
per il suo ordine
Merci beaucoup
pour votre commande
Thank you
for your order
Gracias
por su pedido
Hartelijk bedankt
voor uw bestelling

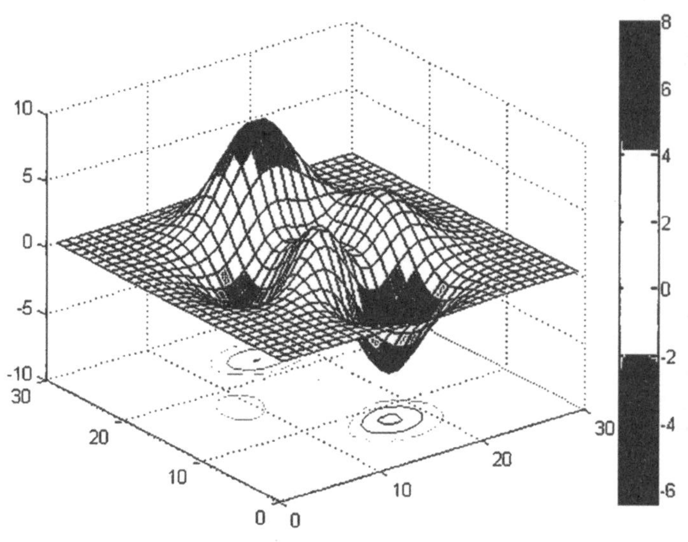

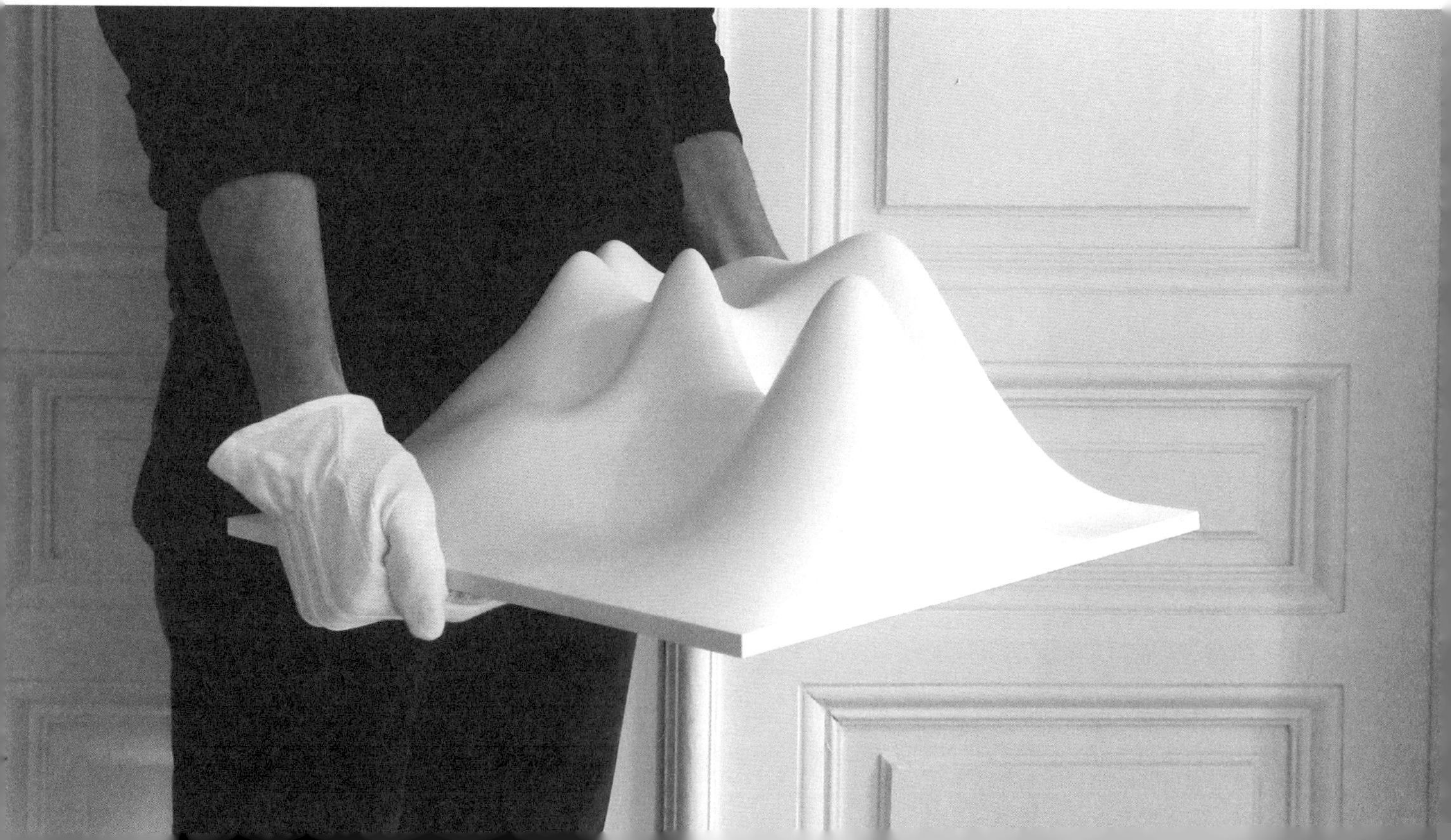

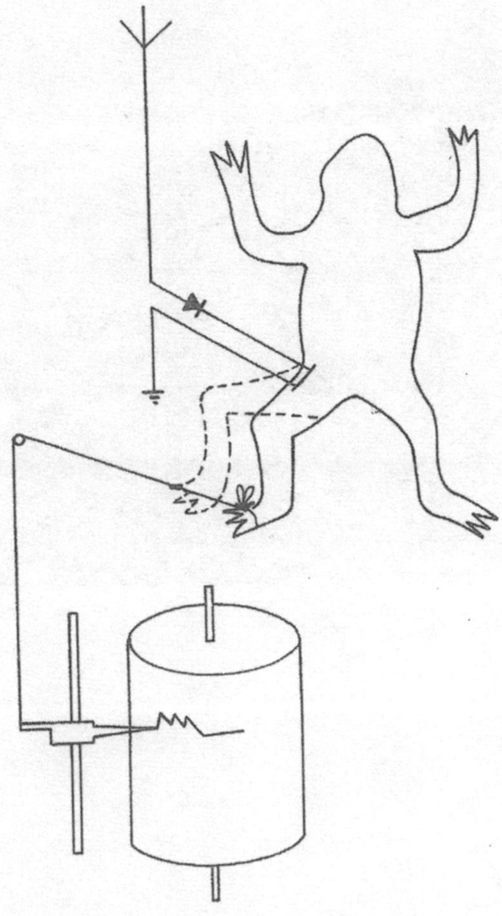

Figure 6.5 Long before radio energy was used to carry an acoustic signal, many ingenious devices were invented to detect radio energy. Lefeuvre's "physiological" receiver, for instance, uses the electrical sensitivity of a frog's leg.

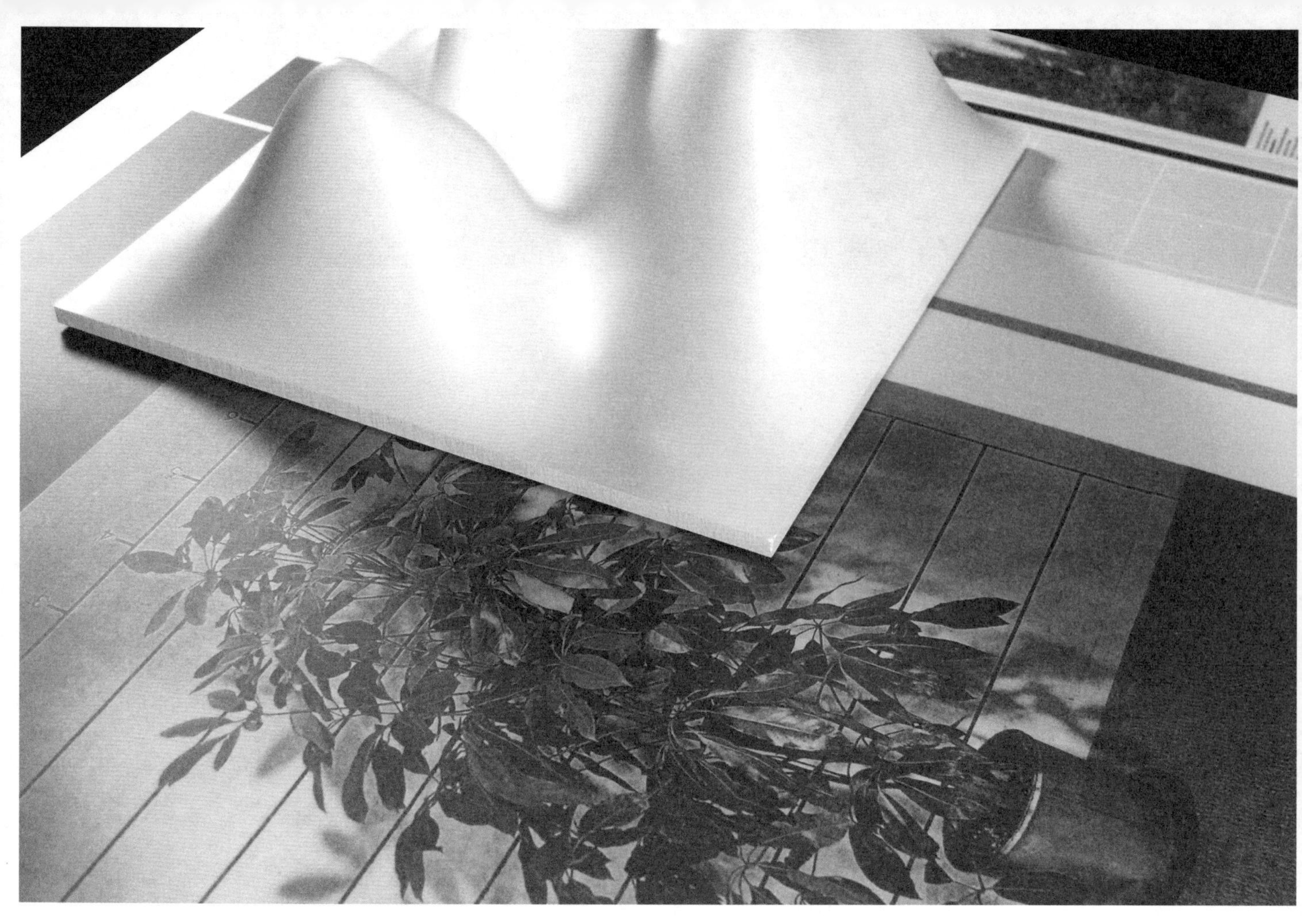

Weather Systems

Sébastien Pluot

"No one would deny that the painter has nothing to do with things that are not visible. The painter is concerned solely with representing what can be seen."[1] This blunt, surprising statement made by Leon Battista Alberti in *Della Pittura* reveals a repressed phenomenon analyzed by Hubert Damisch about the unsettled role played by the cloud in this paradox that consists in representing invisibility in Renaissance painting. Damisch asks:

> Do the rules of perspective lend themselves to the representation of phenomena that break through the ordinary bounds of the human order? Or, to put that another way, do divine interventions, which open up this world to the beyond and, more generally, mystical—or even physical—exchange between the earth and the sky provide matter suitable for representation despite the fact that depiction seems to be subject to an organizational principle for the pictorial field that seems to imply, as its corollary, that the illusionistic space constructed by geometrical means is governed by rules analogous to the laws that operate in the empirical universe: body and objects are subject to gravity, and this imposes limitations upon the manner in which they move around, and so on? Can such representations even have a place in this system, unless supernatural manifestations or miraculous events allow themselves to be reduced to the common norms of perception, or vision?

Simultaneously revealing and veiling, showing and dissimulating, clouds—bound to this paradoxical status that is also that of writing—play the visible and metaphorical roles in the perspective system of the material yet unfathomable,[2] the physical yet ethereal, the static yet moving matter, all that may correspond to the ungraspable mystic dimension and the mystery of the divine. As soon as the world becomes visibly and structurally governed by a rational grid, how can the mystery of the incommensurable be represented, if not by a plastic sign that questions representation itself? Clouds do not only represent a climatic phenomenon, but are primarily the sign of the impossibility of representing the presence of God, the mystical presence

1 Leon Battista Alberti, *De Pictura*, Book II, 78, also in Hubert Damisch: *A Theory of Cloud, Toward a History of Painting* (Stanford: Stanford University Press 2002), 112.

2 From the old English *fæthm*, that represented the span of outstretched arms.

of infinity. It plays the role of the difference between the profane and the sacred, meaning what might resist representation.

Let us raise the hypothesis that this dilemma, as transposed today, now concerns the combined power of radio waves and algorithm systems. The cloud for Renaissance painting would entail the same kind of mystery as what lies behind the Cloud© of the digital age. Something like an ethereal, godlike presence/absence that stores, circulates, and computes data with the help of algorithms, and that ultimately governs everyone's lives. The organic and unpredictable cloud as opposed to the rational mathematical grid being the two systems and episteme that have generated an ongoing dialectical crisis up to now.

Since "technological media turn magic into a daily routine,"[3] as Friedrich Kittler stated, how does one organize a critical representation of these pervasive powers—both visible and invisible, rational and irrational, familiar and uncanny—that surround us and populate our daily digital unconscious?[4] This is precisely the question raised by the work of Peter Jellitsch.

Data clouds

STB, the title of a series of drawings he initiated in 2011, is an acronym for Stream Body Drawings, a motion algorithm software generally used by architects for simulating wind directions and air forces that occur around high-rise buildings. These drawings of nebulous forms are obtained through a rigorous method that Jellitsch elaborated using computer screens[5] broadcasting different scientific digital patterns of radio frequencies, air streams or data clouds. He affixes a drawing paper on these images, enabling him to trace the shapes that he breaks up into small arrows, a plastic transformation that we can analyze on various levels. Peter Jellitsch remarks that architect Lebbeus Woods describes the way Leonardo da Vinci used curly human hair in order to draw the curves of clouds. The STB drawing method does

3   Friedrich A. Kittler, *Gramophone, Film, Typewriter*, trans. Geoffrey Winthrop-Young & Michael Wutz (Stanford: Stanford University Press 1989), 35–36.

4   The first transatlantic wireless transmission took place in 1901, one year after Freud published *The Interpretation of Dreams*, and the realm of the uncanny and presence of ghosts became effective through the new media.

5   The size of the drawings corresponds to the size of the computer screens.

not rely on this conception of correspondence between any fragments of nature: rather, it paradoxically inserts a highly human subjective and material feature in which the virtual scientific model is expected not to betray any expressive affect. The arrows become visible signs as well, they not only describe physical phenomena that can be mathematized, but also refer to linguistic systems. These indexical shifters continuously transform themselves. Like a Möbius strip, they bend on themselves, never revealing their hidden sides, endlessly pointing to another direction and some other visible or invisible adjacent sign. The clusters of individual arrows may therefore reflect and contradict a history of parameterization of behaviors that connects Gustave Le Bon's theory of the crowd[6] to the algorithms, invented in the 1980s, allegedly able to predict the stochastic movements of bird swarms, also called "bird clouds," later applied back to human behavior by experimental physiology with the help of cybernetics.

After the Second World War, Norbert Wiener clearly explained the goals of cybernetics:

> Besides the electrical engineering theory of the transmission of messages, there is a larger field which includes not only the study of language but the study of messages as a means of controlling machinery and society, the development of computing machines and other such automata, certain reflections upon psychology and the nervous system…[7]

Therefore, the world should not be only a book written in the language of mathematics, as Galileo stated, this book should be easily rewritten. Alberti already described his map of Rome as an extremely powerful tool incorporating the control of space and time:

> The man who possesses them [the numbers] can so record the outlines and position and arrangement of the parts of any given body in accurate and absolutely reliably written forms that not merely a day later, but even after a whole cycle of the heavens, he can again at will situate and arrange the same body.

Such declarations testify to the extreme plasticity of the algorithm that can be used to analyze,

6   Gustave le Bon's *The Crowd: A Study of the Popular Mind* (1895) was aimed at identifying human behavior in collective situations. Many aspects of his theories rely on racist, pseudo-scientific conceptions.

7   Norbert Wiener, *The Human Use of Human Beings: Cybernetics and Society* (Boston: Houghton Mifflin 1954), 15.

"predict" and control, almost indifferently, everything from the motion of local air streams and weather systems, to the trajectory of bird swarms, collective behaviors, language, and the speculations of financial markets,[8] with the success we all know. The pervasive circulation of data through electromagnetic waves (radio, the Internet…) seems to connect everything with everything.

Once the obsolete notion of ether was incorporated into the rational theory of electromagnetism, science and art already envisioned various interconnections of the senses. Light, sound, electricity, and heat were composed by the same phenomenon, invisible radio waves going through space and matter. The nineteenth-century discovery of electromagnetic fields — which pushed occult speculations about the ether into the realm of positivism — and its consequences on technical tools such as X-rays or distant communications through radio waves, already organized another paradigmatic regime of representation that structurally reshuffled the relations between proximity and distance. Literally immersed into a magnetic bath, reality is not submitted to what is visible, but to the presence of scientifically validated ghosts. Modernity, according to Karl Marx, is compelled by a recurrent uncanny phenomenon according to which "everything that is solid melts into the air." Imbued by its exchange value, the commodity was transformed, fetishized into an occult, magical phenomenon. Henceforth, the intangible became the rule for immaterial exchanges affecting and controlling reality.

Prompted by a critical relation with the political and economical capitalist system, many artists from the 1960s dealt with the complexity of invisible systems. Hans Haacke gave instructions by phone to a museum in order to modify the temperature of an exhibition space,[9] and presented climatic control devices in an exhibition as a way to show — as the title of the work suggests[10] — how the art institution was controlling the atmosphere into a highly conditioned environment echoing the power of invisible phenomena in the age of cybernetics and information theory. These two works were proposed at a time when Haacke had rejected the term "system" — around which he had

8   High-speed trading functions with algorithms that are generating billions of immaterial values, circulating independently from human control from one databank to another.

9   Hans Haacke proposed this work for the exhibition *Art by Telephone* (1969, MCA Chicago). This exhibition consisted in inviting artists to transmit their works through a telephone conversation. Their works would be activated, interpreted, and constructed by the staff of the museum on their behalf.

10   Hans Haacke's *Recording of Climate in Art Exhibition* (1970) was presented in New York for the exhibition *Conceptual Art and Conceptual Practices*.

previously based his whole work—because of its use in warfare and by global corporations.

This fantasy of immediate and invisible communication was one of the features on which Robert Barry critically speculated with *Telepathic Piece*, the *Inert Gas Series* or the *Radio Waves* pieces (all c. 1968–1969). Rather than criticizing these new invisible influences, Barry was dealing with the affinity between invisible phenomena and the imaginary. The use of invisible phenomena aimed at reducing the artist's determination over the forms. One of the consequences being the ability to delegate the power of representation to the "viewer-interpreter." These two kinds of position reveal how invisible phenomena and linguistic systems are shaping people's behavior in coercive or emancipatory ways.

Indeed, Barry's and Haacke's invisible yet intelligible proposals coincided with the unprecedented deployment of new possibilities for economic, administrative, communicational, and relational immediacy operated by electromagnetic environments. Already, the social and physical bodies were permeated by invasive radio waves that claimed to calculate and configure behaviors. Today, clouds of data controlled by algorithms govern preferences and desires. A computer native like Peter Jellitsch knows how much these invisible systems can be as acutely glorious as they are appalling: they arouse fantasies of omnipotence, transparency, wealth, empowerment and freedom, they also raise anxieties of intrusion and dispersion, they produce stock market crashes, allow the spread of computer viruses and ubiquitous spying… One of the critical dimensions of Peter Jellitsch's drawings resides in the way they reveal what lies behind the construction of scientific representation. How science broadcasts mesmerizing evidence of mystery. Jellitsch's fascinating, hypnotic, haptic, and ungraspable drawings are analyzing these ambivalent, dazzling feelings. Such ambivalence toward an invisible power—the origin of which may indifferently arise from technology, God, or the id—was represented four centuries ago in Correggio's *Io* (1531). In this painting, Jupiter, taking on a vaporous grey, cloudy form, grabs Io's waist. The turmoil of the cloud simultaneously represents Io's sexual drive, supposedly aroused by Jupiter, and a terrifying ghostly presence threatening to overshadow her pale, reckless body.

Free circulation of signs

For the exhibition *Breaking News from the Ether* [11], Peter Jellitsch showed a series of STB drawings, the installation *Bleecker Street Documents* (the electromagnetic portrait of the New York studio he stayed in), as well as *Reference Table (the way you moved through me)*, a site-specific work he did for this exhibition in Montpellier. For this last project, Peter Jellitsch did not only consider electromagnetic fields [12] but also the fields of meaning emanating from the other artworks on display in the exhibition. The installation *Reference Table (the way you moved through me)*, on which he was working during his one-month residency, was placed on the exact same spot as Laurie Anderson's *Handphone Table* after it was removed from the exhibition to be shown elsewhere. Anderson's work is a wooden table that generates sound as soon as two people sit at each end and place their elbows on the wood while curving their palms on their hears. By installing a table that he designed with the exact same measurements as *Handphone Table*, Jellitsch's work embodied a spectral presence of the absent work.

The electromagnetic portrait of the space included detailed notes of his mapping process as well as a series of facsimile of works that resonated with the relations between ideas informing his work and crucial topics he identified in the exhibition that formed a wide, indexical set of artistic references that one can interpret as a mental space of the context.

Jellitsch covered the table with an enlarged photographic scale reference (a grid with a color chart) on which he displayed a large reproduction of Mel Bochner's *Measurement: Plant* from 1969 (that shows a ficus tree in front of a measurement grid). At the intersection of these two images a handwritten inscription, "Demonstration (it could be like this)," [13] is in dialogue with an image

11   Dernières Nouvelles de l'Ether (curated by: Franck Bauchard & Sébastien Pluot) 07.02.–22.06.2014, La Panacée, Montpellier, FR / Artists: Dominique Blais, Will Potter, Vincent Betbeze, Ugo La Pietra, Trevor Paglen, Superstudio, Sharon Kulik, Robert Barry, Ralf Baecker, Philippe Deloison, Nicholas Knight, Peter Jellitsch, Martin Ratniks, Maria Loboda, Marcel Duchamp, Liam Gillick, Laurie Anderson, Laurent Grasso, Lawrence Weiner, John Cage, Günther Domenig & Eilfried Huth, Hugo Brégeau, Haines & Hinterding, Hans Hollein, François Curlet, Dunne & Raby, Don Burgy, Dominique Blais, Dan Graham, Christina Kubisch, Brian O'Doherty, Bettina Samson, Berdaguer & Péjus, Bat, Alvin Lucier, A Constructed World.

12   More specifically the mobile phone intensities filling the exhibition space and its surrounding in the historic center of the city.

13   This sentence is part of a work called *Methodology* (1969) in which Bochner wrote three statements: 1. Hypothesis (What if…) 2. Demonstration (It could be like this…) 3. Theory (Therefore it seems that…).

of a tree antenna camouflage Jellitsch borrowed from Dunne & Raby's *Design Noir: The Secret Life of Electronic Objects*, as well as another Xeroxed image of *Perspective Insert, Collapsed Center*, a 1967 work by Bochner resulting from the photographic deformation of a grid. Over this arrangement, the notebook including Jellitsch's mapping of the area surrounding the exhibition site as well as a map reporting electromagnetic measurements was also displayed. Browsing the booklet, viewers could discover the work's process, reading a quotation he borrowed from Laurie Anderson: "the way you moved through me," a sentence that qualifies both the radio waves and semantic fields he gathered and combined from the atmosphere.

Four milled objects in coated ureol representing the invisible electromagnetic mapping of the space floated spectrally above all this iconographic material like a pale — allegedly harmless — ghostly body.

Sébastien Pluot is an art historian and independent curator. He is the co-director with Maud Jacquin of *Art by Translation*, International Research and Exhibition program for Art and Curatorial practices (ESBA TALM, ENSAPC, CNEAI=). He is the editor of two recent publications, *Art by Telephone Recalled* (Mix, 2014) and *A Translation From One Language to Another* (Les presses du Réel, 2015).

He has co-curated numerous exhibitions, including: *The House of Dust by Alison Knowles*, James Gallery, New York; Cal Arts, Los Angeles; Cneai= and La Galerie, Noisy le Sec, Paris; A.I.R 351; Villa Croce ; *Art by Telephone Recalled* CNEAI, Paris, CAPC, Bordeaux, Emily Harvey Foundation, New York, ESBA TALM, Angers, SFAI, La Panacée, Montpellier ; *Breaking News From the Ether* and *A Letter Always Arrives at Its Destinations*, La Panacée ; *A Translation From one Language to Another*, CNEAI, Paris ; *Double Bind, Stop Trying to Understand Me*, at Villa Arson, Nice. *Anarchism Without Adjectives, On the Work of Christopher D'Arcangelo*, at CAC Bretigny, 2011; Montehermoso Art Center, Vittoria; Artists Space, New York; Extra City, Anvers; Leonard and Bina Ellen Art Gallery, Concordia, Montreal; MAK Center, Los Angeles. He was guest teacher at the SFAI, Barnard College and CUNY in New York, Sorbonne Université, Lyon Post-Master and has lectured in many seminars, conferences and symposiums, among them Princeton University, University of Florida, Centre Georges Pompidou, Jeu de Paume, INHA, Paris, HEAD of Geneva. He has developed the project *Living Archives*, a research exhibition exploring the uses of the document and archives in contemporary art in partnership with Renée Green at the SFAI. He received the "Hors les Murs" grant from the Villa Médicis, the research grant of the CNAP and several grants for the research program In Translation. He holds a master's degree in art history and theory from the EHESS. He is a member of the International Board of Selection AiR351.

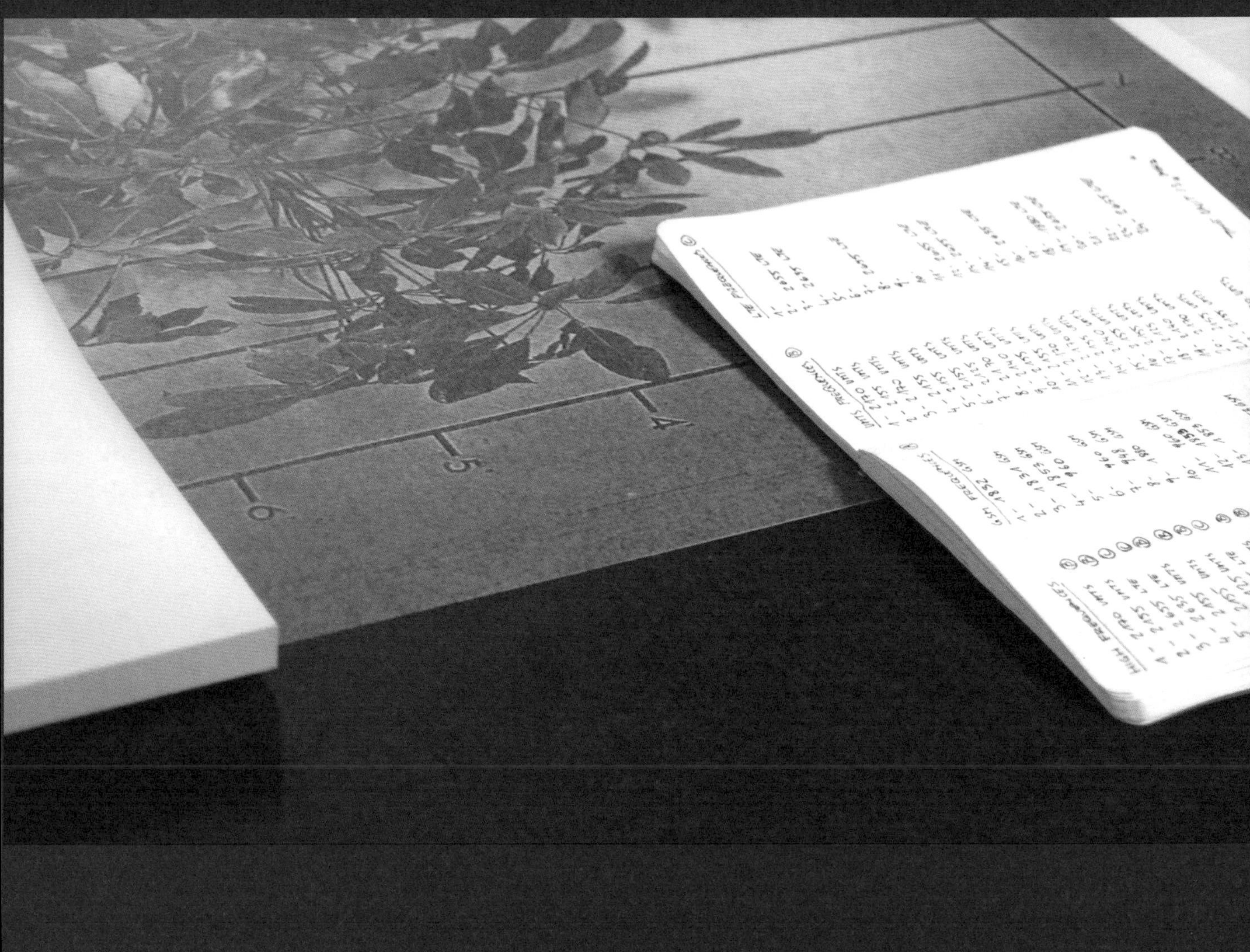

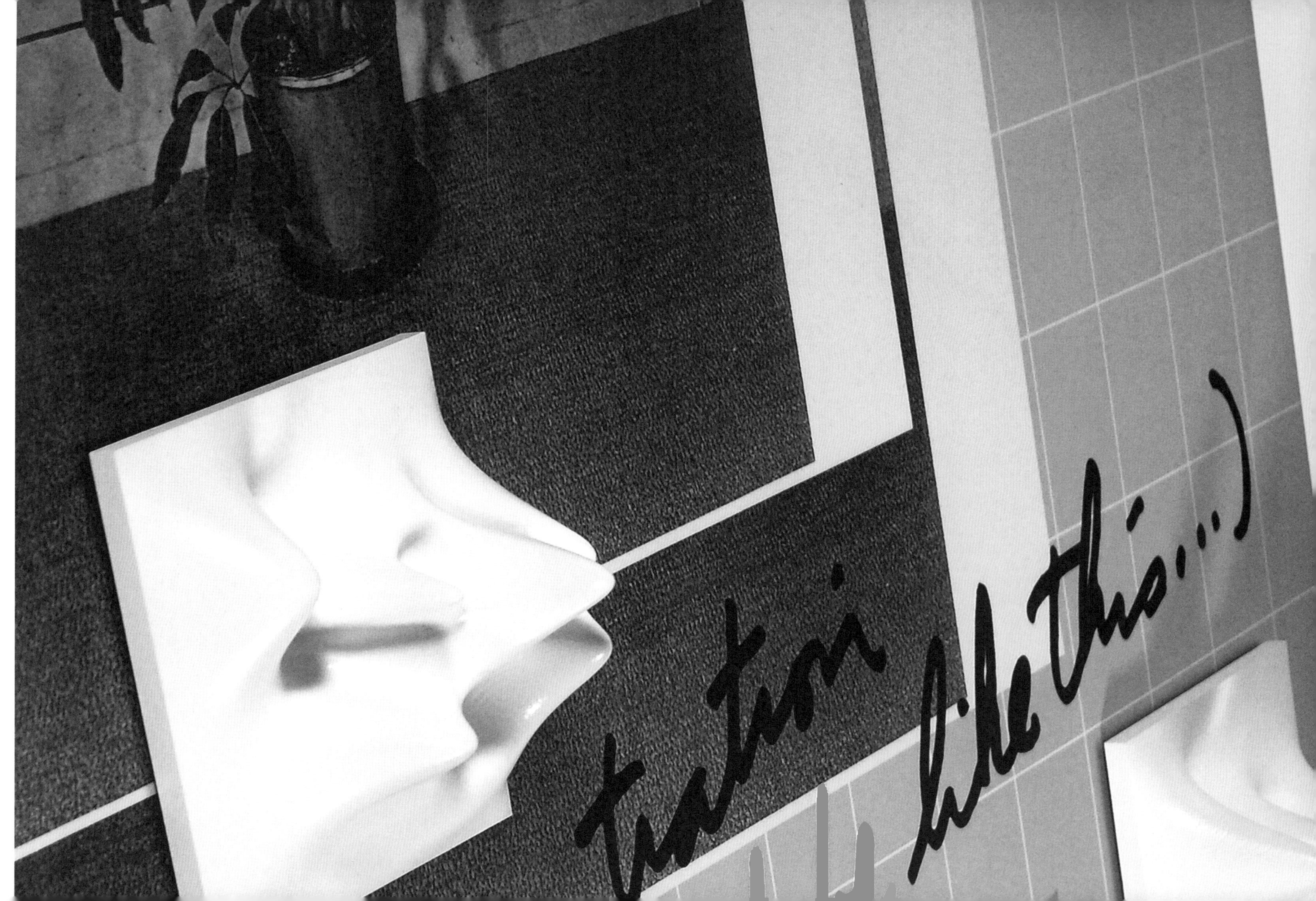
...tration like this...)

Reference Table
(the way you moved through me), 2014
Mixed media
91×79×152,5 cm

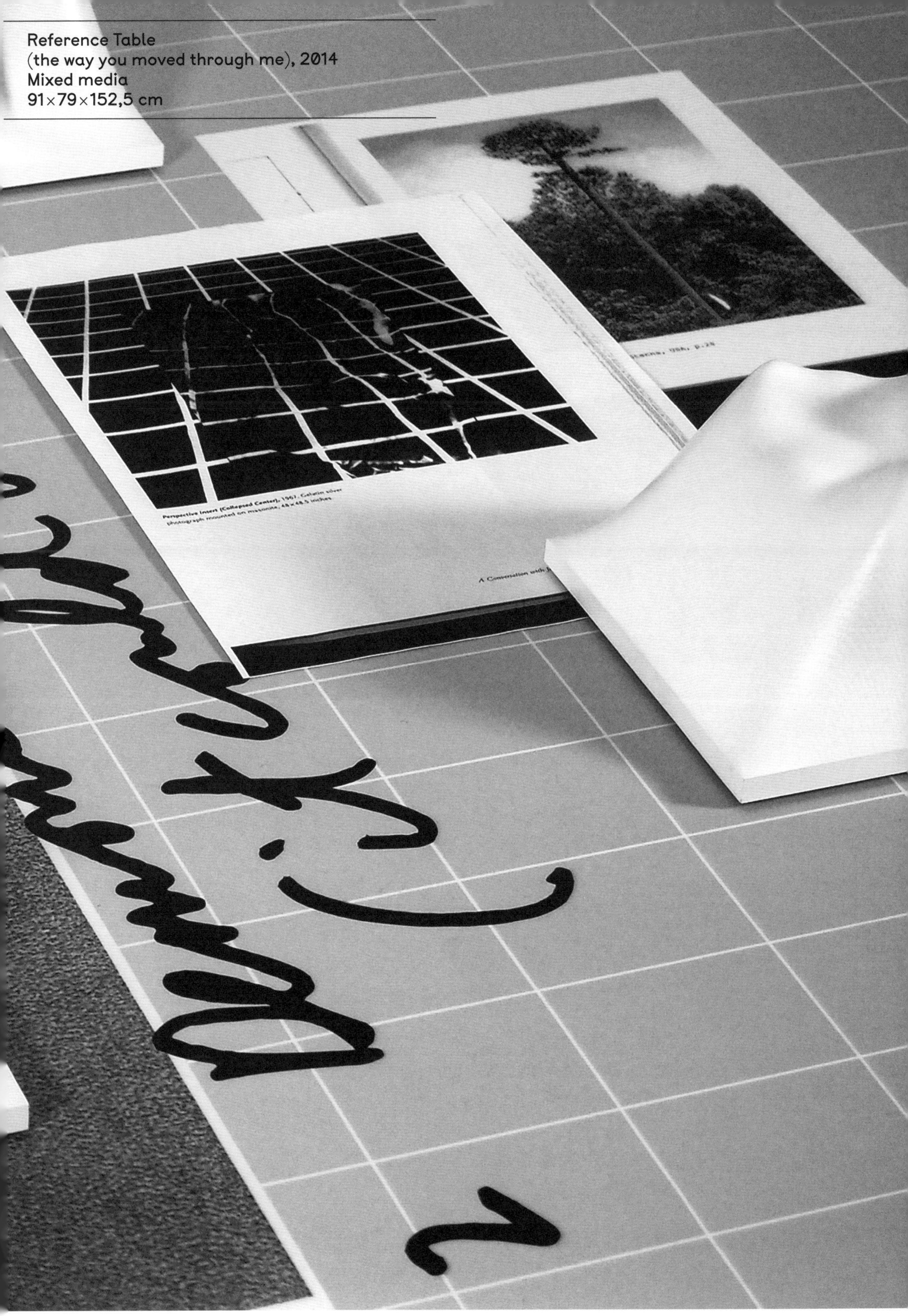

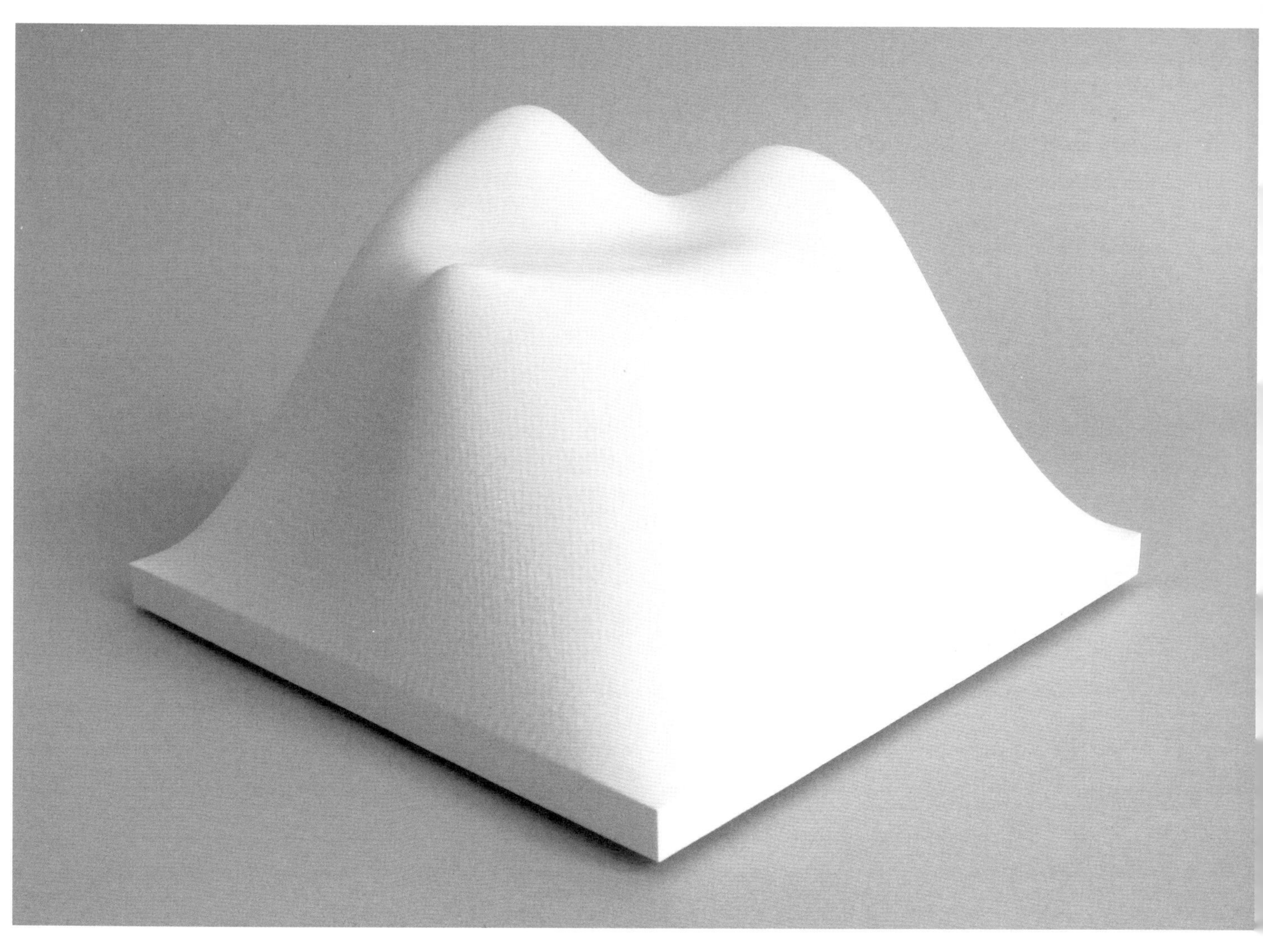

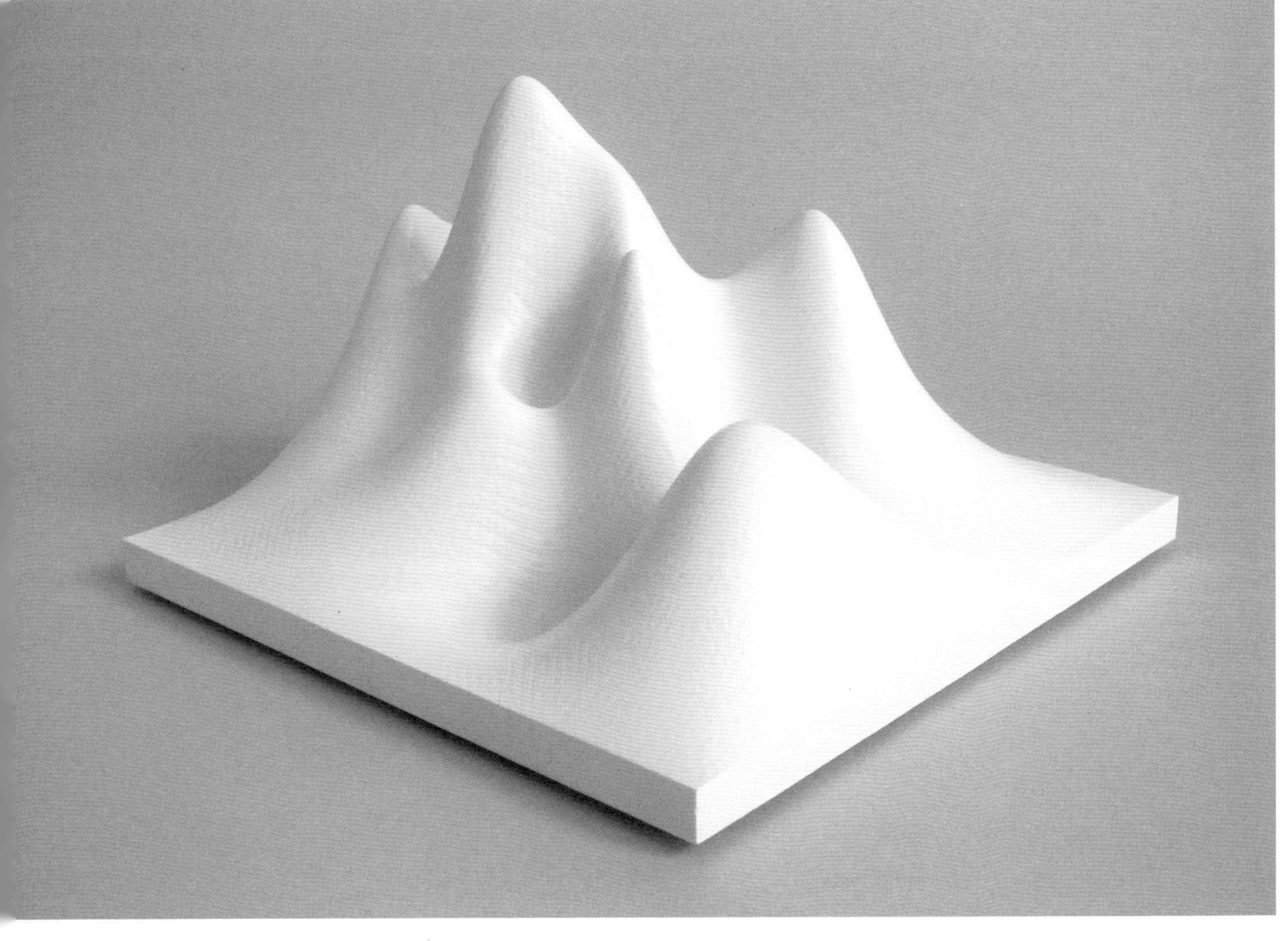

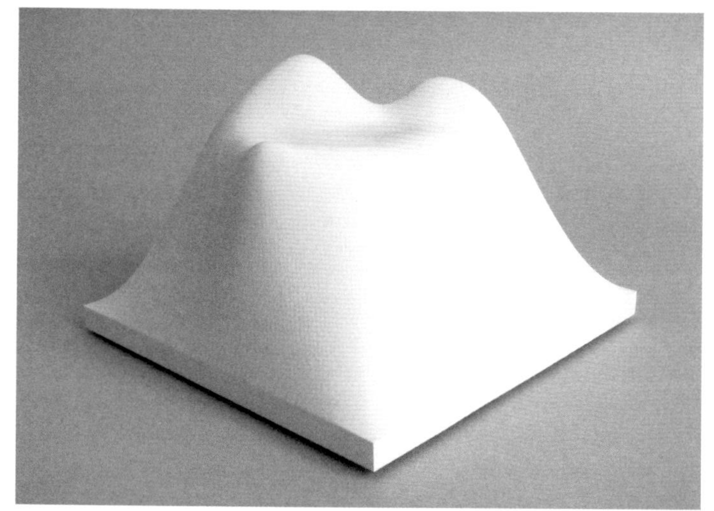

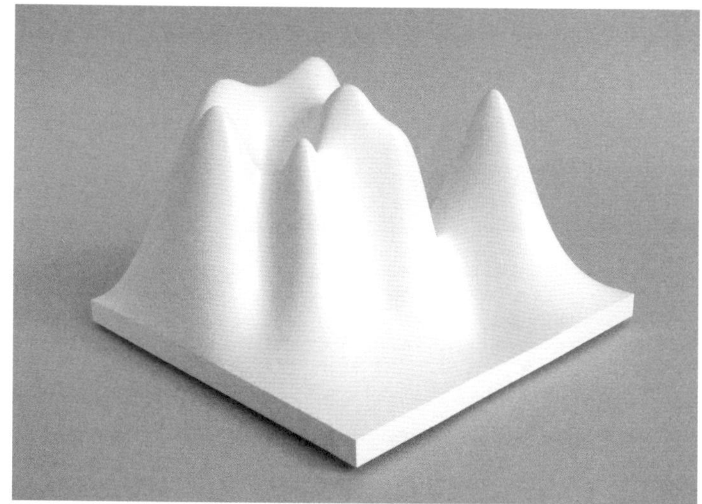

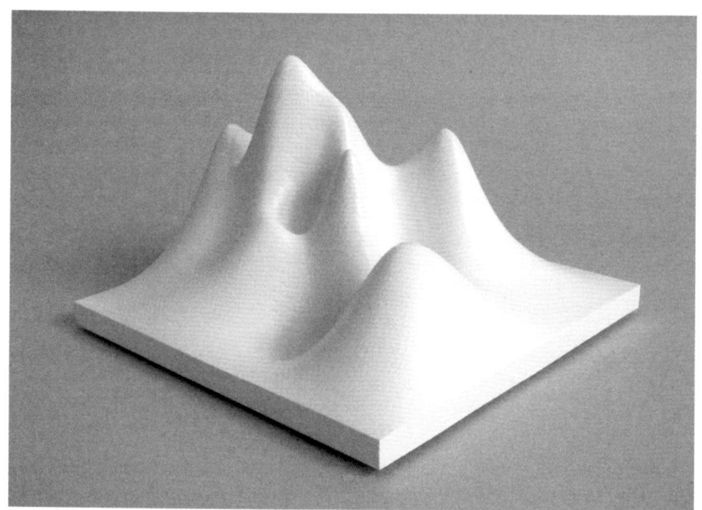

Data Objects Montpellier (UMTS, GSM, LTE), 2014
Coated ureol
Each 15×8×15 cm

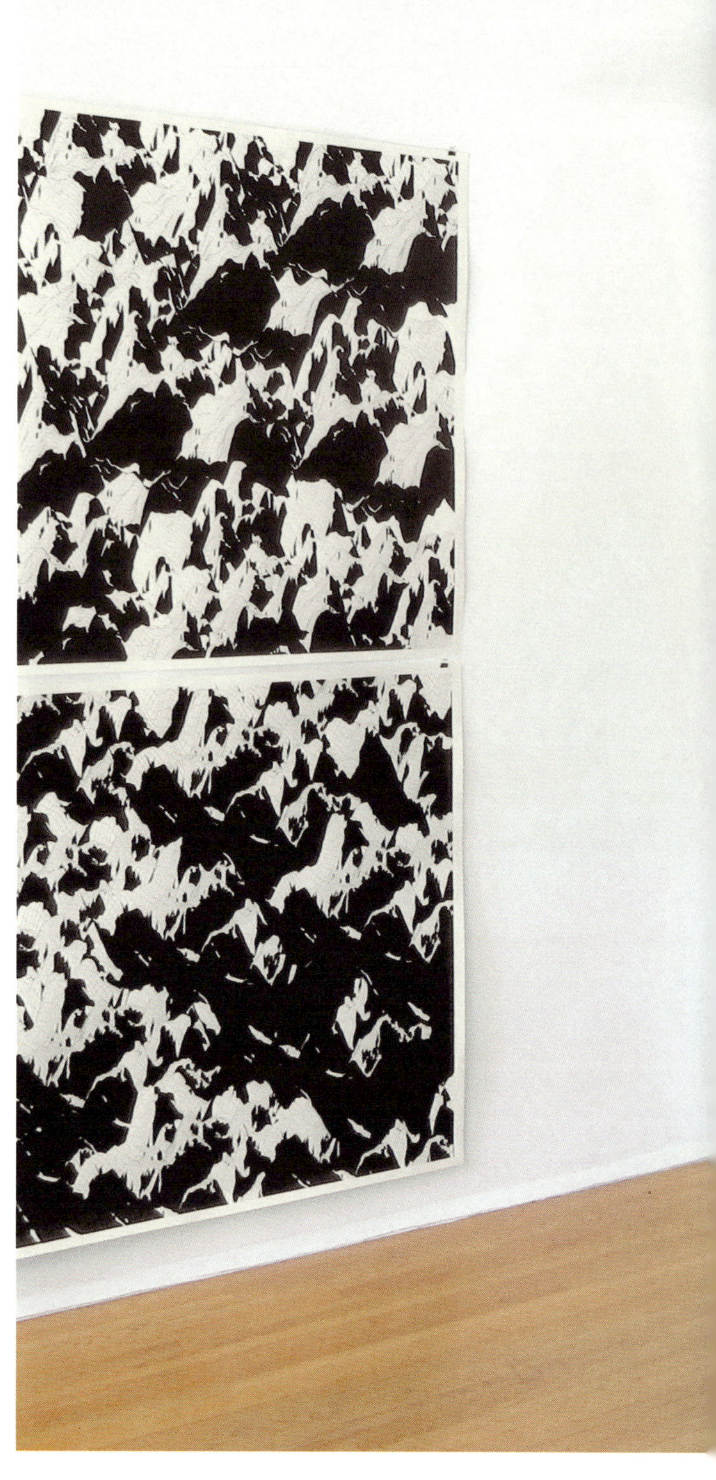

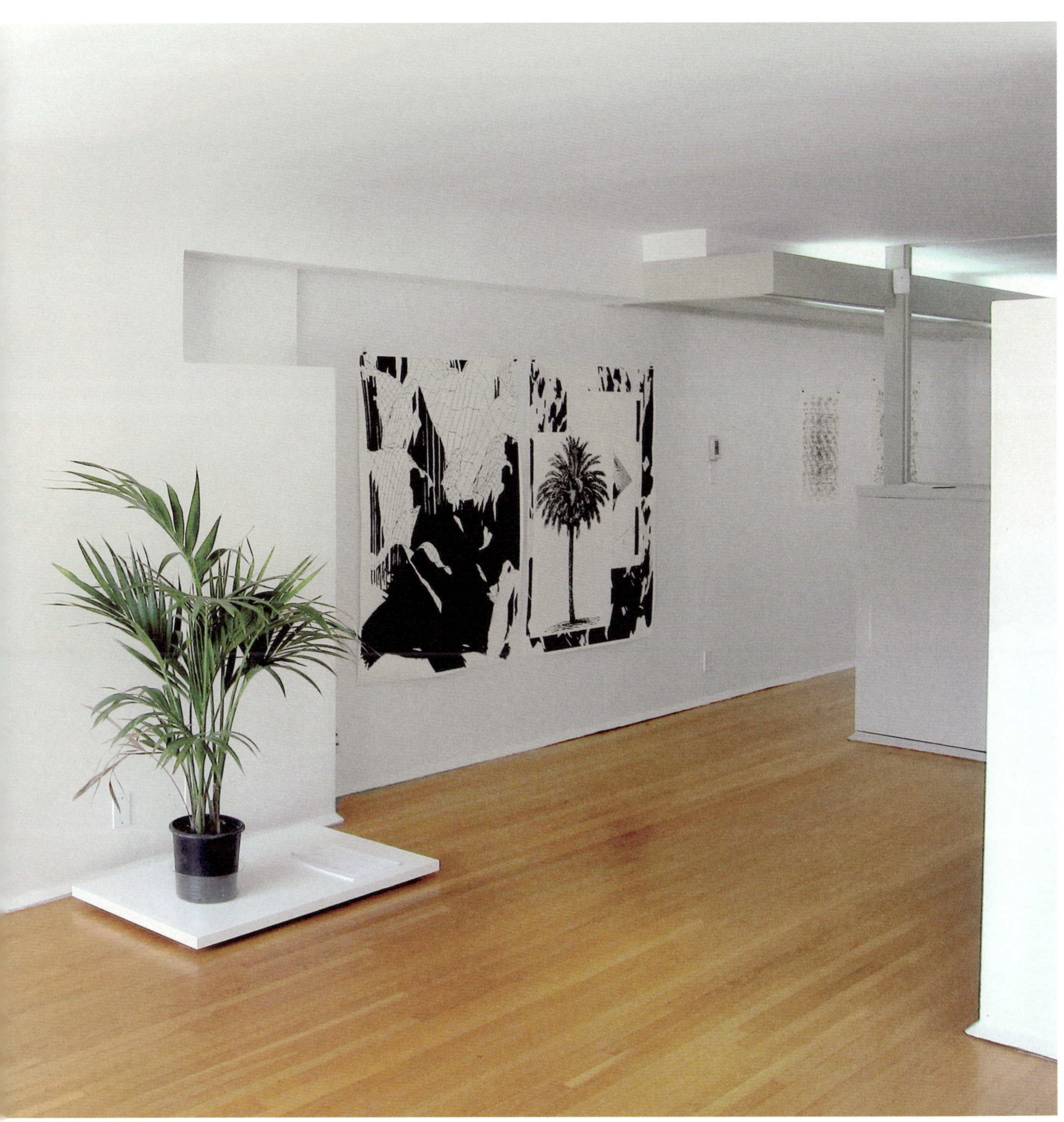

Exhibition
Group 38, 2014
Maria von Hausswolff, Peter Jellitsch,
Björn Kämmerer, Pradeep Devadass
& Sushant Verma
MAK Center, Artists and Architects-
in-Residence Program
Mackey Apartments
Los Angeles, US

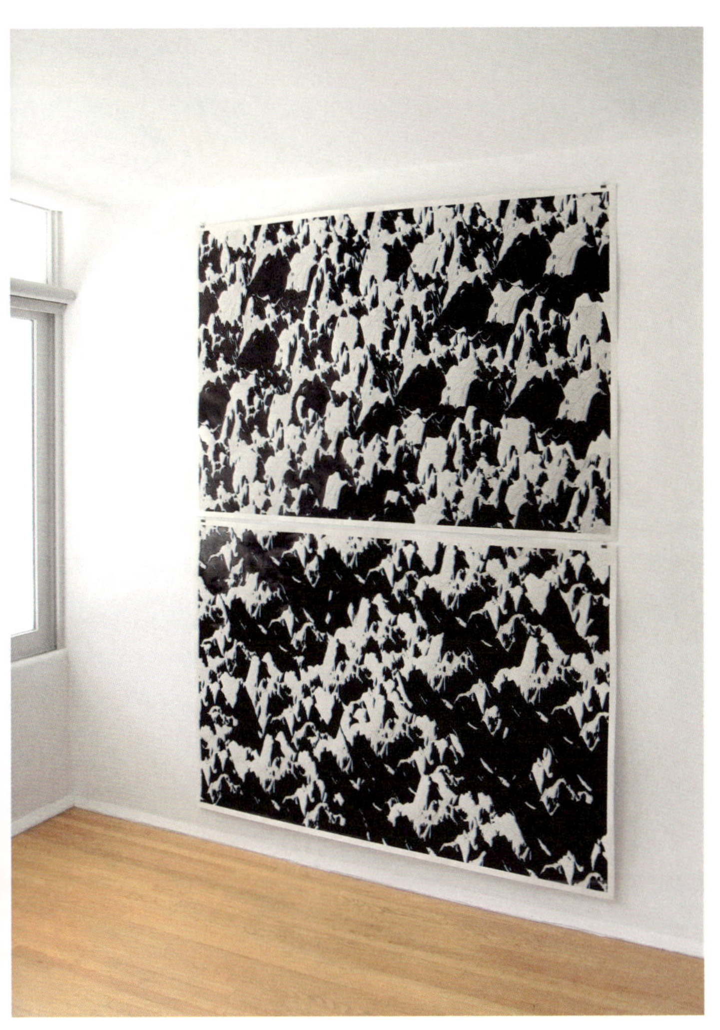 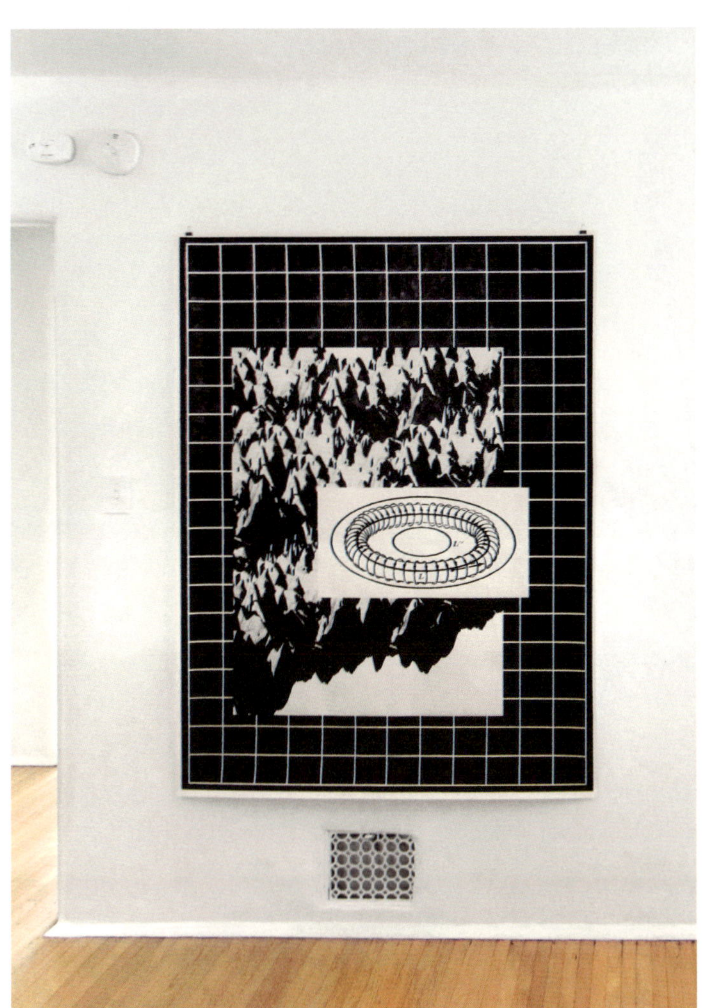

Data Drawing 18, 2014 (left)
Pencil, acrylic, crayon, lacquer on paper
110×152 cm

Data Drawing 23, 2014 (left)
Pencil, acrylic, crayon, lacquer on paper
110×152 cm

Data Drawing 21, 2014 (right)
Pencil, acrylic, crayon, lacquer on paper
160×116 cm

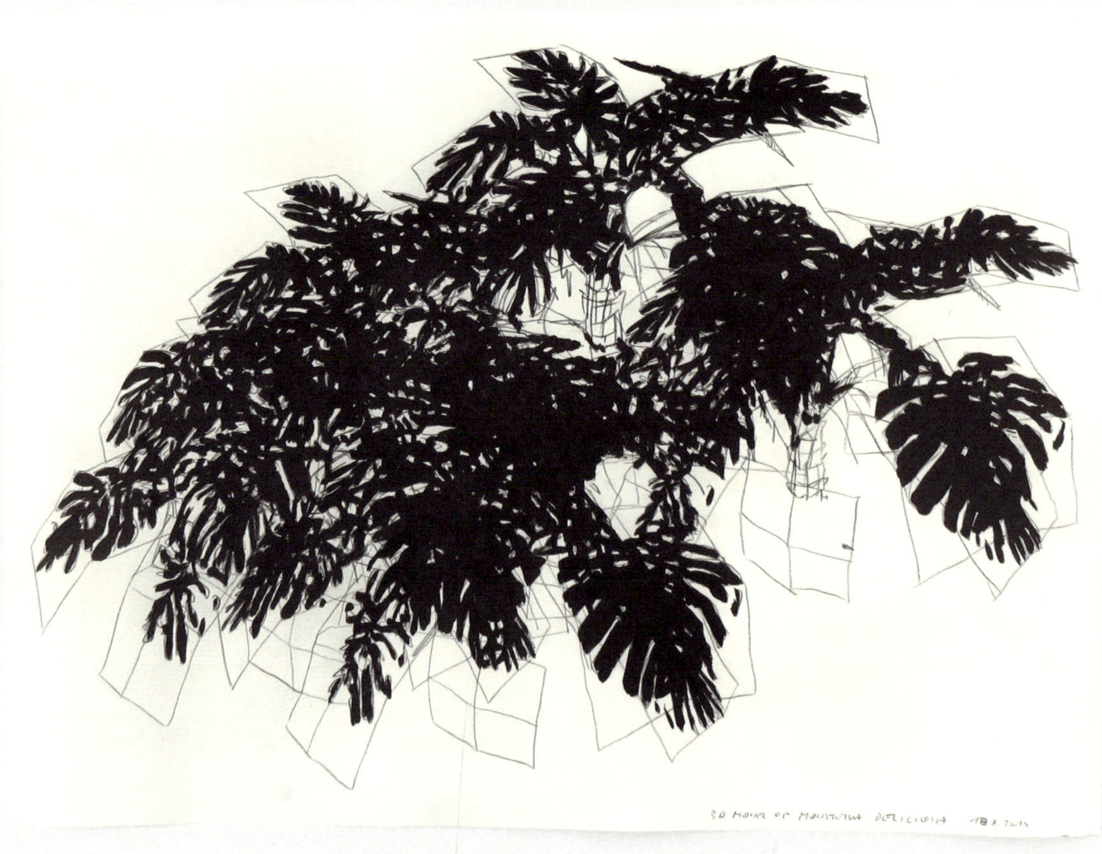

Monstera Deliciosa (after SketchUp), 2014
Pencil, crayon, acrylic on paper
37×50 cm

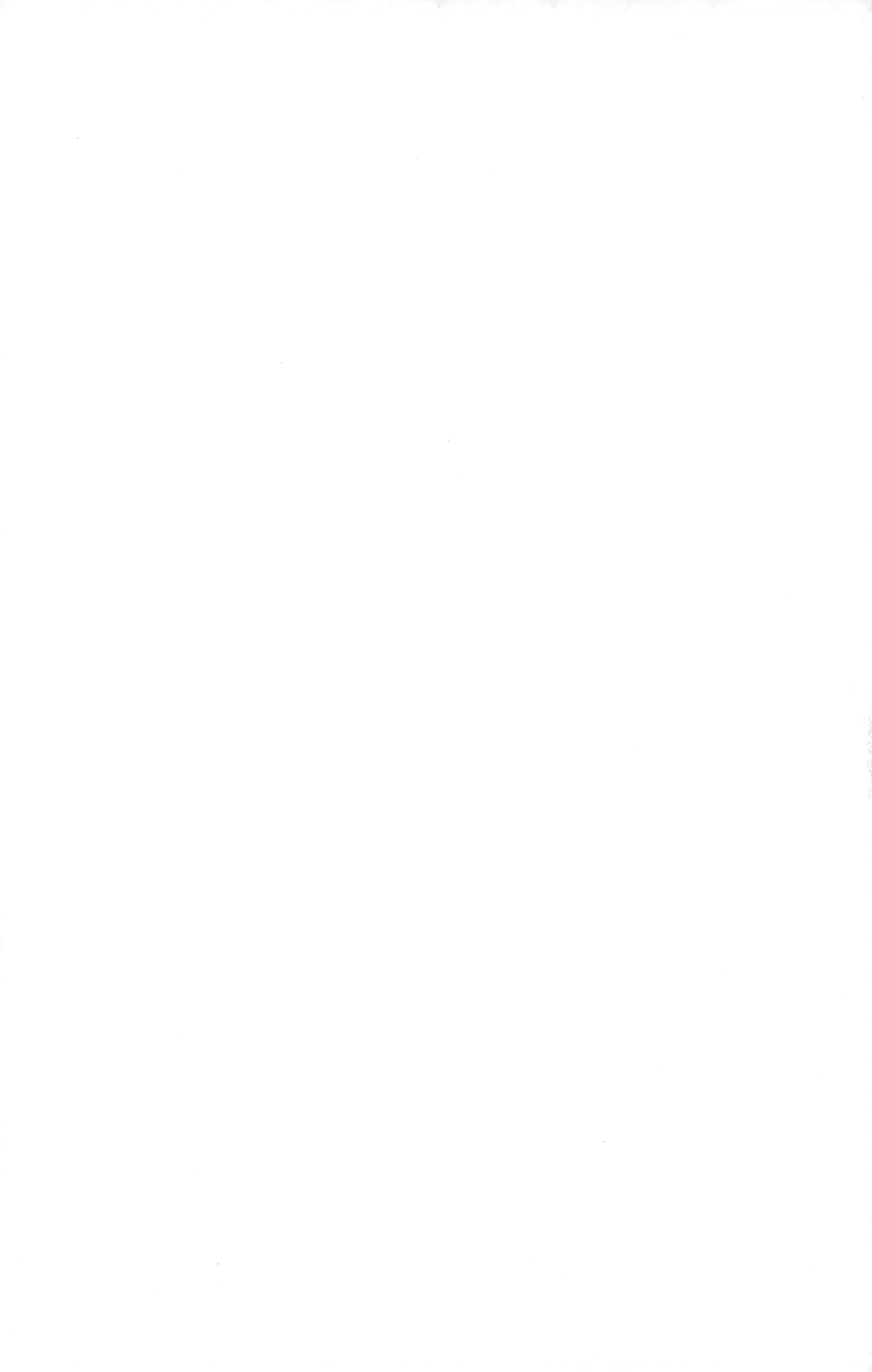

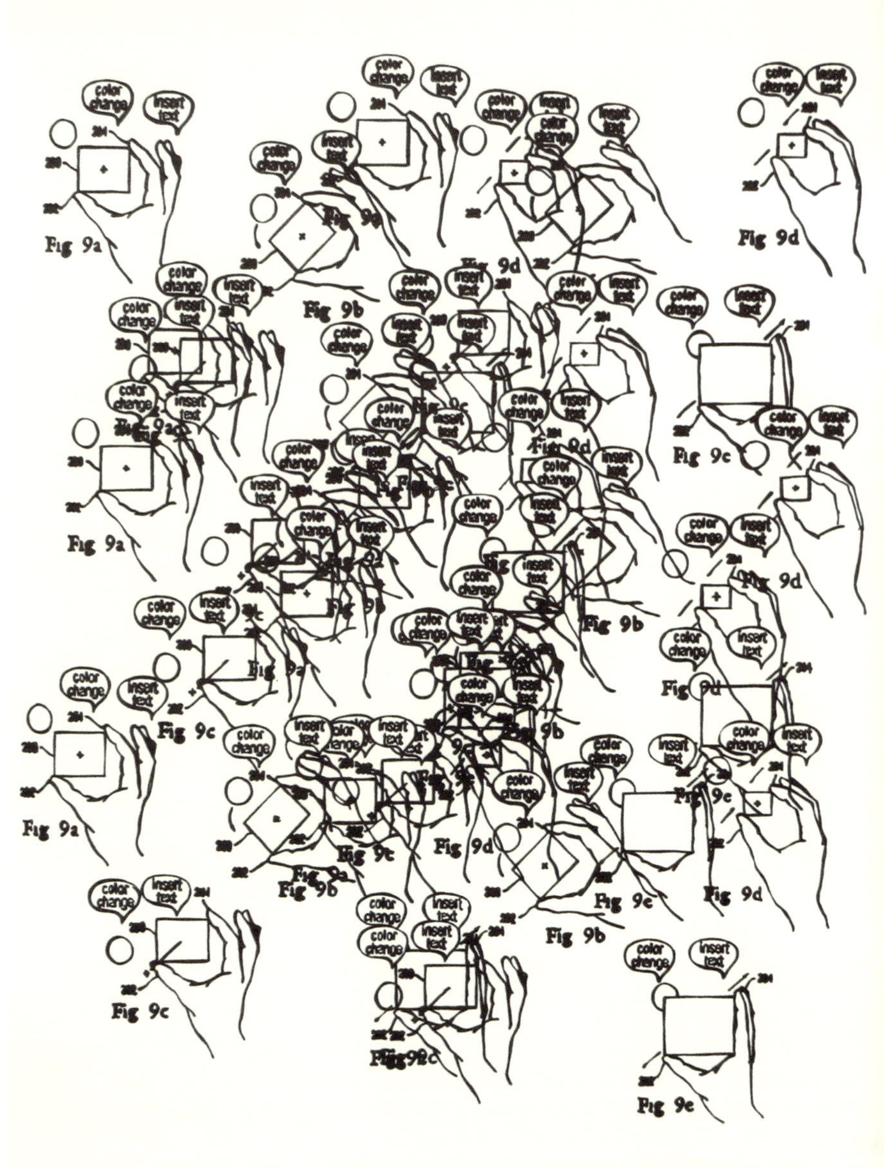

color change
insert text
Fig 9a
Fig 9b
Fig 9c
Fig 9d
Fig 9e

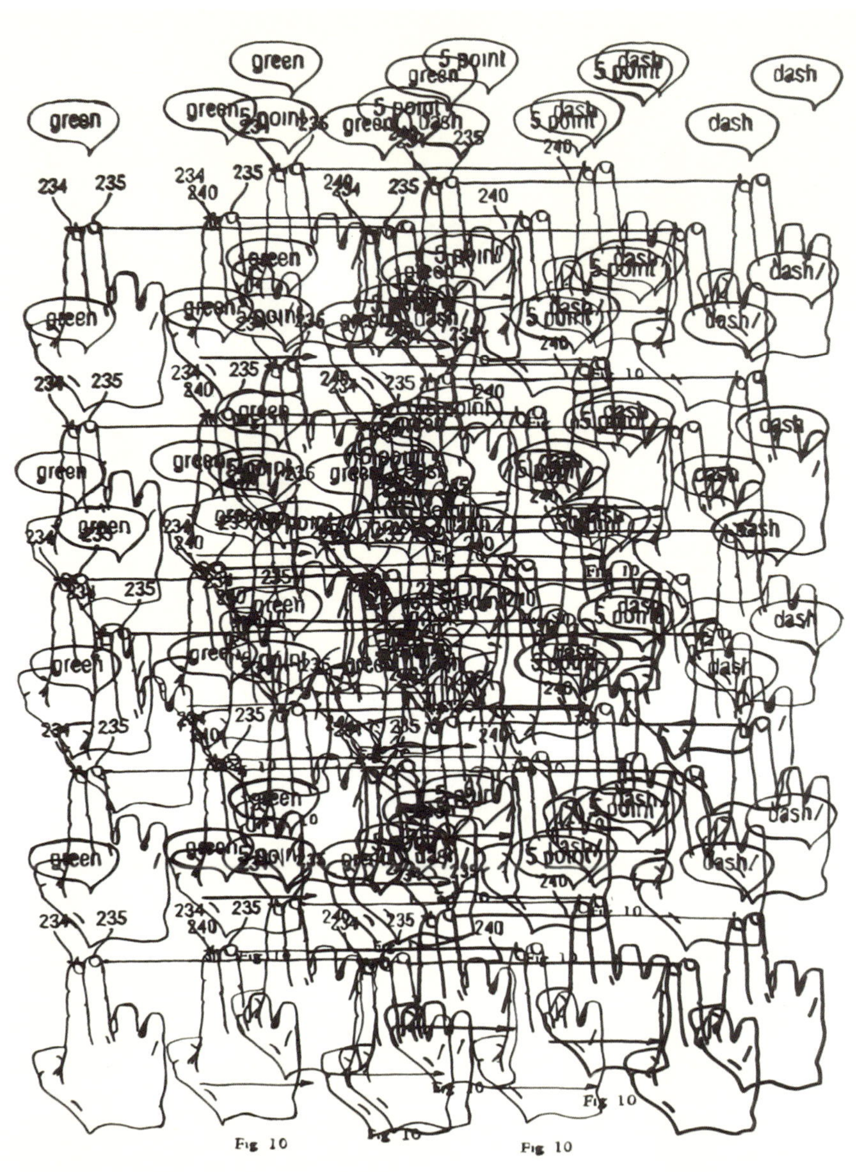

Apple Patent (multi-touch gesture), 2014 (left page)
Ink, lacquer on paper
98×72 cm

Apple Patent (slide to unlock), 2014
Ink, lacquer on paper
70×50 cm

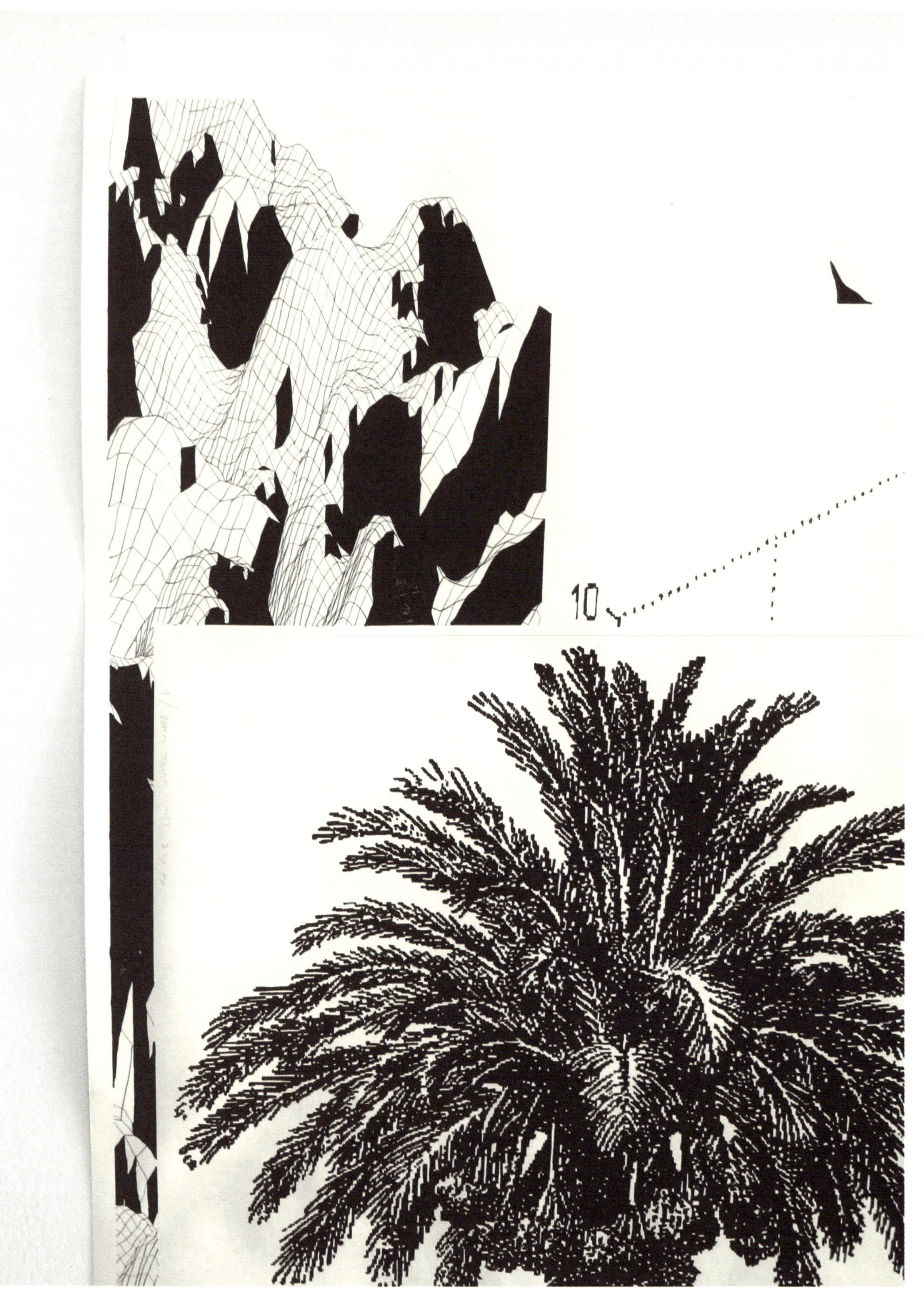

(Detail)
Data Drawing 22, 2014

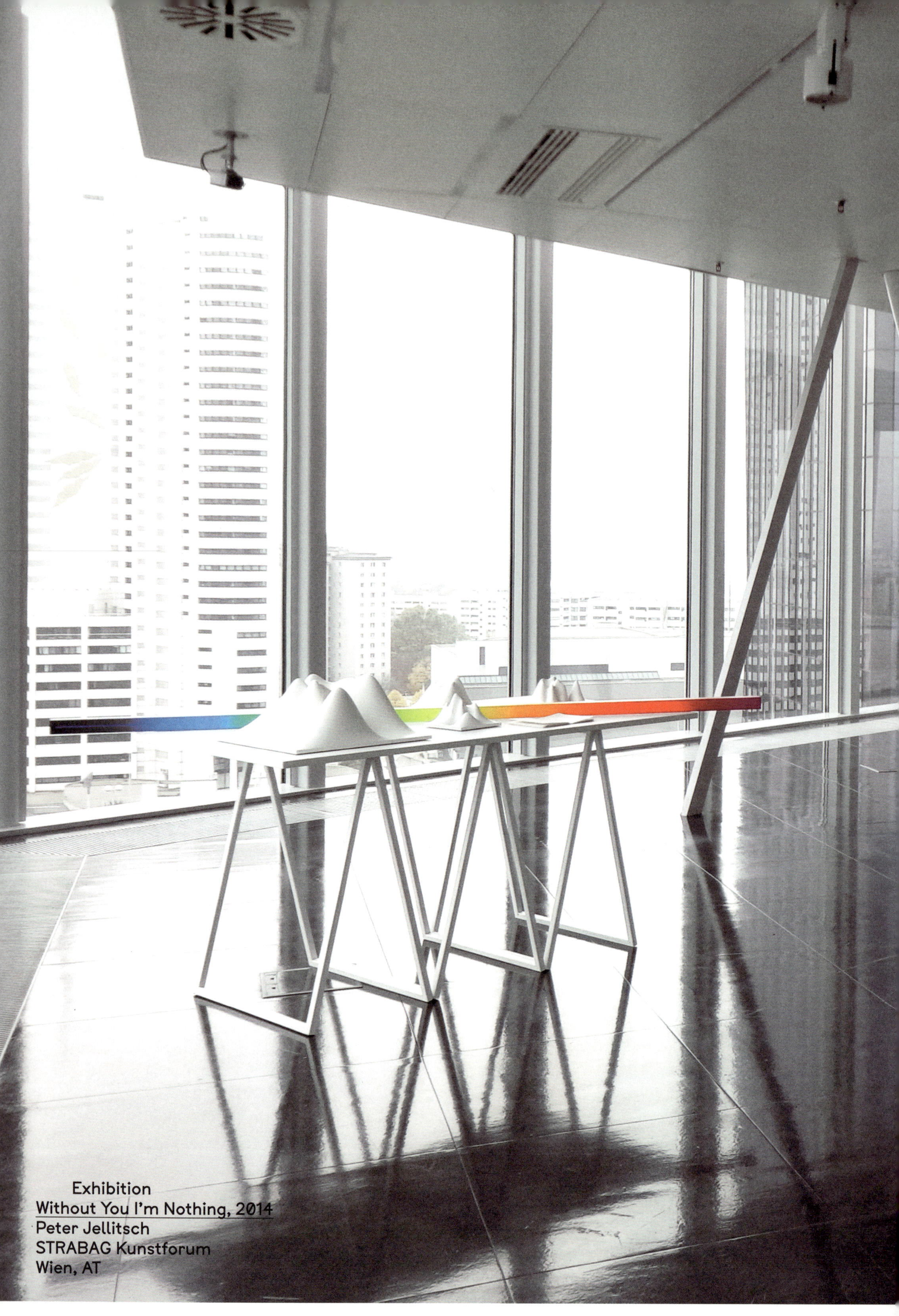

Exhibition
Without You I'm Nothing, 2014
Peter Jellitsch
STRABAG Kunstforum
Wien, AT

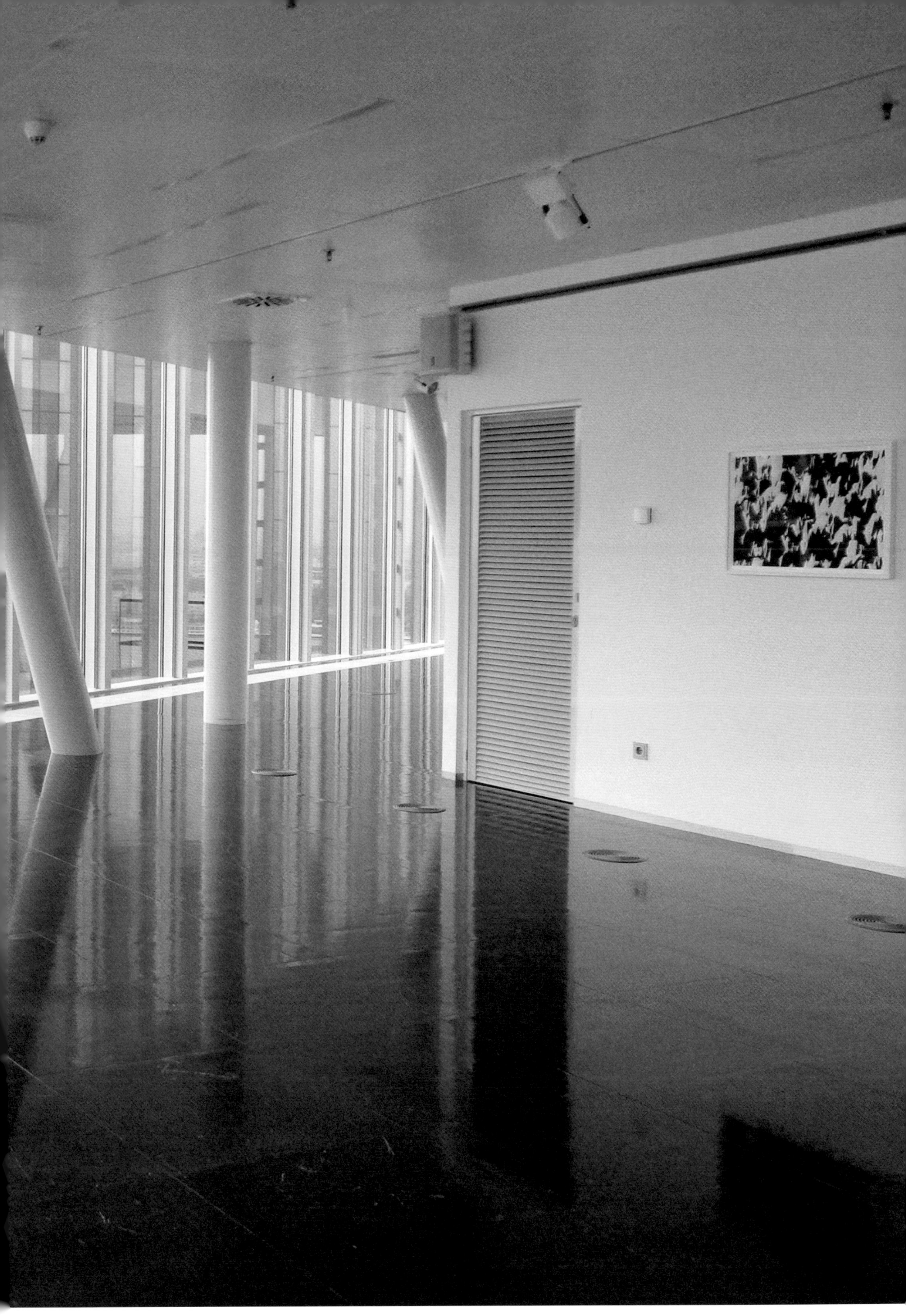

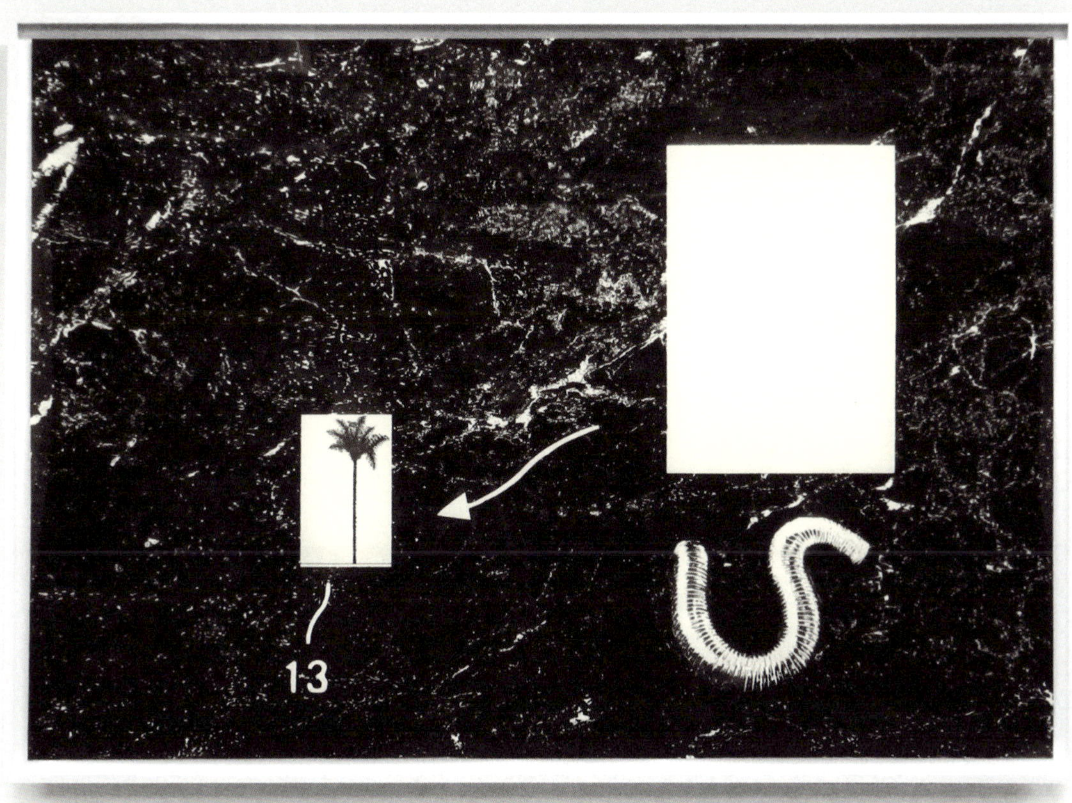

Today in North America, 2014
Ink, pencil, lacquer, acrylic on paper
117×161 cm

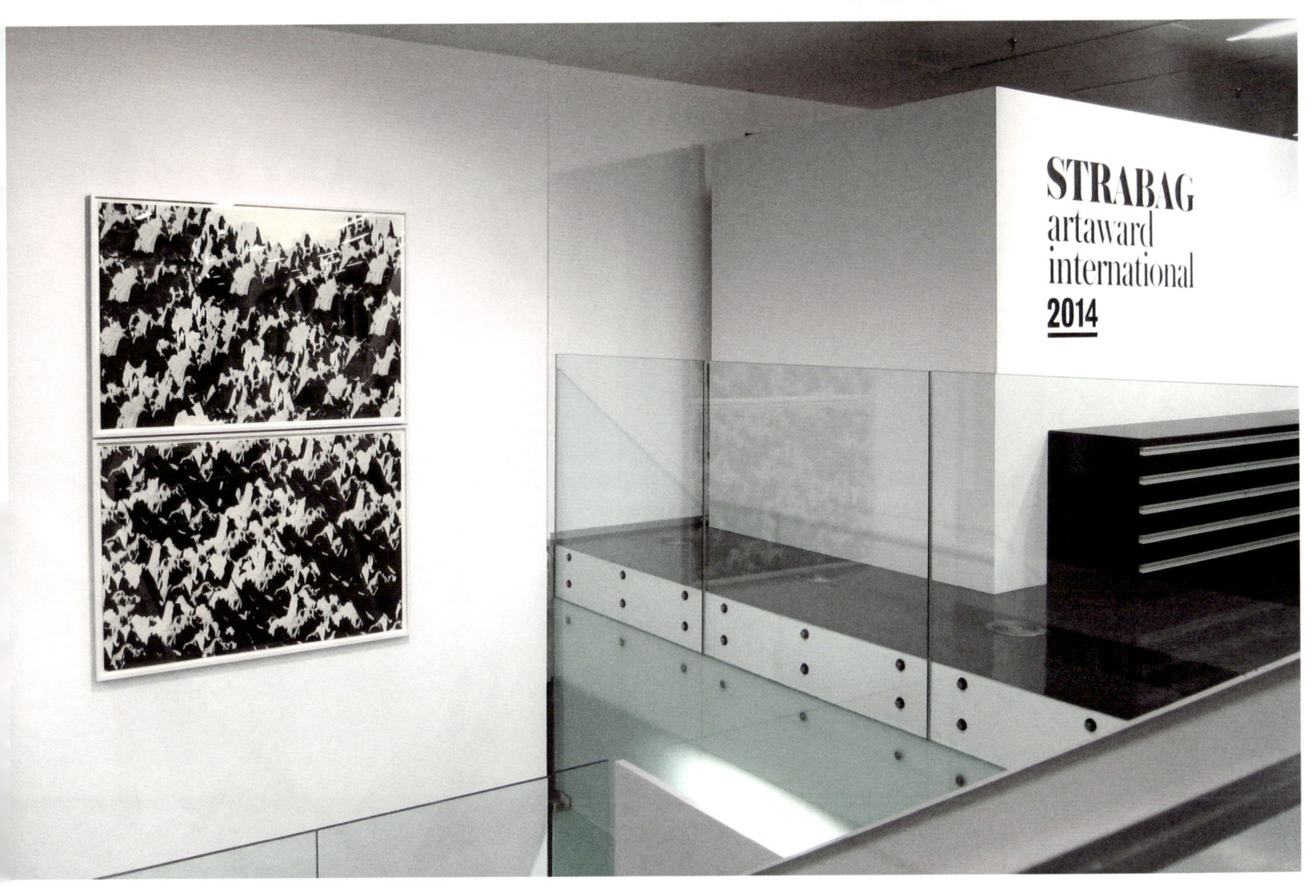

Data Drawing 19, 2014
Pencil, acrylic, crayon, lacquer on paper
110×152 cm

Data Drawing 23, 2014
Pencil, acrylic, crayon, lacquer on paper
110×152 cm

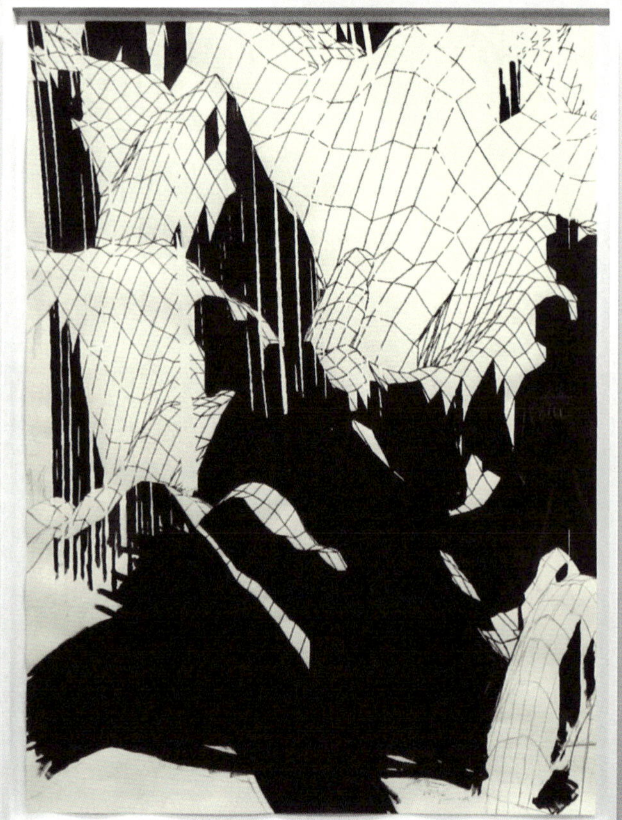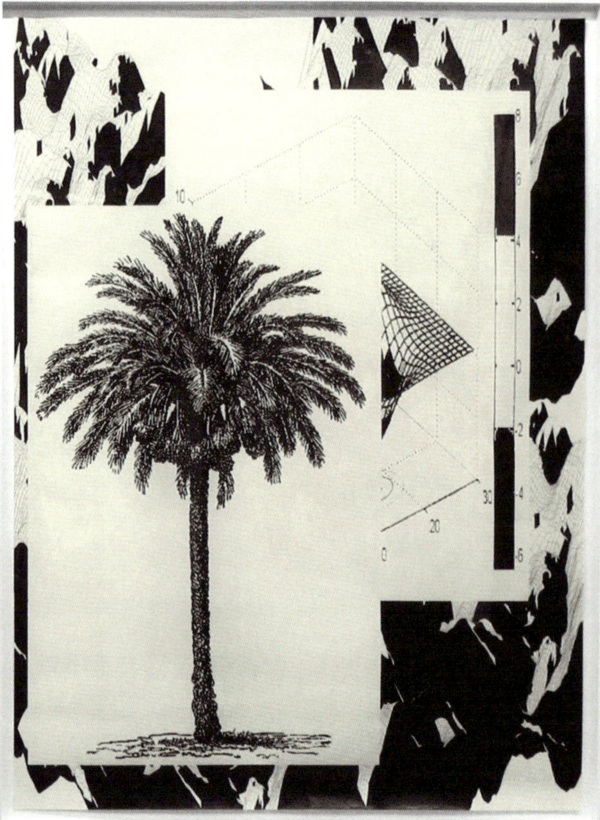

Data Drawing 24+22, 2014
Pencil, acrylic, crayon, lacquer on paper
Each 140×102 cm

(Detail)
Data Drawing 24, 2014

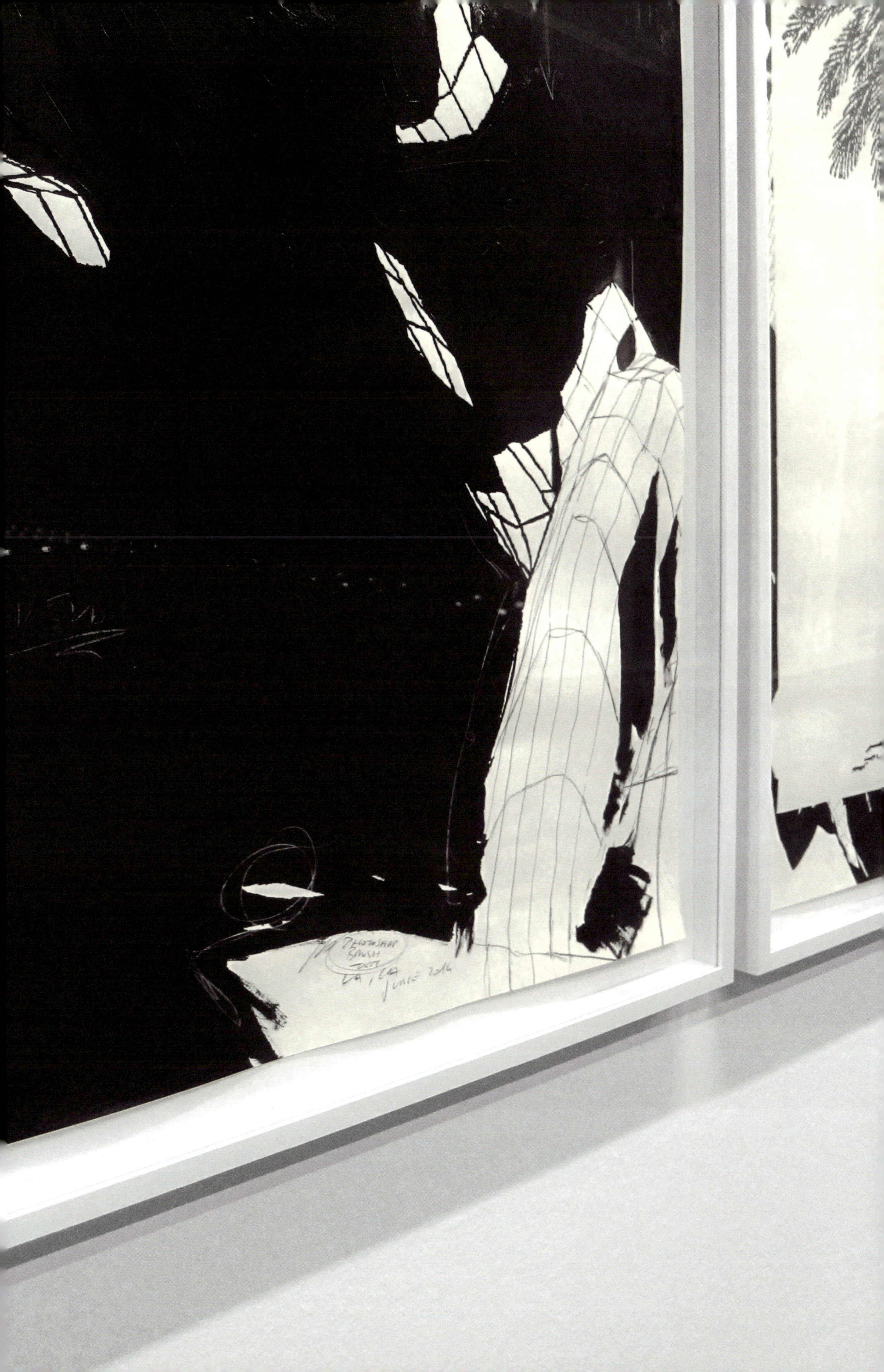

PHOTOSHOP
BRUSH
TEST
LA, CA   JUNE 2016

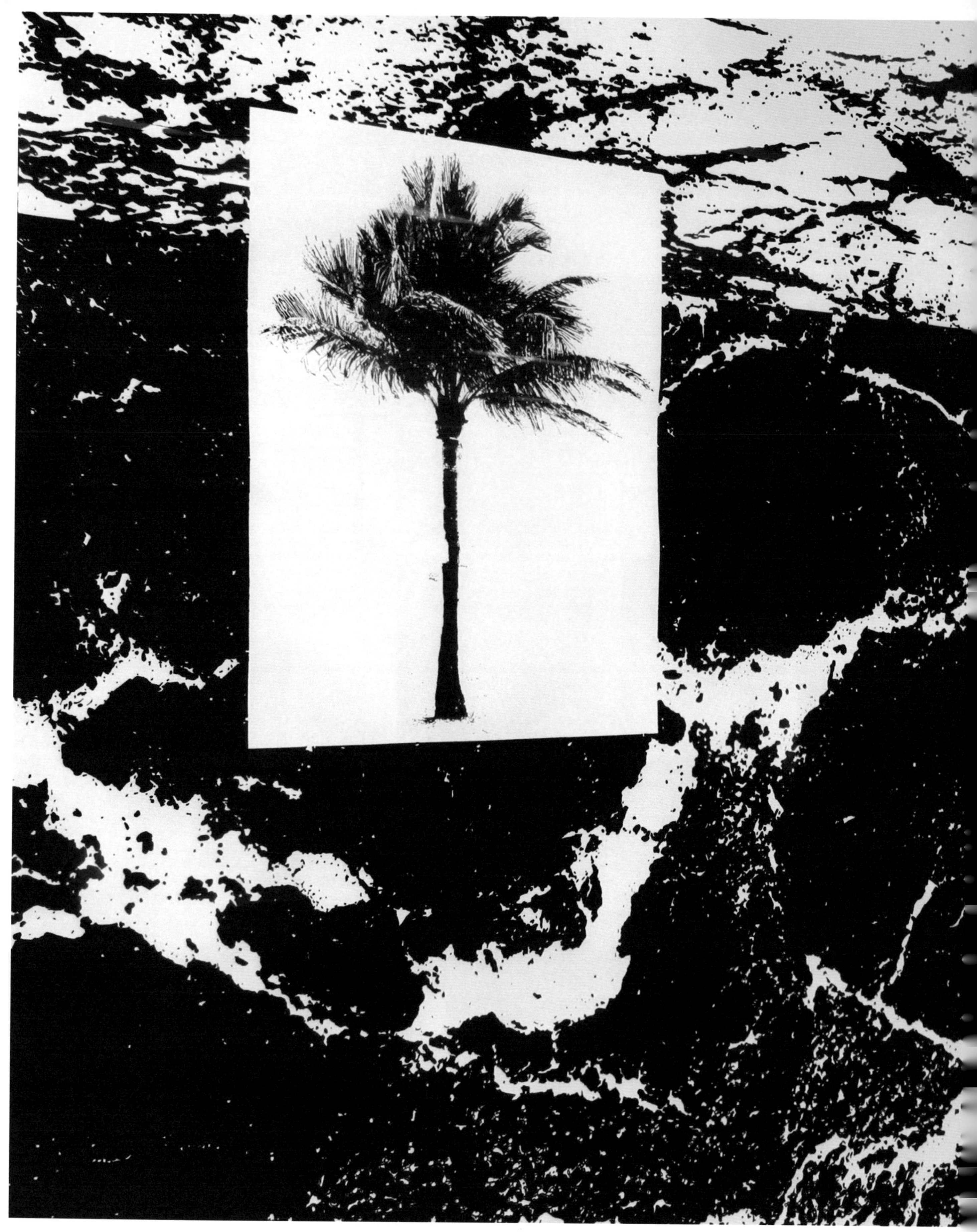

(Detail)
Without You I'm Nothing, 2014

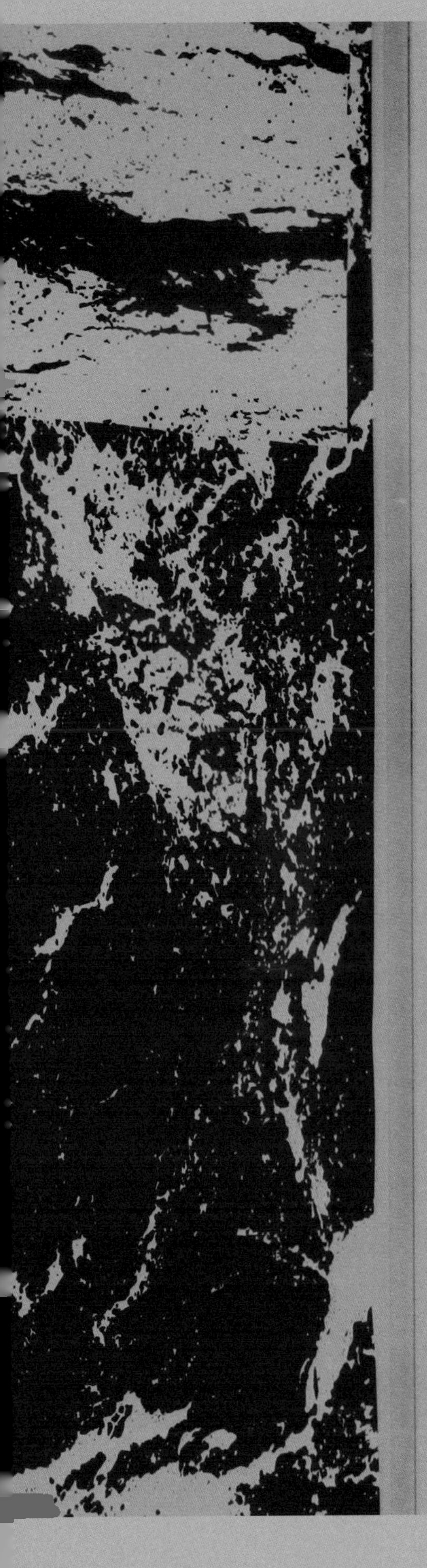

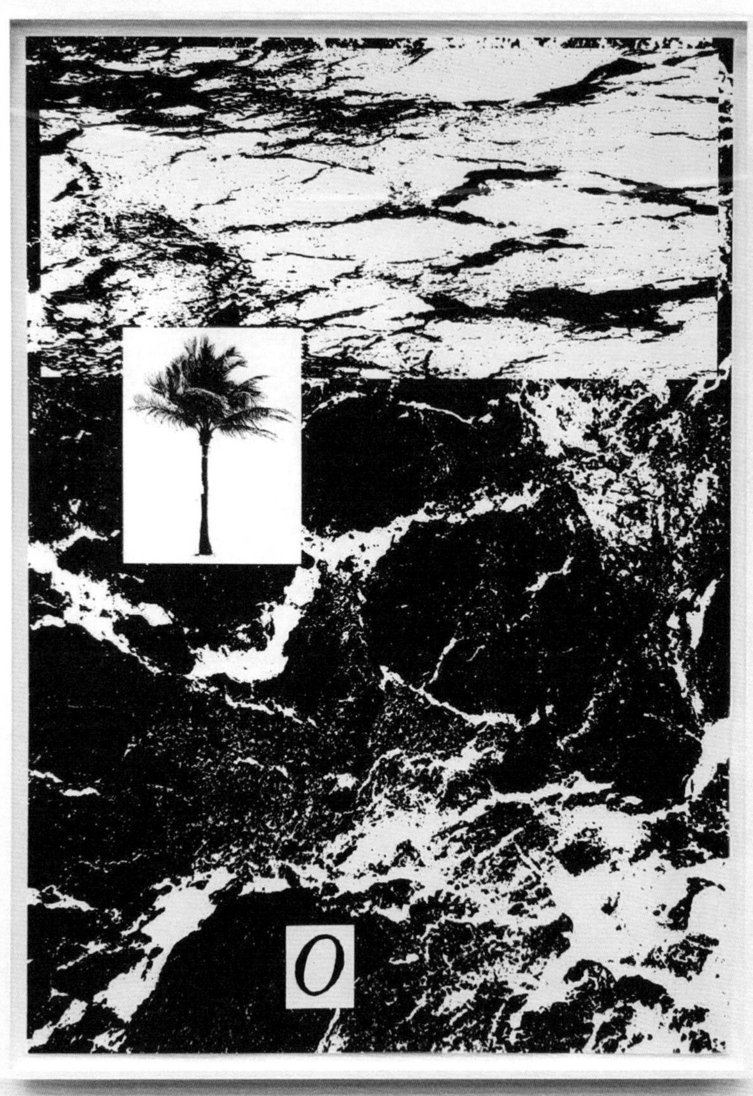

Without You I'm Nothing, 2014
Ink, lacquer, acrylic on paper
157×113 cm

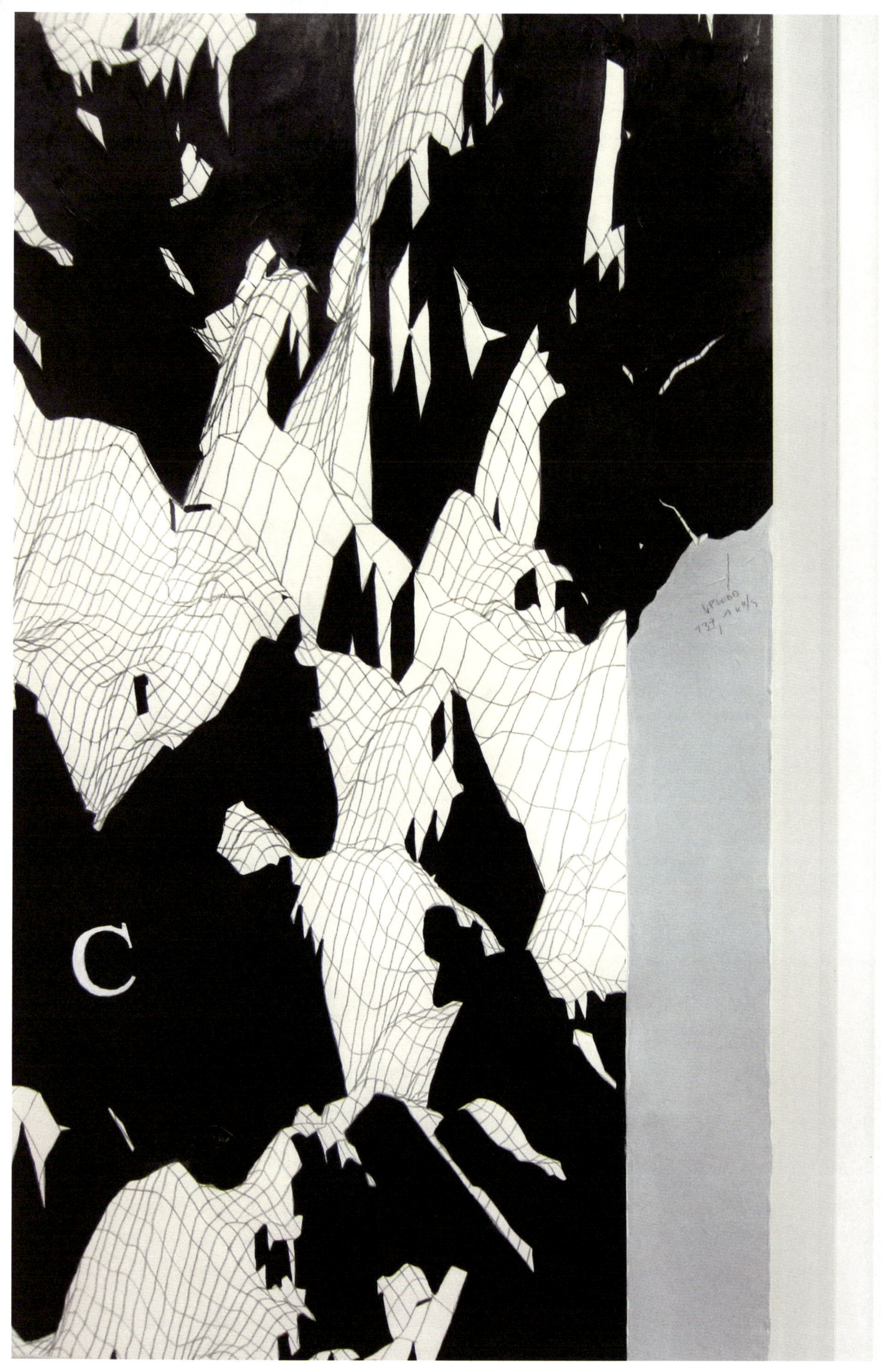

(Detail)
Data Drawing 20, 2014
Pencil, acrylic, crayon, lacquer on paper
161×117 cm

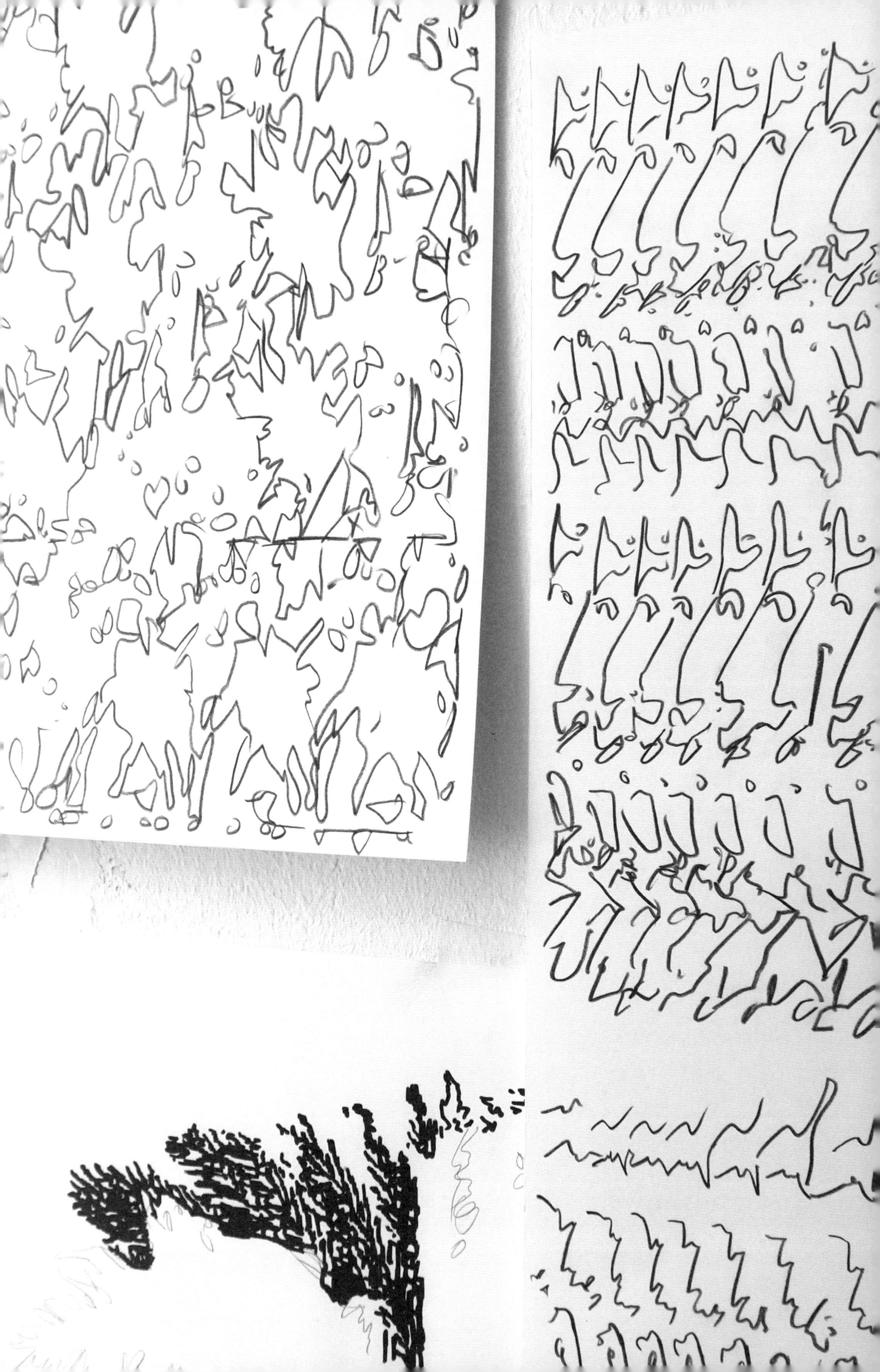

A perpetual and potentially never-ending creation of value from nothing.

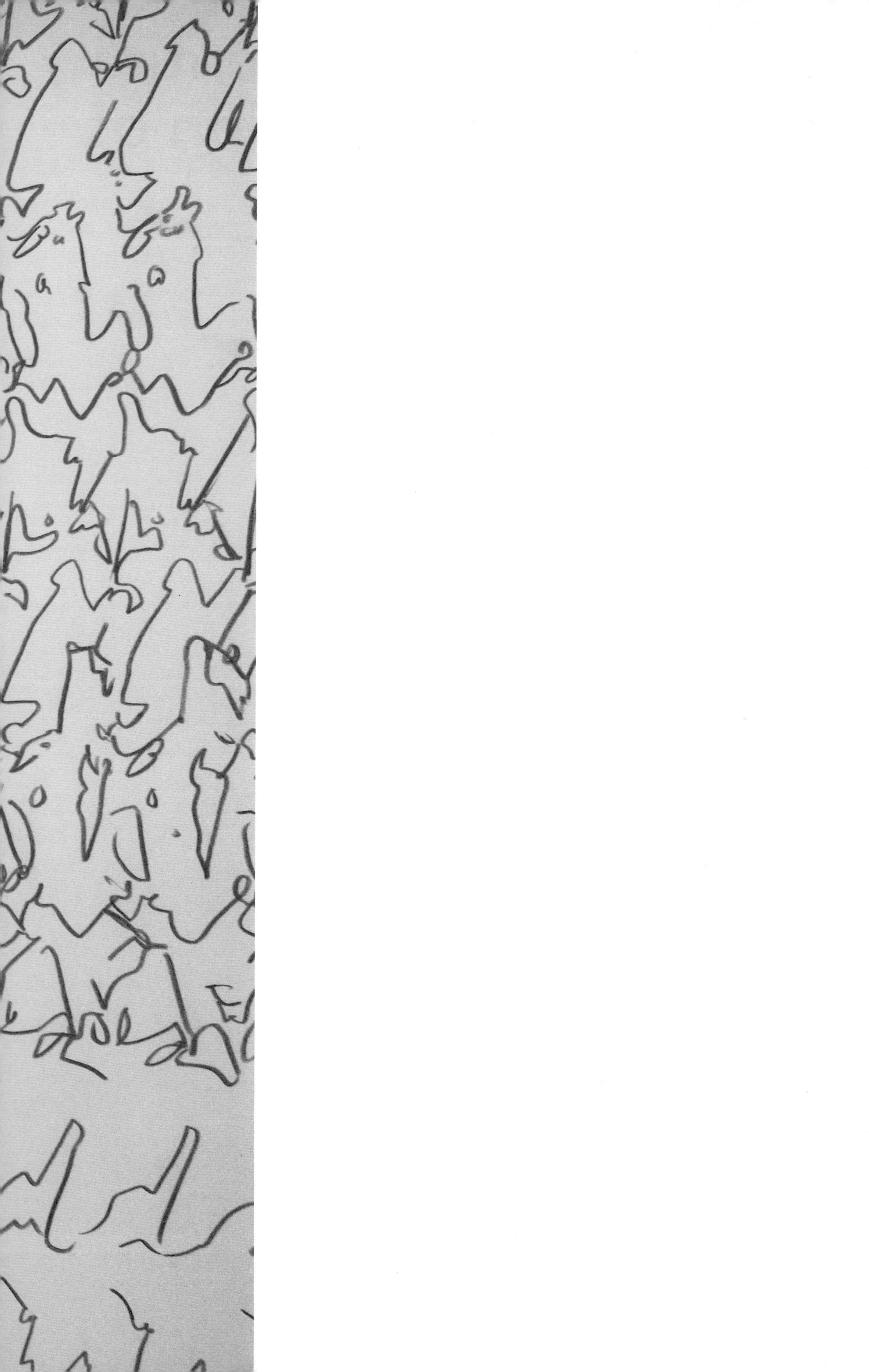

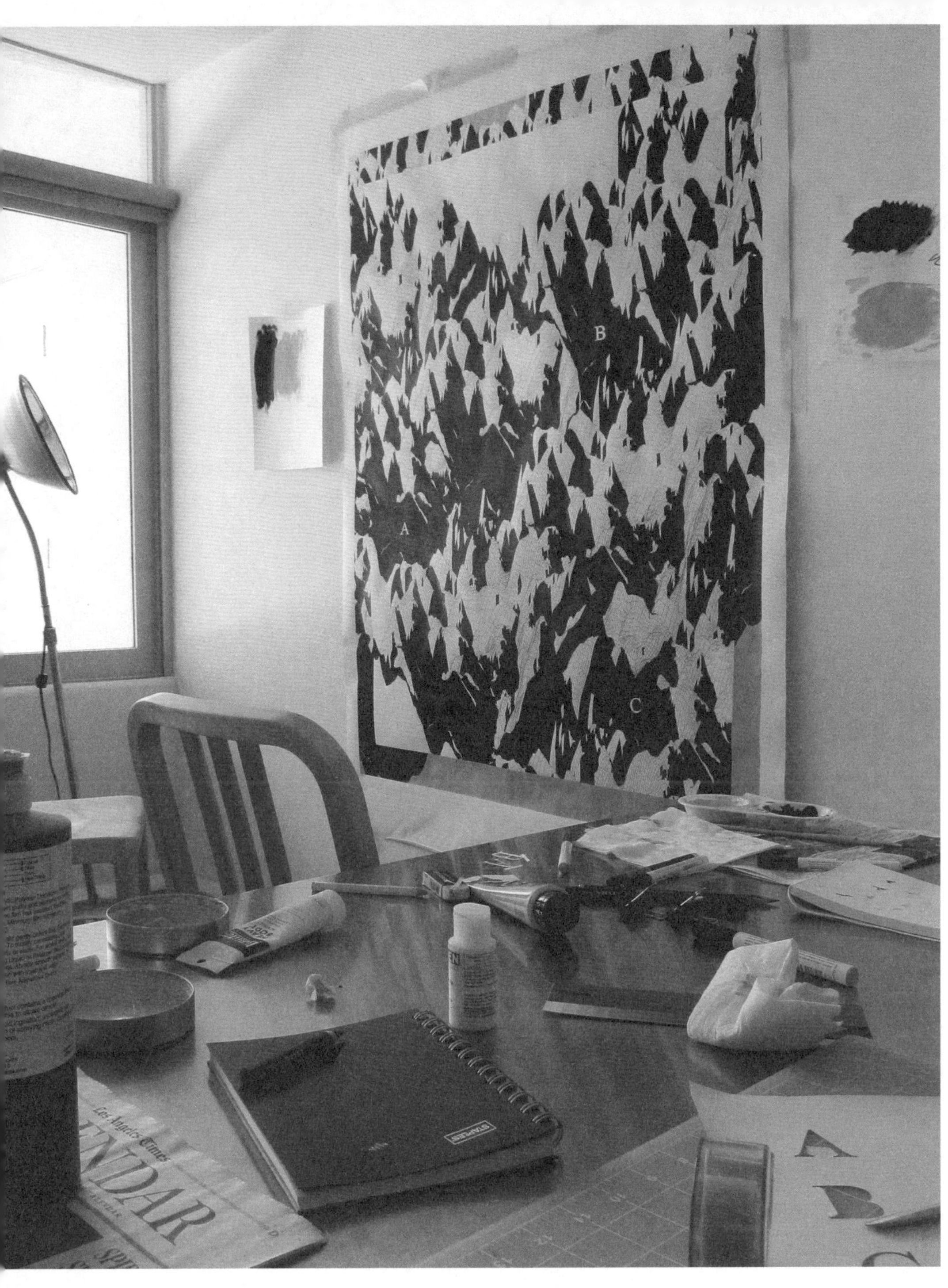

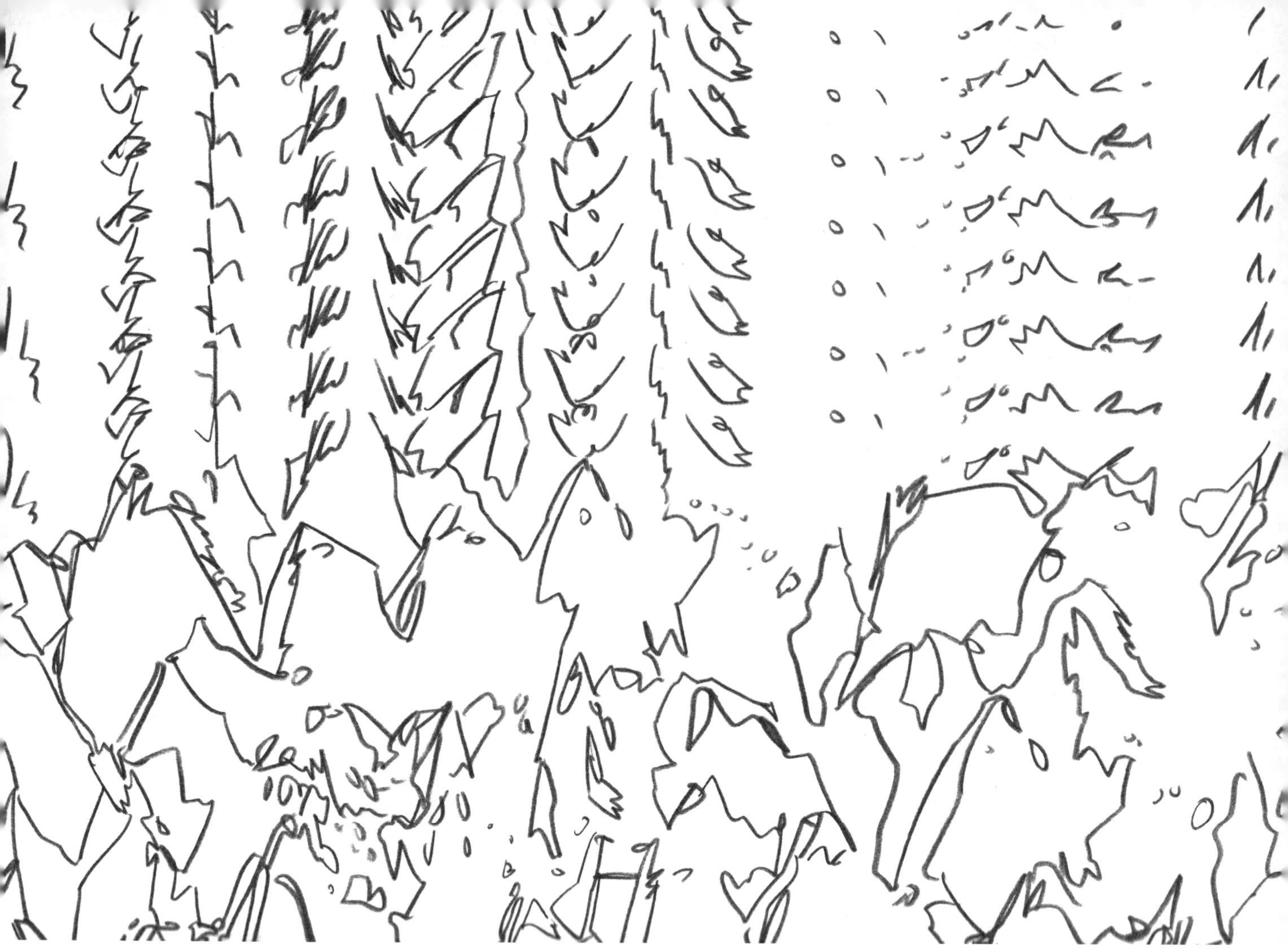

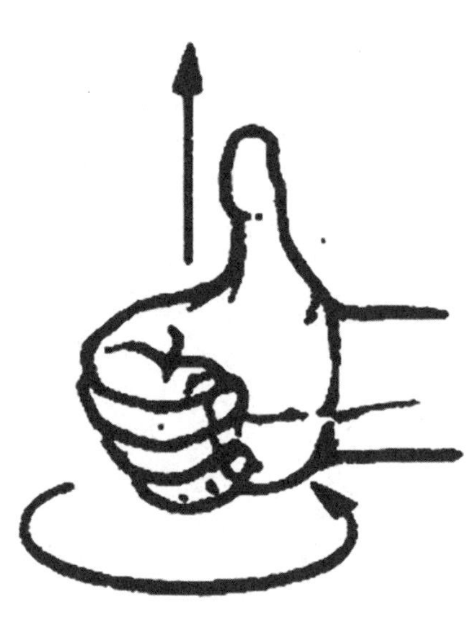

17.22

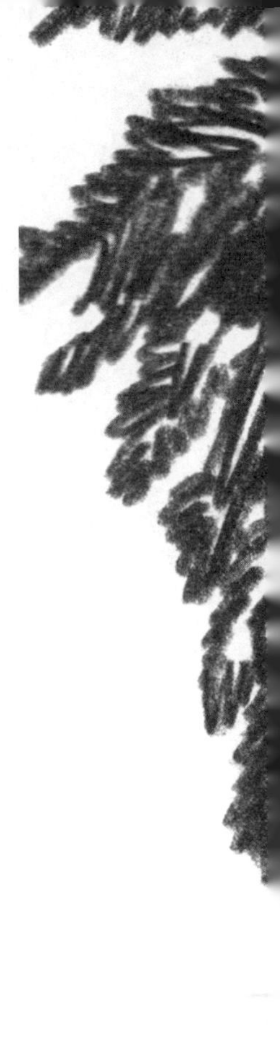

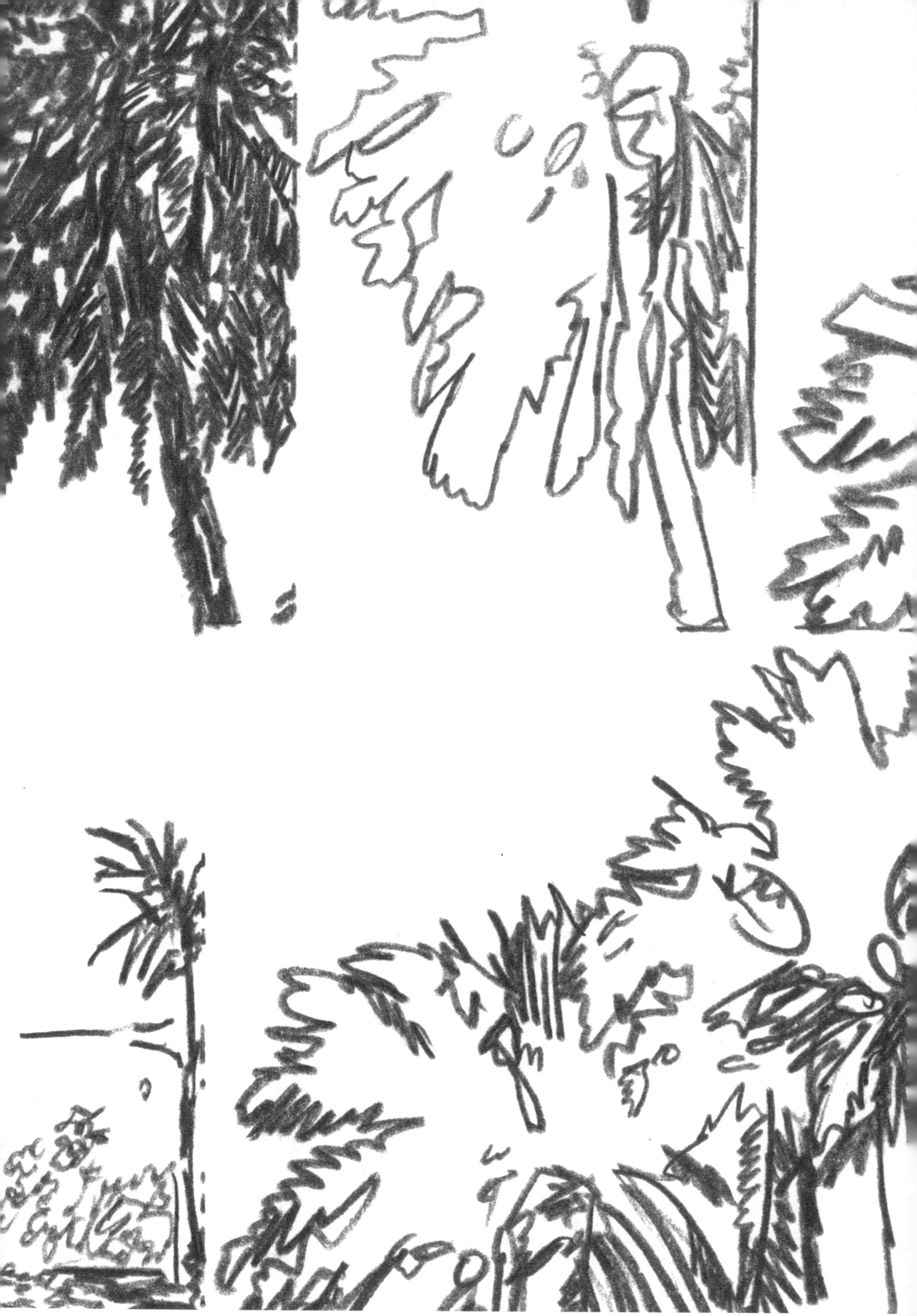

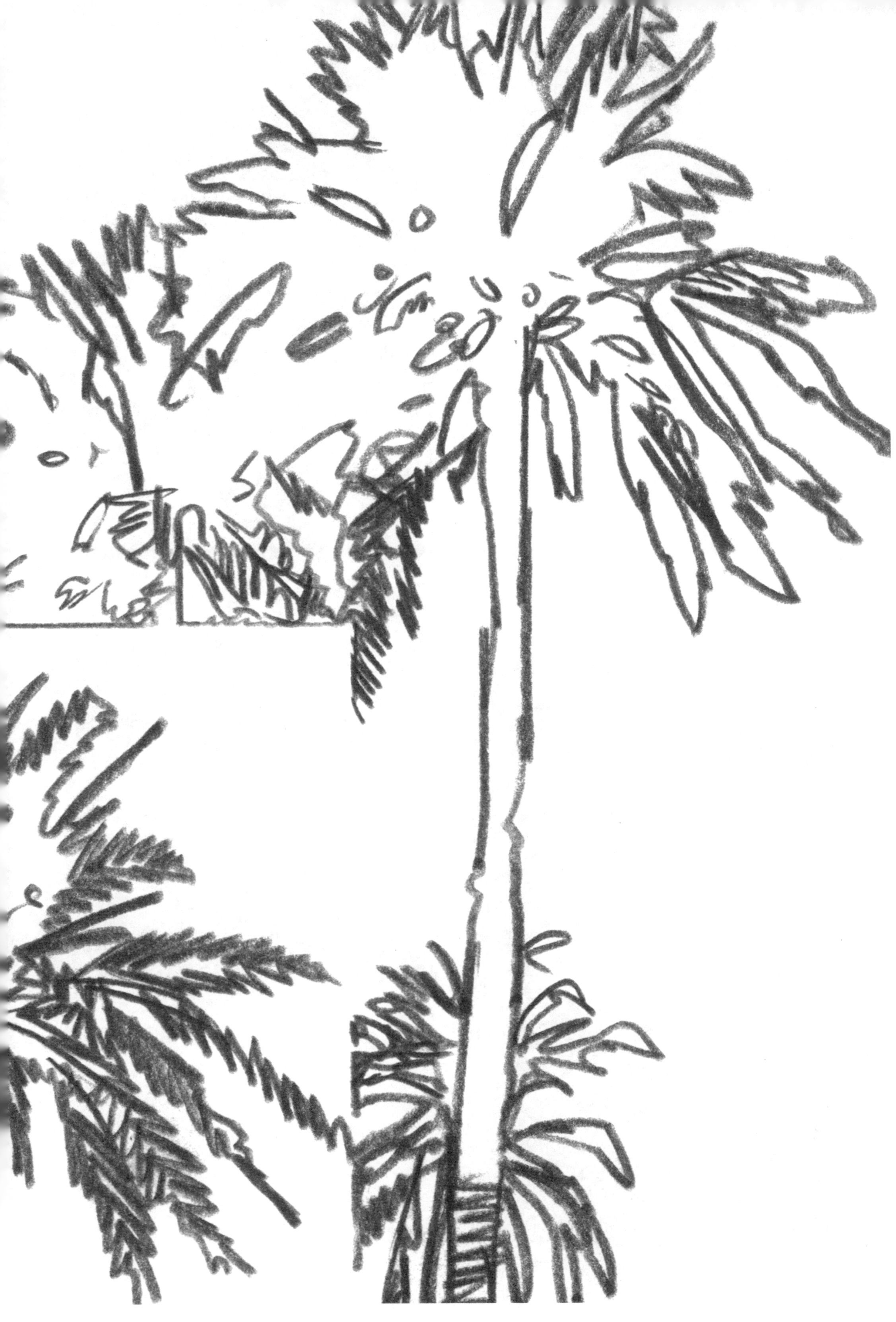

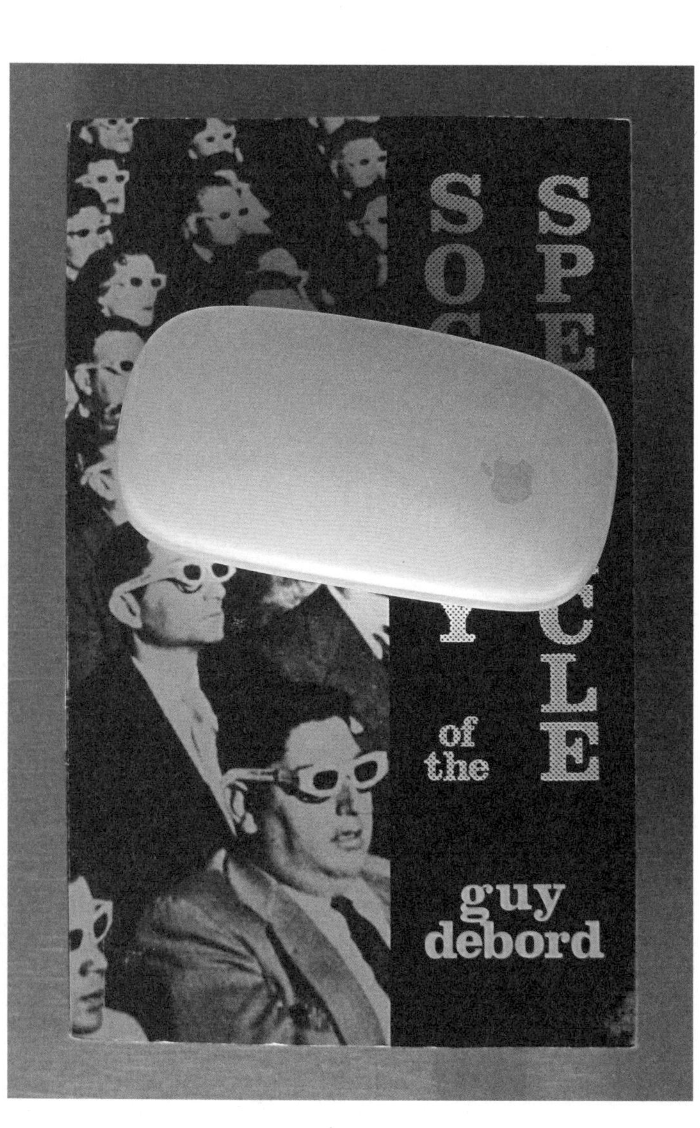

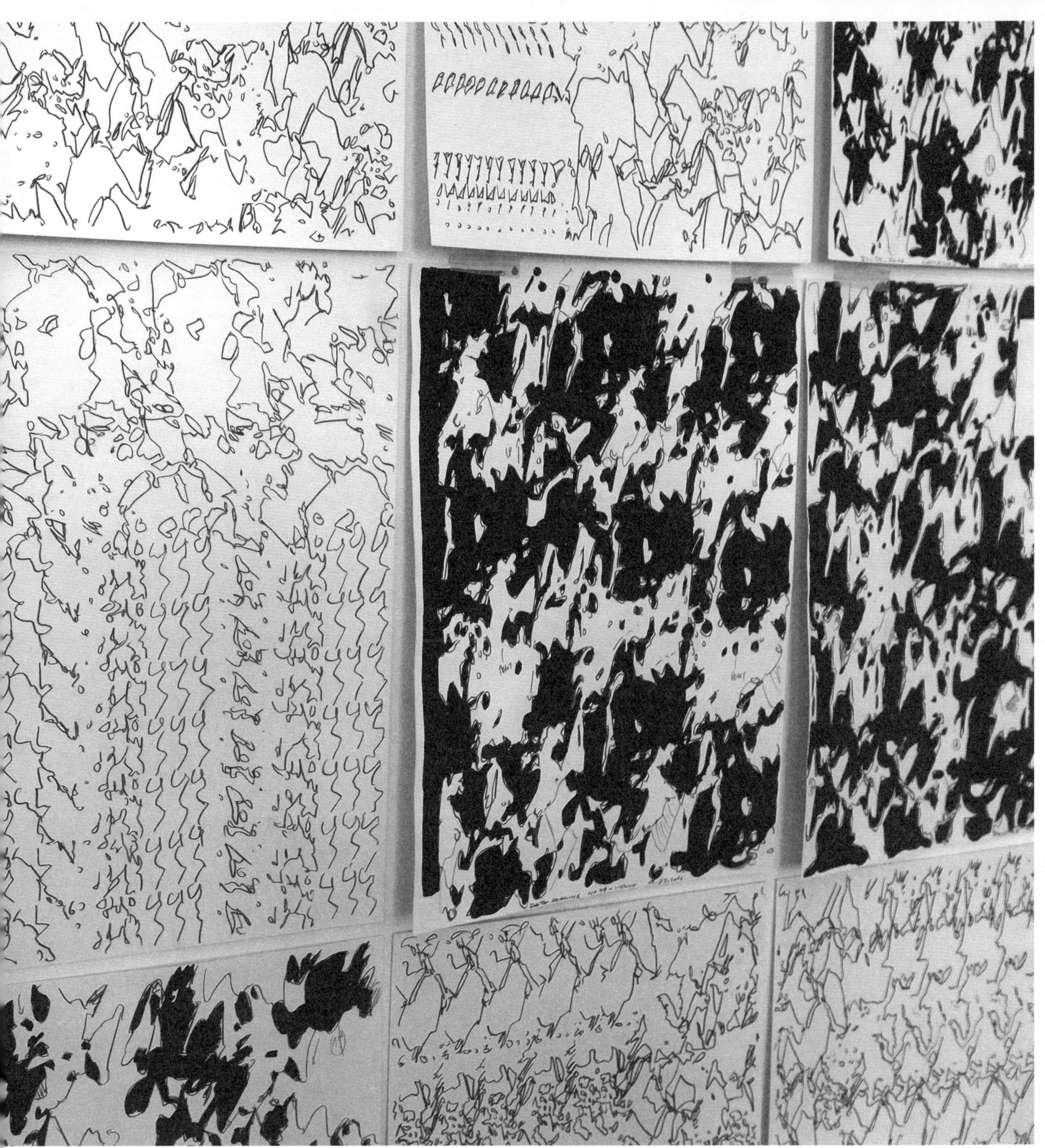

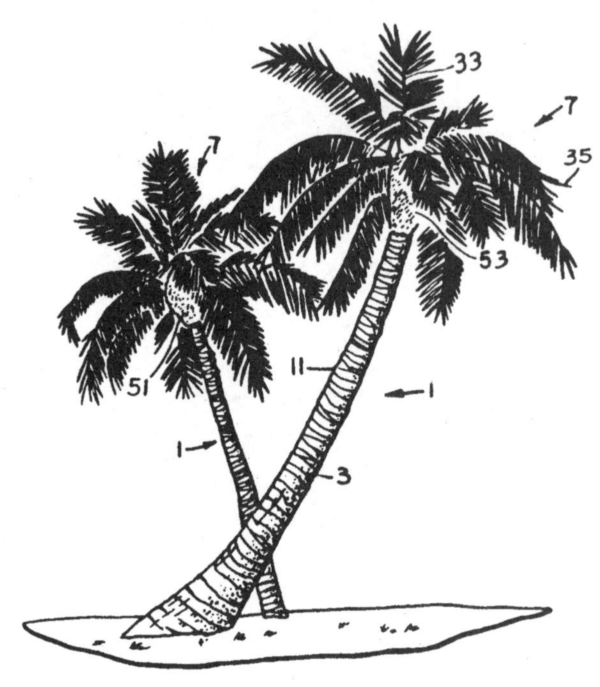
33
7
35
7
53
11
51
1
1
3

"Without You
I'm Nothing" or:
The Relevance
of the Invisible

Marlies Wirth

The first view of Planet Earth from outer space was an important historic event. The technology behind space travel enabled humanity to occupy a new collective vantage point, one that visually anchored what had previously been invisible. The very first, and most famous, color photograph of Earth "from the outside" that Apollo 8 astronauts Borman, Anders, and Lovell took from space on December 24, 1968 entered history with the title *Earthrise*.[1] It became a pictorial icon for an era of new technological possibilities, a point of departure, and simultaneously a symbol for the burgeoning environmental movement because it revealed the finite living space of humanity.

In 1966, after Lunar Orbiter 1's first successful mission to the moon, Stewart Brand — author, activist, and inventor of the term "personal computer" — had already mounted a major campaign challenging NASA to publish a photo of Planet Earth from space. He was convinced that such an image would change our worldview, and not only in the literal sense. In the fall of 1968, he launched the first edition of the *Whole Earth Catalog*, an image of the "whole earth" on the cover. The catalog listed assorted useful and independent tidbits of information about products that support a sustainable lifestyle. Brand's notion of the term "tools" was intended to lead to an understanding of complex "whole systems." He conveyed ideas of global unity, environmental protection, affinity for technology, and cultural networks. Thus, the *Whole Earth Catalog* was eventually cited as a precursor to search engines such as Google[2] and is now considered one of the most important documents of California's counterculture.

The consequences of this event are remotely, yet still concretely, related to the concept underlying the work of Peter Jellitsch, which can be interpreted as a reflection on the socio-cultural transformation process set into motion by the Internet. The *Data Drawings* are premised on a fundamental, and now indispensable, component of life and work today: the Internet, or World Wide Web, whose origins can be found in the continuation of the media discourse that began in the 1960s.[3] If nothing else,

1 According to NASA audio recordings, the image was de facto an unplanned snapshot taken by astronaut William Anders; a short time prior, his colleague, Commander Frank Borman, had taken a similar black and white photo from a different angle. Nowadays this color photograph counts as the most influential environmental photograph ever taken. A black and white photograph taken in August 1966 by the Lunar Orbiter 1 satellite was not publicized by NASA at the time it was taken.

2 The comparison stems from Steve Jobs, who in his 2005 commencement address at Stanford University called the *Whole Earth Catalog* "one of the bibles of [his] generation." "Stay hungry. Stay foolish." (the slogan he frequently quoted later), was from the back cover of the 1974 edition of the *Whole Earth Catalog*. In the 1980s, Stewart Brand's idea of the *Whole Earth Catalog* gave rise to the project The WELL ("Whole Earth 'Lectronic Link"), one of the first virtual social communities lasting to the present.

3 Cf. Marshall McLuhan, *Understanding Media: The Extensions of Man* (1964); Marshall McLuhan & Quentin Fiore, *The Medium is the Massage* (1968).

the stylized icon of the globe is a symbol for "the Internet" and our networked world, the only material prerequisite being the constant availability of an online connection. Against a background of technological and digital achievements since the first view of Planet Earth, the *Data Drawings* illustrate our present time in a formal-aesthetic way as the pervasive chronicling and analysis of people, goods, and data across the global network. Through the physical act of drawing, Peter Jellitsch makes the invisibility of data discernable in a visual symbolization of what the global network produces: a perpetual and potentially never-ending creation of value from nothing.

The quintessential success of the Internet, which has significantly changed our society, rests upon the possibility of exchanging data at high speeds, whereby the increasing rapidity (bandwidth) of this exchange has been the most significant driver of its development and possibilities. Such network connections' data is the foundation and starting point for Peter Jellitsch's artistic work. In his *Data Drawings*—large-scale, topographical drawings—he gives physical form to the invisible digital processes that surround us. Using application software, the artist recorded measurable data off of WLAN connections—ping, download and upload rate. After noting the actual numerical values, Peter Jellitsch creates an initial pictorial representation by diagramming the deviations in the Internet connection along the axes of time and intensity. He then repetitively translates the diagrams into formally complex drawings (pencil, colored pencil, paint, and acrylic) evocative of landscape topographies. With this process, precise numerical values are translated into an abstract artistic gesture, whereby the invisible manifests itself in a tangible object—the drawing—with the unmistakable variability of human imprecision.

A quasi homage and wink in reference to On Kawara's famous *Date Paintings* is given not only by the choice of title of Peter Jellitsch's *Data Drawings*: every *Data Drawing* is simultaneously a snapshot and a mapping of the Internet connection of the artist's whereabouts at the time of the measurement. The day of the measurement is the day of the drawing, therewith combining concept and repetition. The act of (re)counting invisible data at the artist's immediate location becomes process-contingent self-monitoring and makes a statement about the status quo of the networked world. In the surveillance society of the 21st century, the Internet's trove of data is tapped at central hubs; state power is defined by access to, and ownership of, information as a critical resource. In the sense of a "transparency society," the position of the monitor has shifted and become decentralized. In *The Agony of Power*, Baudrillard describes the end of the perspectival "panopticon": "The eye of the TV is no longer the source of an absolute gaze, and the ideal of control is no longer that of transparency. This still presupposes an objective space (that of the Renaissance) and the omnipotence of the despotic gaze."[4] The "digital panopticon" of the 21st century lacks perspective inasmuch as surveillance is no longer conducted from an omnipotent central point, but from within itself. The omnipresence of voluntary scrutiny is the essence of its efficiency.[5]

One could think of On Kawara as the first "self-tracker" who kept and published precise records of when he got up, where he went, whom he met, and what he read.[6] The surveying and cartography of data in the digital era is a tool for intellectually grappling with the processes underpinning social and political developments. The augmentation of the numeral can be seen as a sign of the ever-increasing measurability and quantification of the human being,[7] who willingly or unwittingly contributes to the sprawling data linkages around the world. Inspired by Edward Snowden's revelations, which raised people's awareness about the overall reach of the global surveillance network, American infographic designer Nicholas Felton, over the course of several years, developed and published his "Personal Annual Reports" wherein he visualized, using graphs, maps, and statistics, an assortment of the personal data and metadata from his communications (such as how frequently he used certain communications platforms, how frequently he emailed, etc.).[8]

4   Cf. Jean Baudrillard, *Agonie des Realen*, (Merve Verlag Berlin, 1978), 48. English translation from Byung-Chul Han, *The Transparency Society*, translation by Eric Butler, (Stanford: Stanford University Press, 2015), 45.

5   Byung-Chul Han, *Transparenzgesellschaft*, (Berlin: Mattes & Seitz, 2013), 49.

6   In his series of works *I Got Up, I Went, I Met, I Read*, On Kawara kept a record of his daily personal activities for twelve years (1968 to 1979).

7   Cf. www.quantifiedself.com.

8   Cf. http://feltron.com.

By chronicling the Internet connection in his *Data Drawings*, Peter Jellitsch also inscribes coded information about his whereabouts into his drawings. In contrast to Kawara or Felton, however, this isn't about the immanence of the information per se, but about the visualization of their intangibility. The Internet is the vector of a new geography; it has conjured up virtual spaces that overlap with real ones and transformed our society and the way we navigate through the world.

Through the process of their genesis, the *Data Drawings* become an interface between knowledge and experience, that enables the artist to uncover the processes of a networked world from an objectivized standpoint. Jellitsch constructs a topography of invisible data, as described in the "map-territory relation": in its translation, measured information is abstracted and utilized for orientation. With digital data, the aura of the original[9] is not lost in repetition—it remains identical over the course of its reproduction and dissemination. In the process of its visualization the data becomes material funneled into a process of aesthetic refinement.

With his symbolic structure of readings from a source of omnipresent WLAN connections, the artist transforms his data recordings into an imaginative topographical overview without a function—the information behind the diagrammatic spikes is no longer decipherable;—big data analyses come to naught in the encrypted poetry of the artistic gesture of drawing.

The artist applies the paradigmatic and inductive thought process of abstraction to the data he has selected for processing. For example, in several of the *Data Drawings*, palm trees stand as significates for the data source: they show the types of palm trees used in the US as models for concealed wireless antennas, also known as "monopalms" based on a word play of monopoly and palm.[10] In Los Angeles, Jellitsch became acquainted with the peculiar camouflaging of cell phone and wireless towers on public land while taking part in the MAK-Schindler Artists and Architects-in-Residence Program. During his six-month stay, he developed the first comprehensive series of *Data Drawings*.

9 Walter Benjamin, *Das Kunstwerk im Zeitalter seiner technischen Reproduzierbarkeit* (1936).

10 This was accompanied in 2016 by Peter Jellitsch's artist book *Palm Tree Antenna*.

11 Cf. Boris Groys, "Entering the Flow," in: C. Cox, J. Jaskey, S. Malik (eds.), *Realism, Materialism, Art*, Center for Curatorial Studies, Bard College, (New York: Sternberg Press, 2015): 79–80.

12 Cf. Boris Groys, "Kosmische Angst," in: 9. *Berlin Biennale für zeitgenössische Kunst*, 2016:112.

13 Cf. Boris Groys, "Kosmische Angst," in: 9. *Berlin Biennale für zeitgenössische Kunst*, 2016:113.

14 Cf. Jean Baudrillard, *Simulacra and Simulation* (1981): http://www.bconrad-williams.com/files/7313/9690/1991/Baudrillard-Jean-Simulacra-And-Simulation2.pdf, https://web.stanford.edu/class/history34q/readings/Baudrillard/Baudrillard_Simulacra.html.

15 The title chosen by Peter Jellitsch for his solo exhibition on the occasion of the STRABAG Artaward — *Without You I'm Nothing* — was the title of a 2011 exhibition in Chicago, where the physical presence of the viewers was incorporated into the artistic works as a condition for their reception. Peter Jellitsch has reinterpreted this statement for his work to signify the immaterial presence of the data, without which his works would not exist.

Every space — physical or virtual — is virtually manifested as a "data packet." The common notion of the "data flows" that stream through the immaterial territories of the networked world must be examined, for digital data production is neither fluid nor immaterial: Across the Internet, every piece of information has its place, its "address," and hence, can be tracked and retrieved at any time.[11] The grid as the central design system of modernity aims at unification and reproducibility, a principle that also can be transferred to the standardization of social systems and sociopolitical developments in general. In a continuously controlled and monitored world, all data and its movements are verifiable and registered in the network — even the Internet is materially and metaphysically inscribed in the earth and will succumb to its fate, like all media up to now, except perhaps in even more radical fashion.[12] Human beings and their data are dependent on everything that happens (politically, economically, and ecologically) on Planet Earth, and even *it* is not isolated in its position within a cosmic whole.[13] "The invisible" in the form of the *Data Drawing* becomes an emblem of Baudrillard's hyperreality: a simulacrum without an example, a model of the real without origin and without reality.[14]

Thus we come full circle to the reference mentioned at the outset. With the image of the whole earth something came into view for the first time that for most of us will always remain invisible — the view of the planet we live on, from the perspective of an indeterminable "out there," which made it very clear that without our planet, there would be no "us," no people, no data, no network, no art: *Without You I'm Nothing*.[15]

Marlies Wirth (*1980) is a curator of MAK — Austrian Museum of Applied Arts/Contemporary Art, Vienna since 2006. She is curating exhibitions, performances, and discursive events in the fields of art, design and architecture, including the *HOLLEIN* retrospective (2014) and the themed group show *24/7: the human condition* for the VIENNA BIENNALE 2015 or the series APPLIED ARTS. NOW with solo exhibitions of a younger generation of artists, designers and architects. With a focus on conceptual, site-specific, research-, and time-based art and a particular interest in the cultural-anthropological contexts of artistic production, she also develops independent exhibition projects with international artists and contributes texts and essays for various publications.

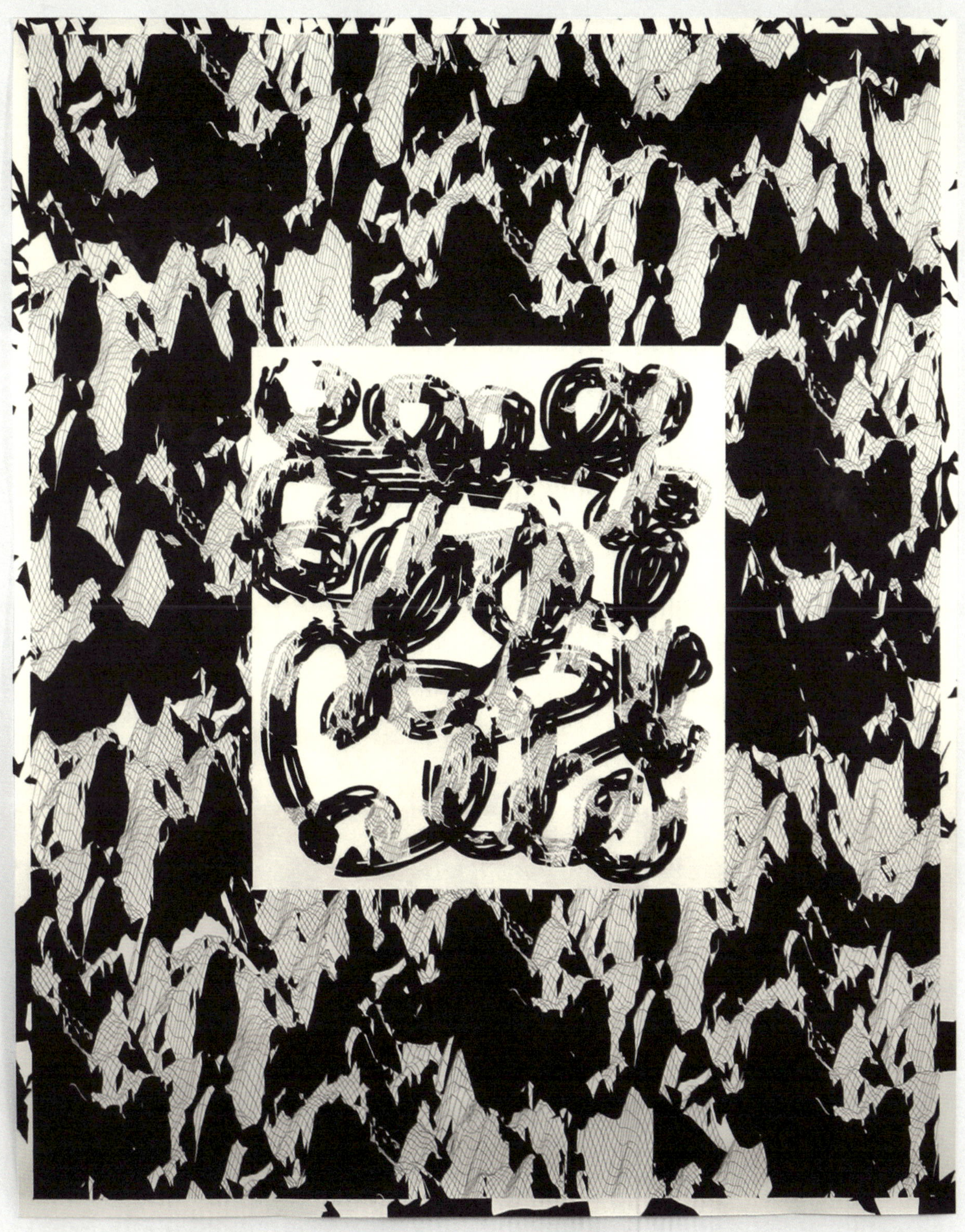

Data Drawing 27, 2015
Pencil, acrylic, crayon, lacquer on paper
155×120 cm

(Detail) (next page)
Data Drawing 27, 2015

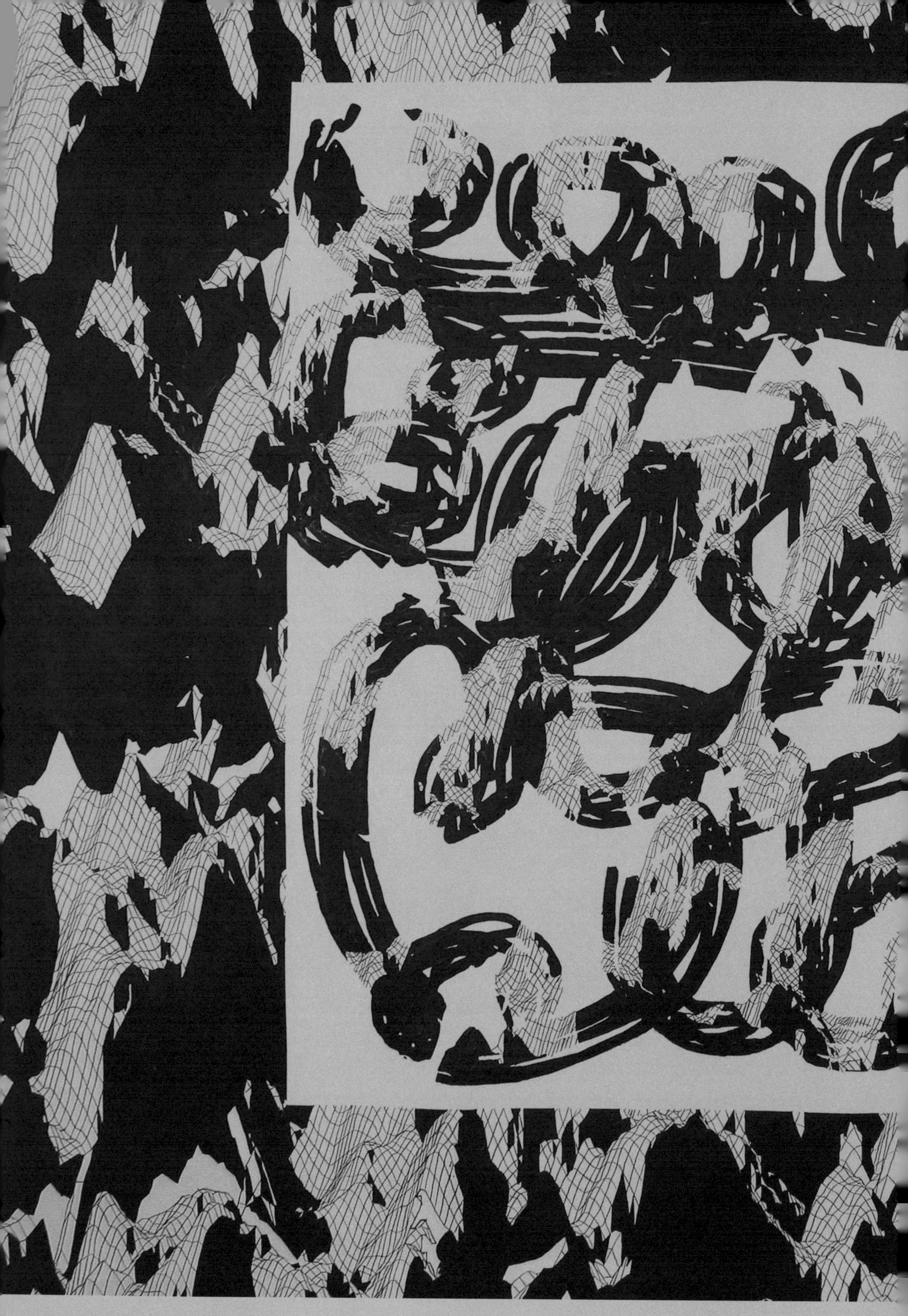

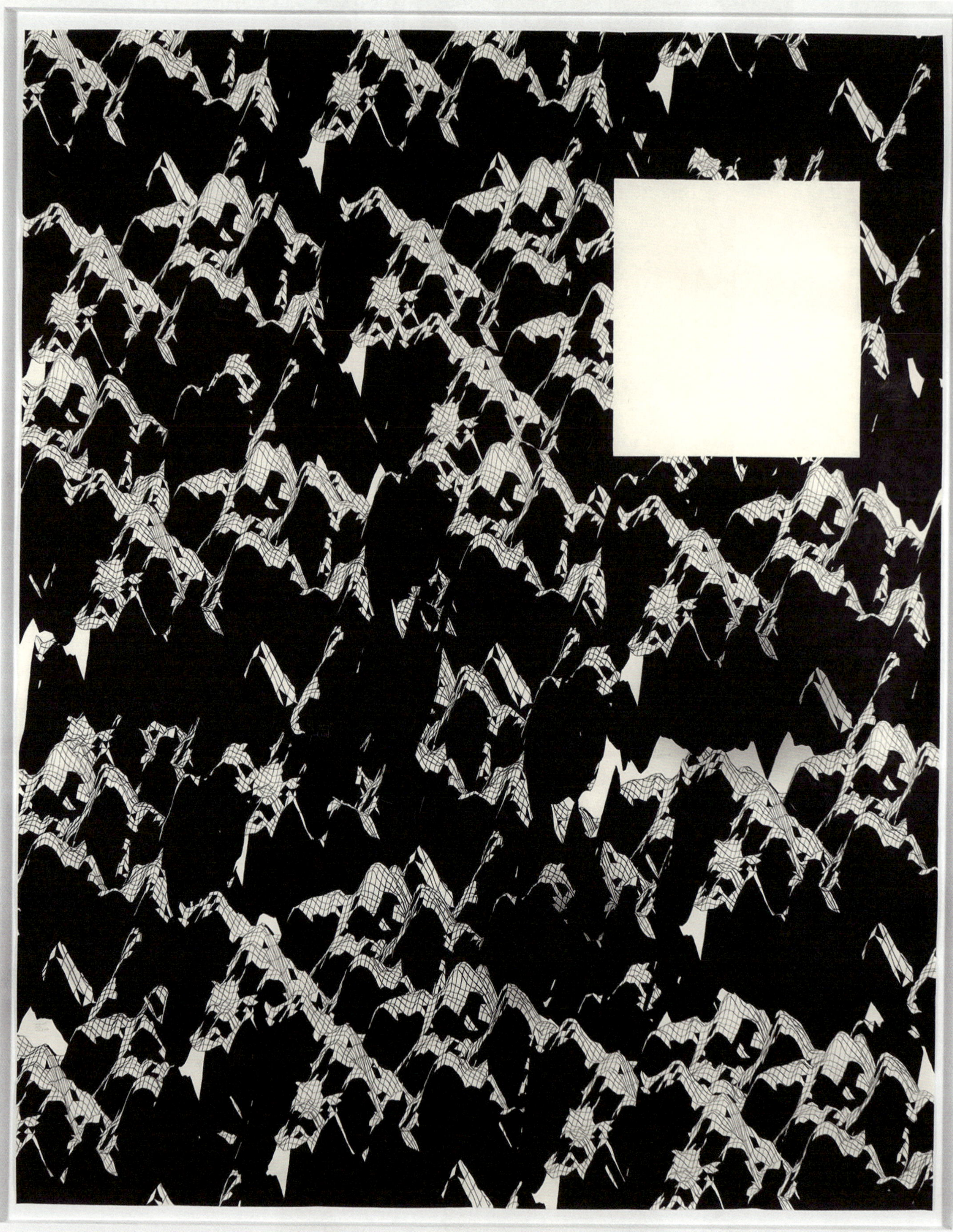

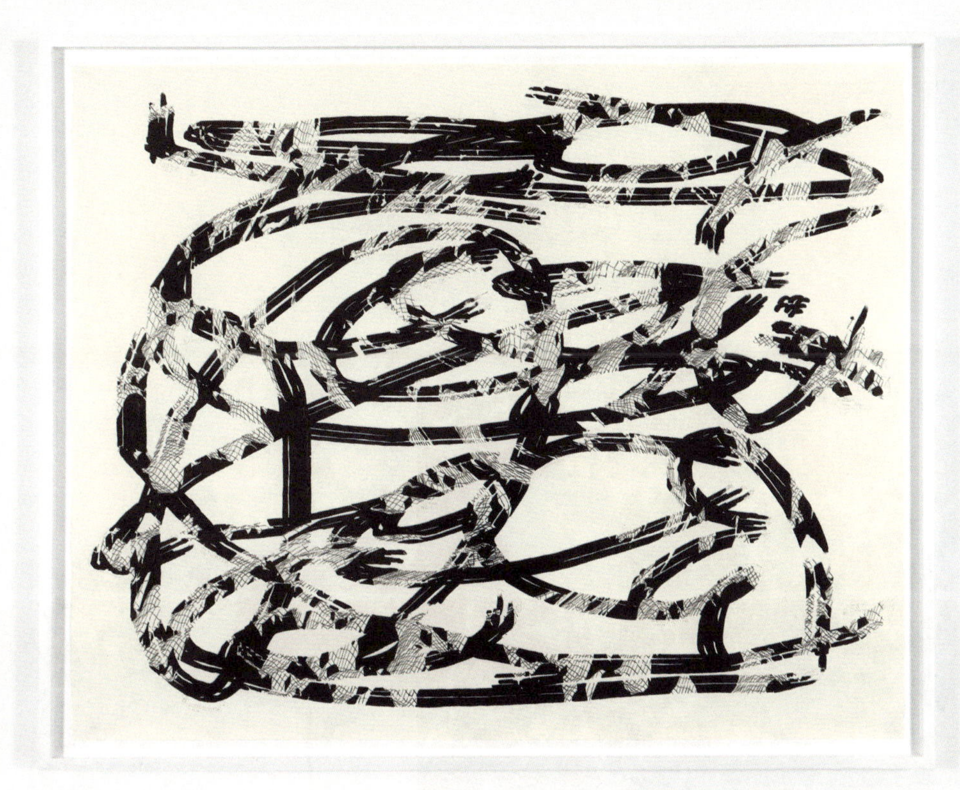

Data Drawing 29, 2015　(left page)
Pencil, acrylic, crayon, lacquer on paper
155×120 cm

Data Drawing 30, 2015　(above)
Pencil, acrylic, crayon, lacquer on paper
86×106 cm

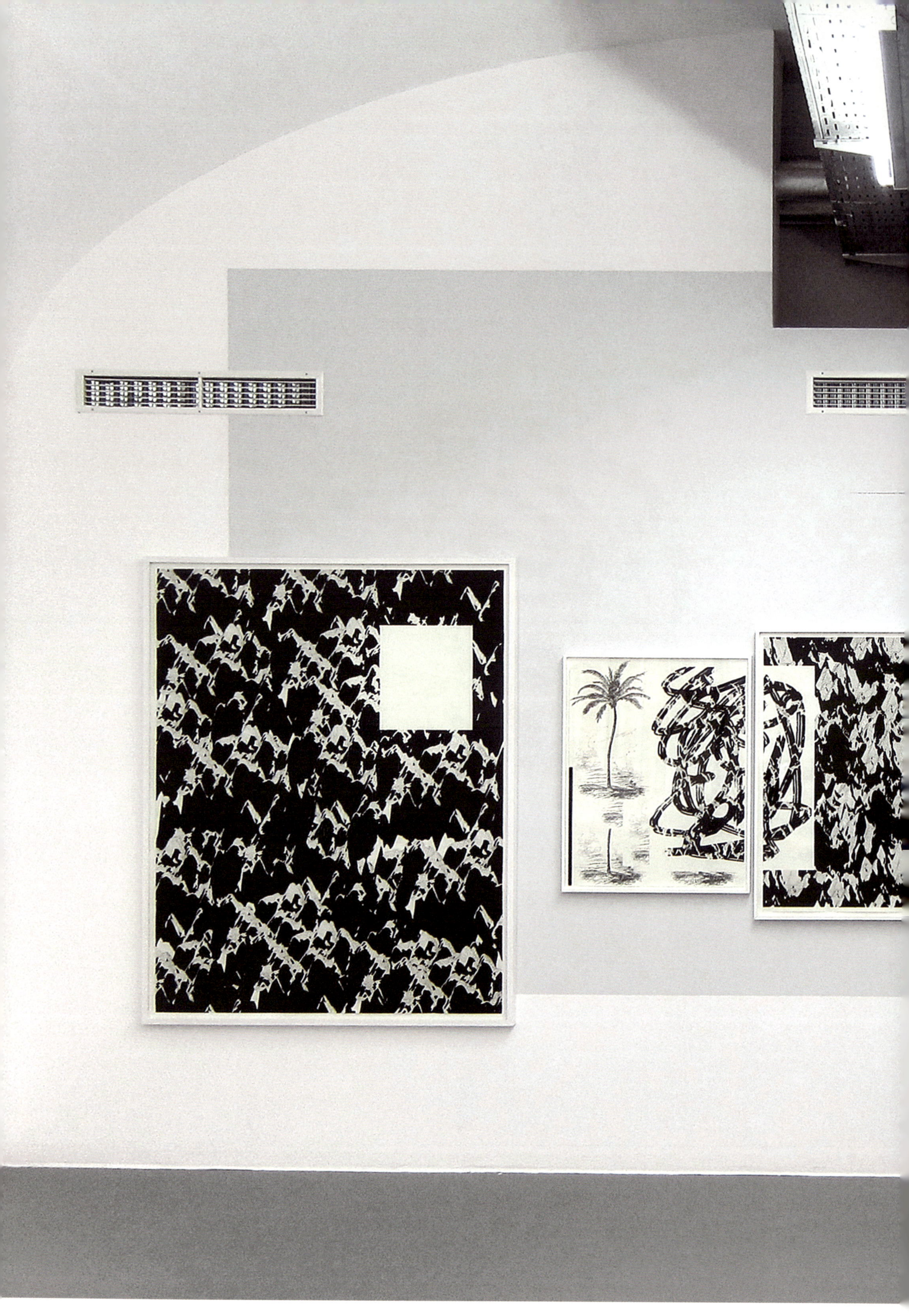

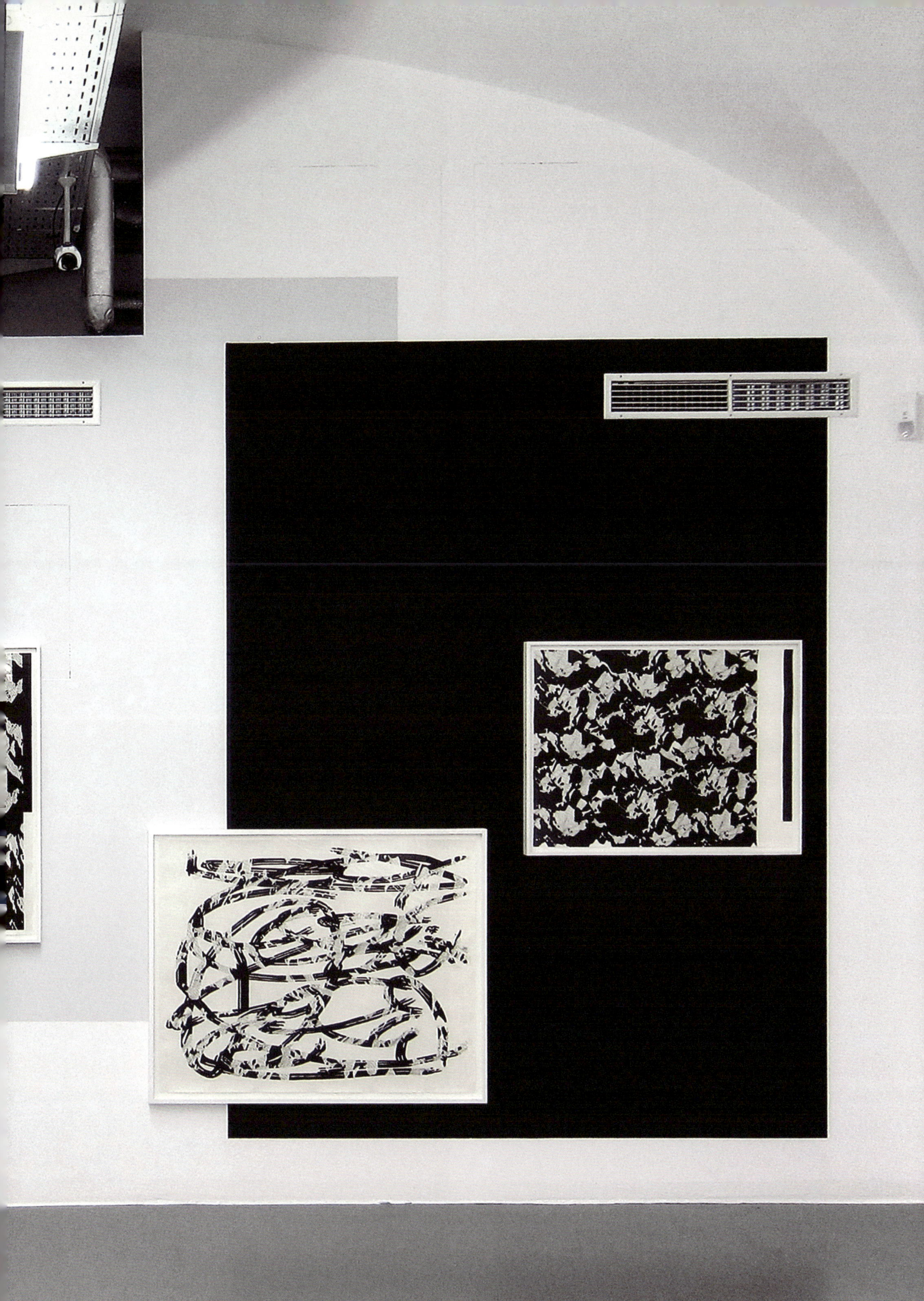

Exhibition (previous page)
<u>24/7: the human condition</u>
(curated by Marlies Wirth)
Ben Thorp Brown, Verena Dengler, Carola Dertnig,
Harm van den Dorpel, Andreas Duscha, Andreas
Fogarasi, Franz Graf, Kathi Hofer, Peter Jellitsch,
Lazar Lyutakov, Mahony, Christian Mayer, Ulrich
Nausner, Danica Phelps, Lili Reynaud-Dewar,
Valentin Ruhry, Seth Weiner, Anna Witt
MAK – Österreichisches Museum für angewandte
Kunst / Gegenwartskunst
Wien, AT

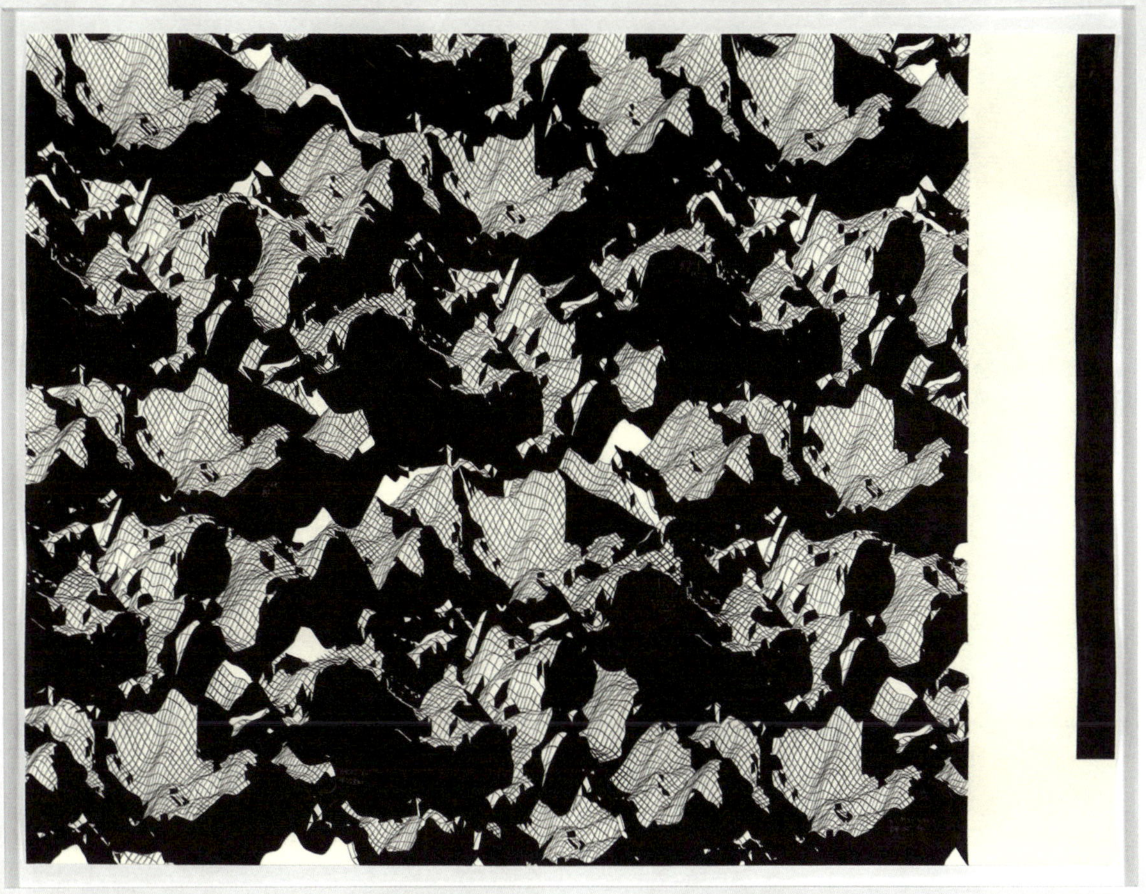

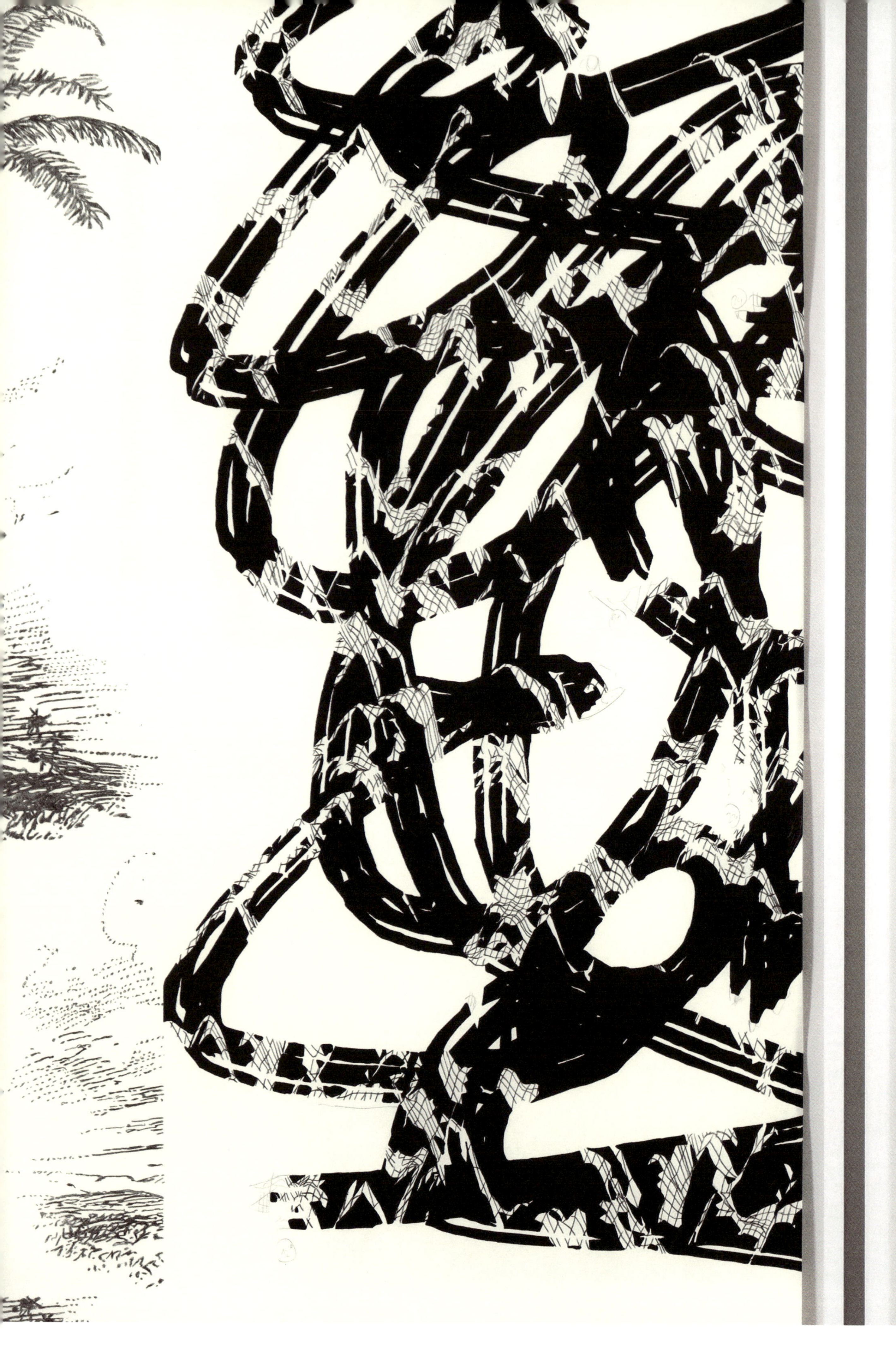

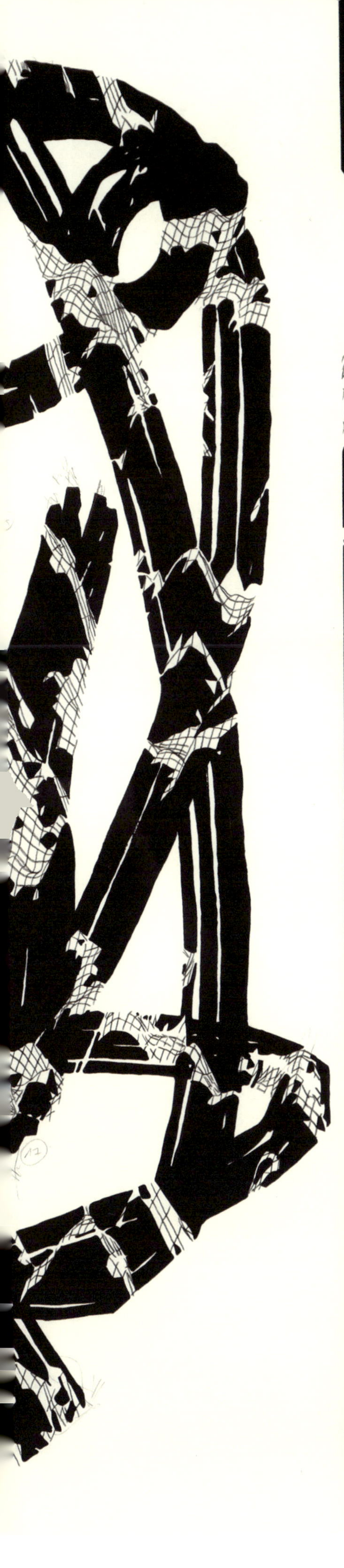

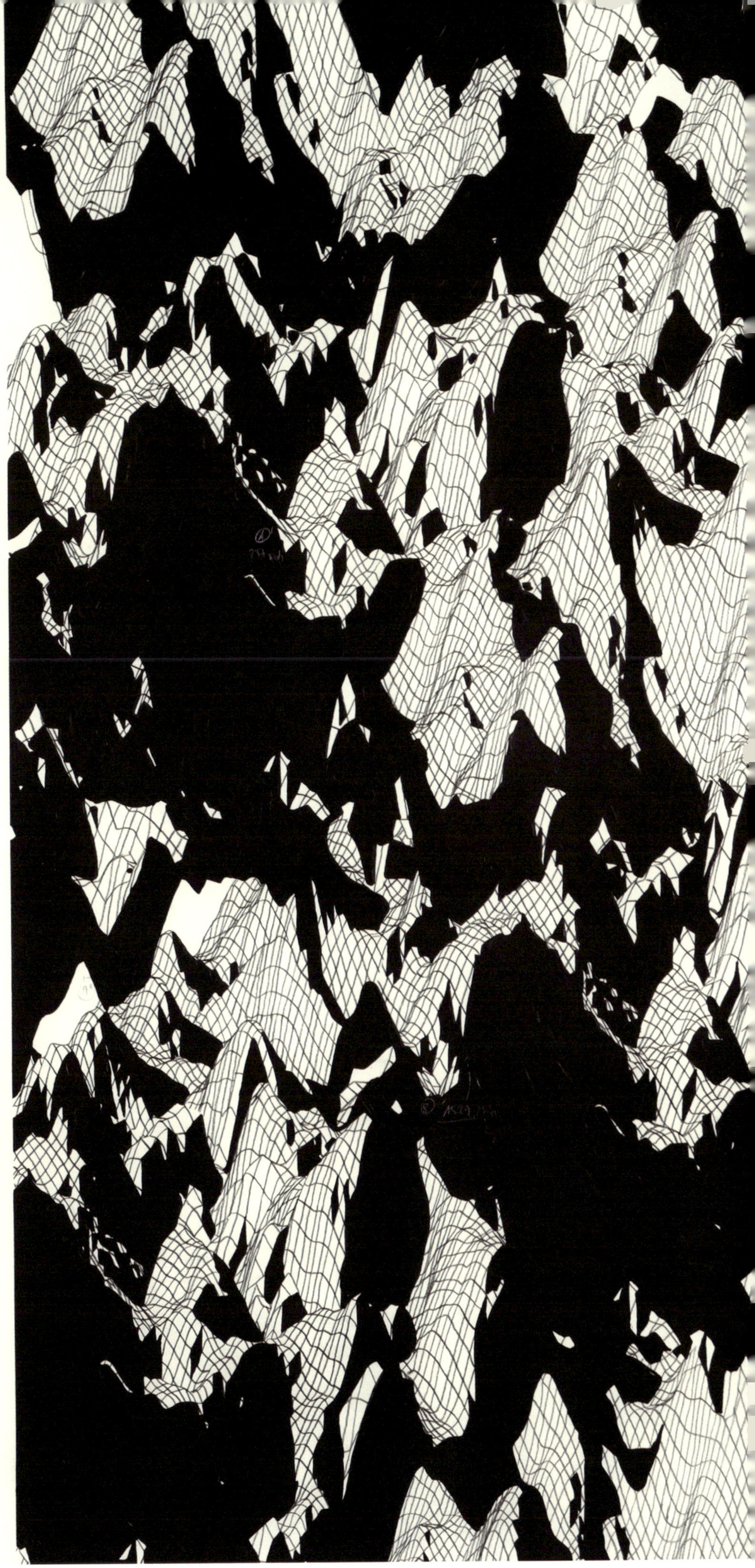

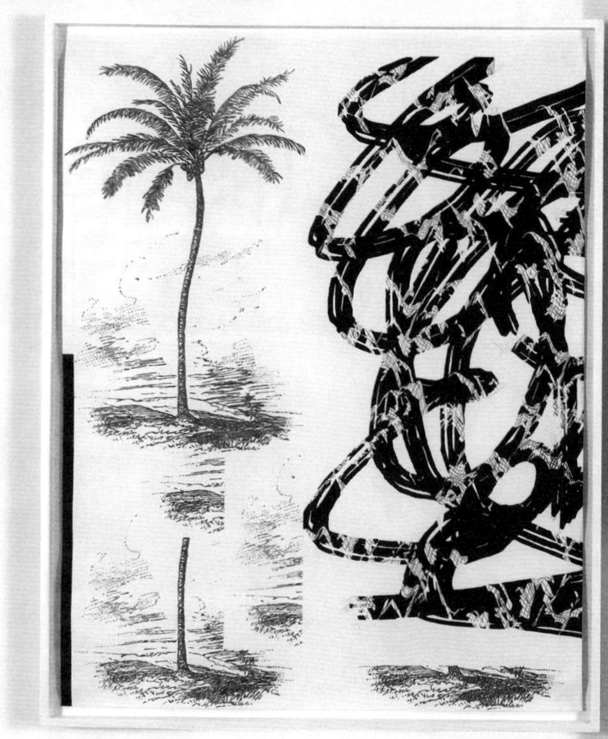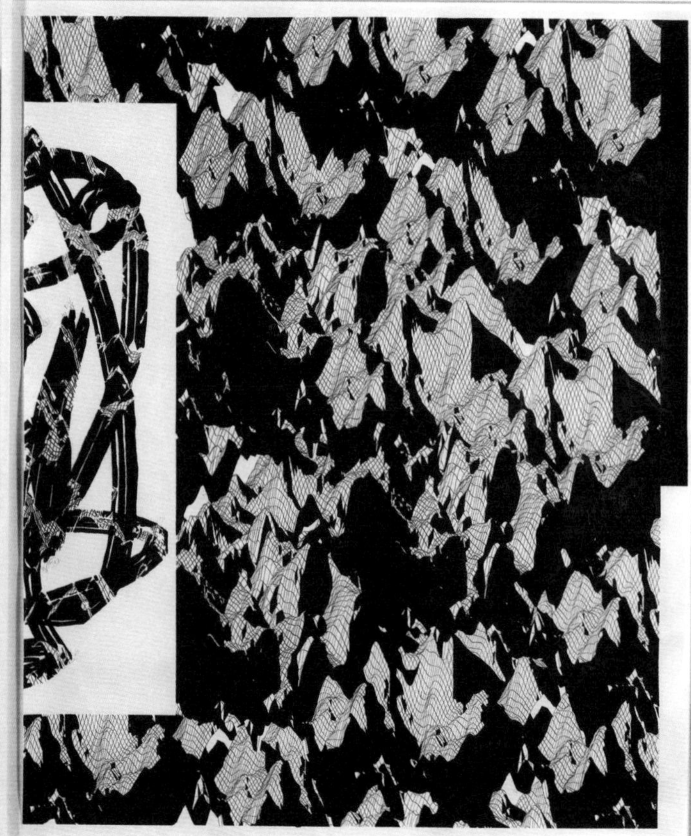

(Detail) (previous page)
Data Drawing 32+33

Data Drawing 32+33
Pencil, acrylic, crayon, lacquer on paper
102×146 cm

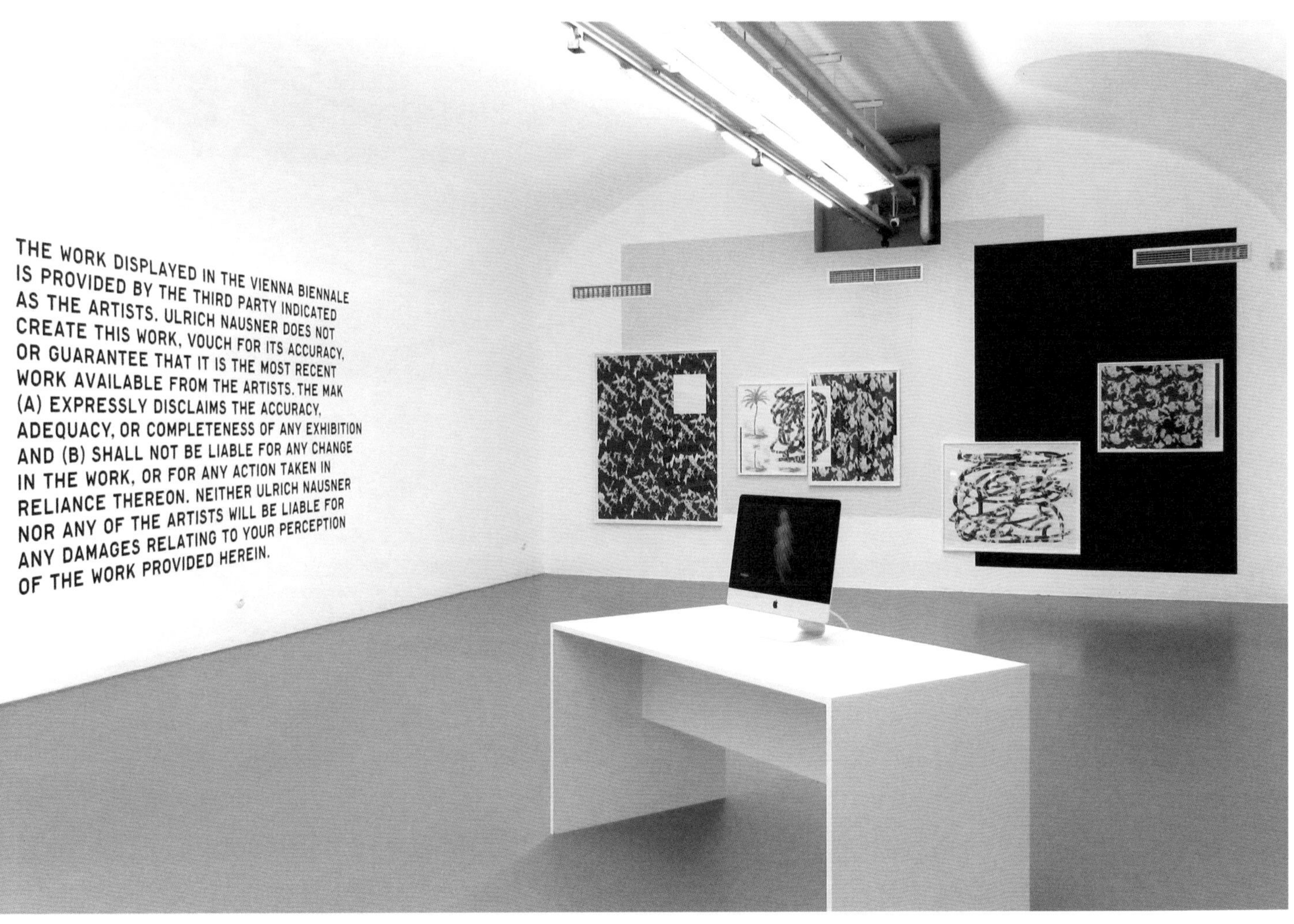
THE WORK DISPLAYED IN THE VIENNA BIENNALE
IS PROVIDED BY THE THIRD PARTY INDICATED
AS THE ARTISTS. ULRICH NAUSNER DOES NOT
CREATE THIS WORK, VOUCH FOR ITS ACCURACY,
OR GUARANTEE THAT IT IS THE MOST RECENT
WORK AVAILABLE FROM THE ARTISTS. THE MAK
(A) EXPRESSLY DISCLAIMS THE ACCURACY,
ADEQUACY, OR COMPLETENESS OF ANY EXHIBITION
AND (B) SHALL NOT BE LIABLE FOR ANY CHANGE
IN THE WORK, OR FOR ANY ACTION TAKEN IN
RELIANCE THEREON. NEITHER ULRICH NAUSNER
NOR ANY OF THE ARTISTS WILL BE LIABLE FOR
ANY DAMAGES RELATING TO YOUR PERCEPTION
OF THE WORK PROVIDED HEREIN.

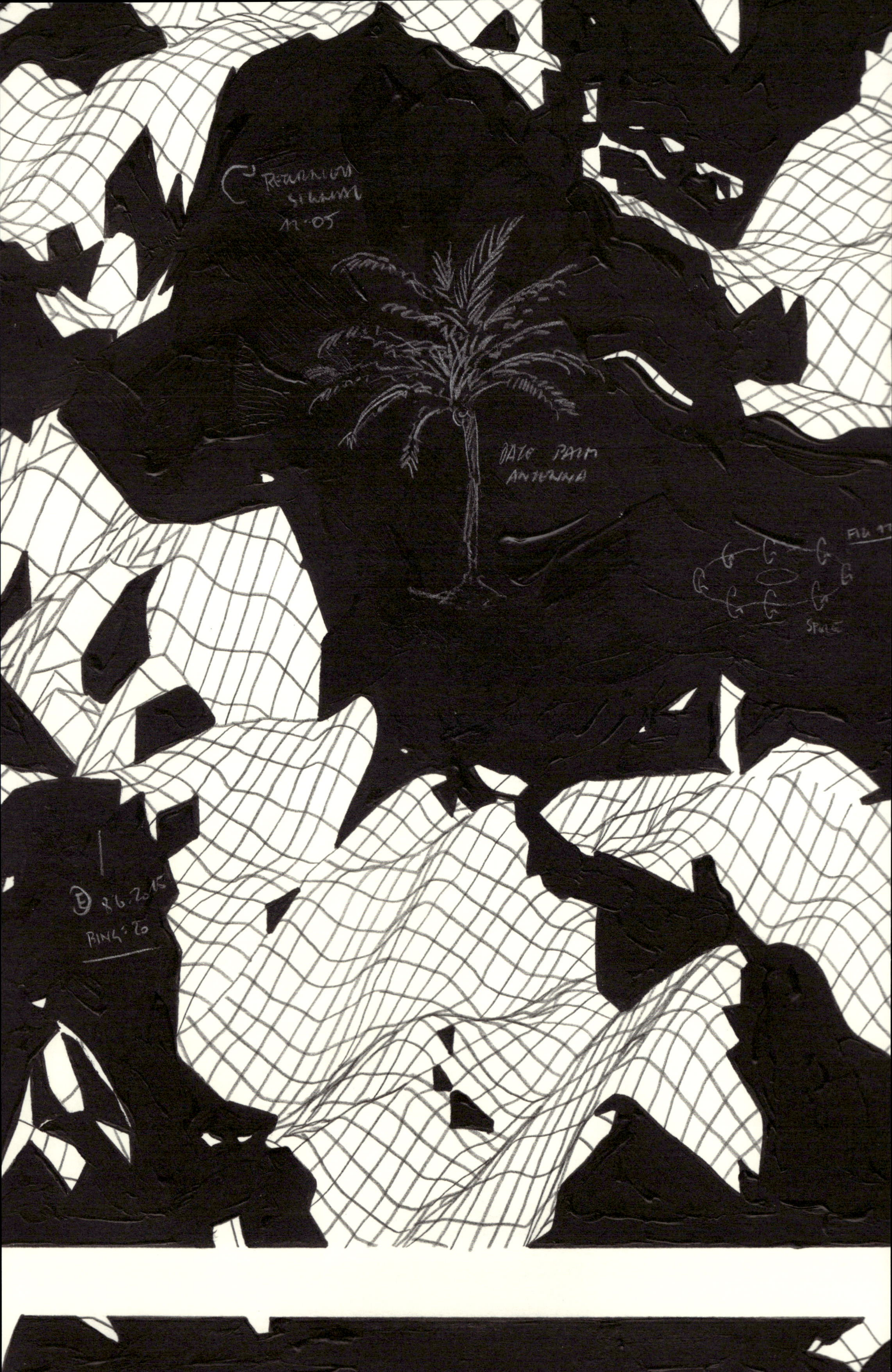
REFERENCE
STRUKTUR
N° 05
DATE PALM
ANTENNA
FIL
SPULE
8.6.2015
RING: 6

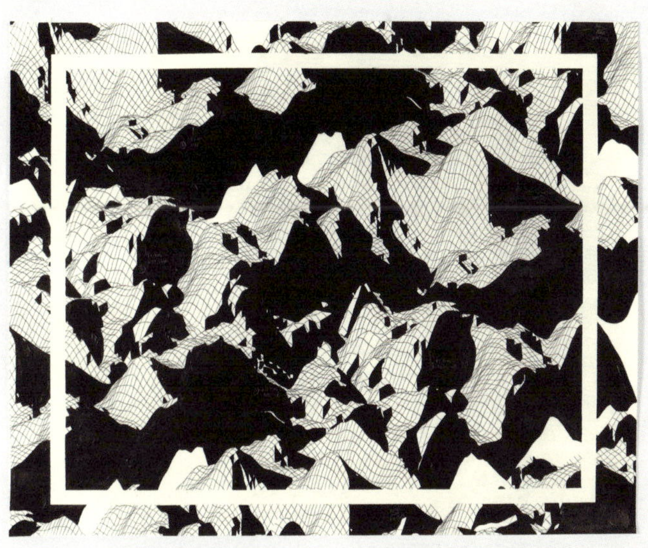

(Detail) (left page)
Data Drawing 36, 2015

Data Drawing 34, 35, 36, 2015
Pencil, acrylic, crayon, lacquer on paper
Each 49×60 cm

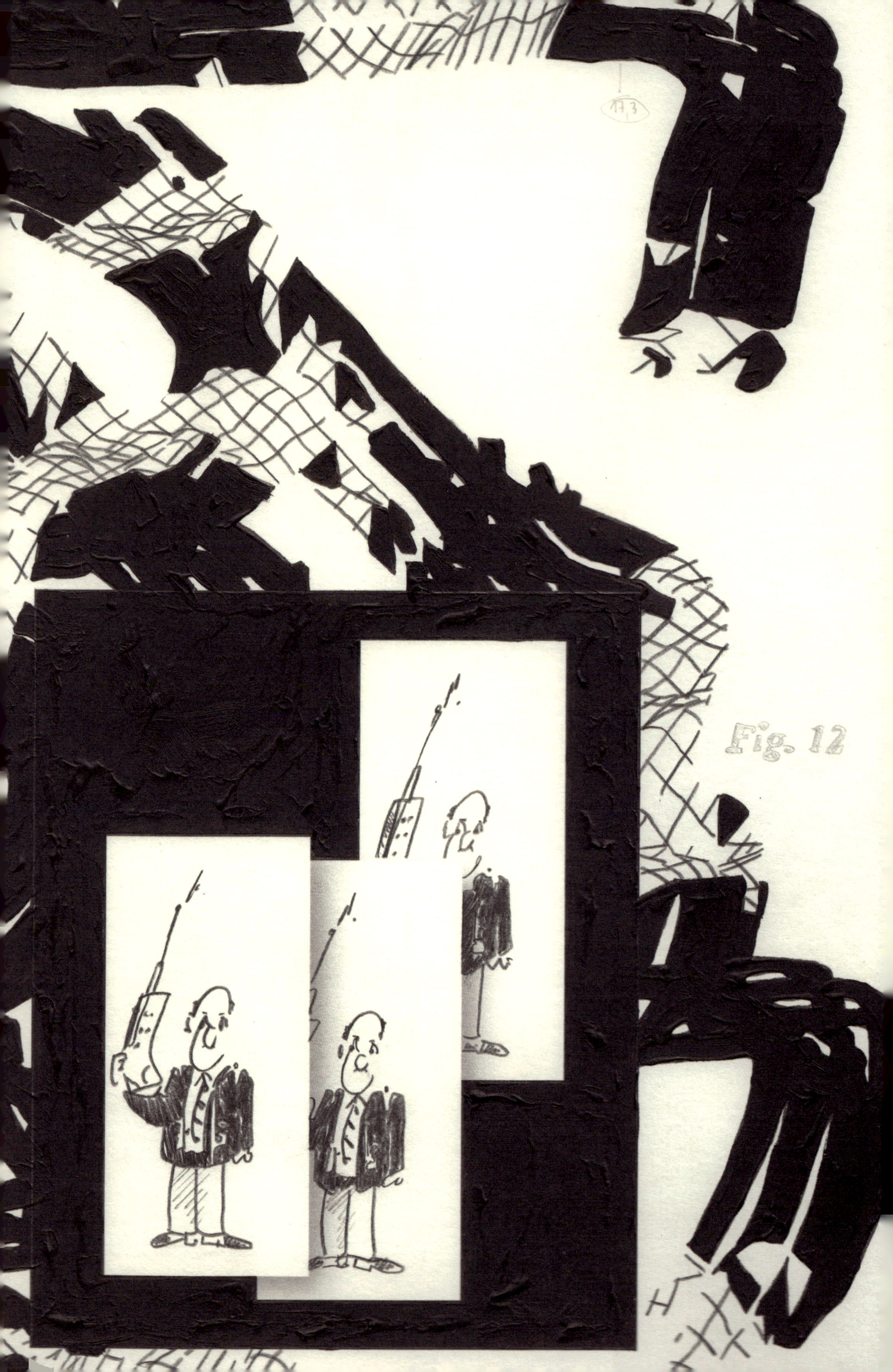
17,3
Fig. 12

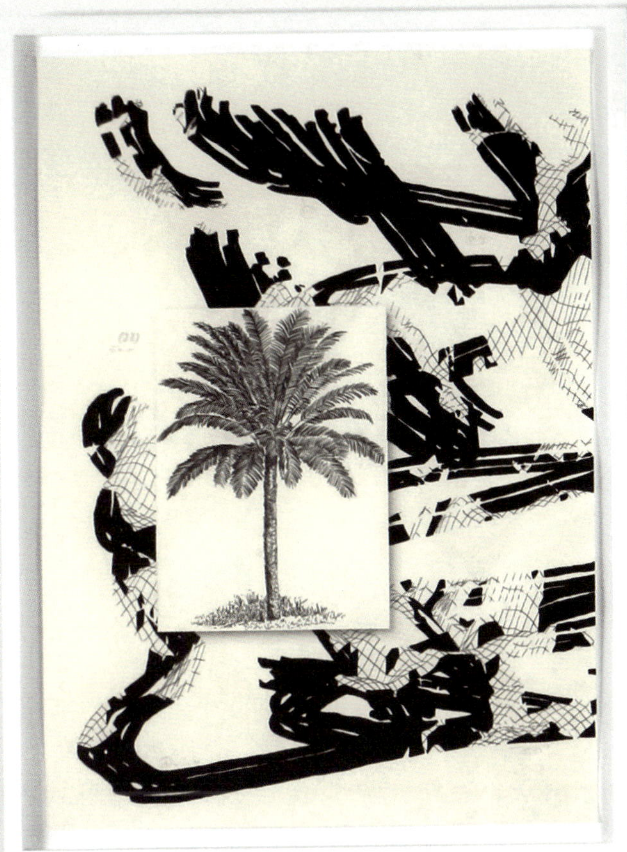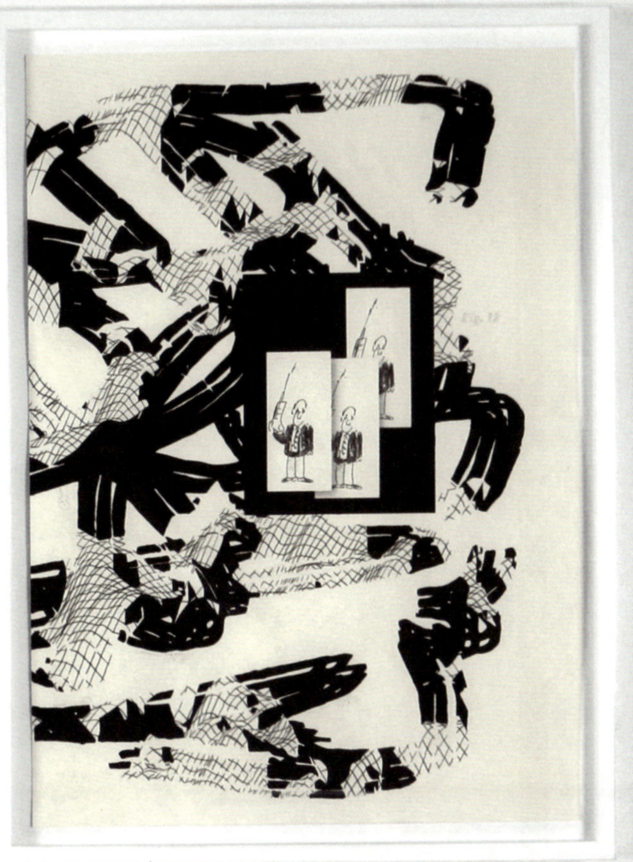

(Detail) (left page)
Data Drawing 40+41 (talking to a palm), 2015

Data Drawing 40+41 (talking to a palm), 2015
Pencil, acrylic, crayon, lacquer on paper
46×70 cm

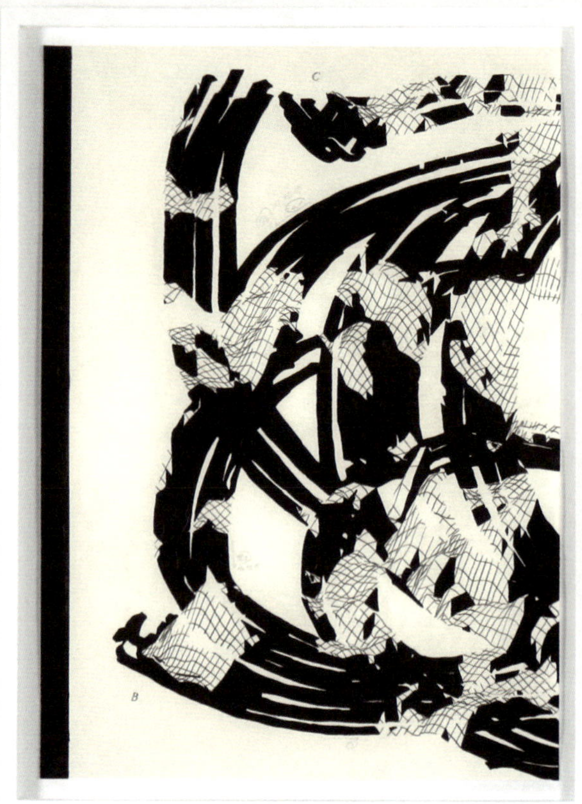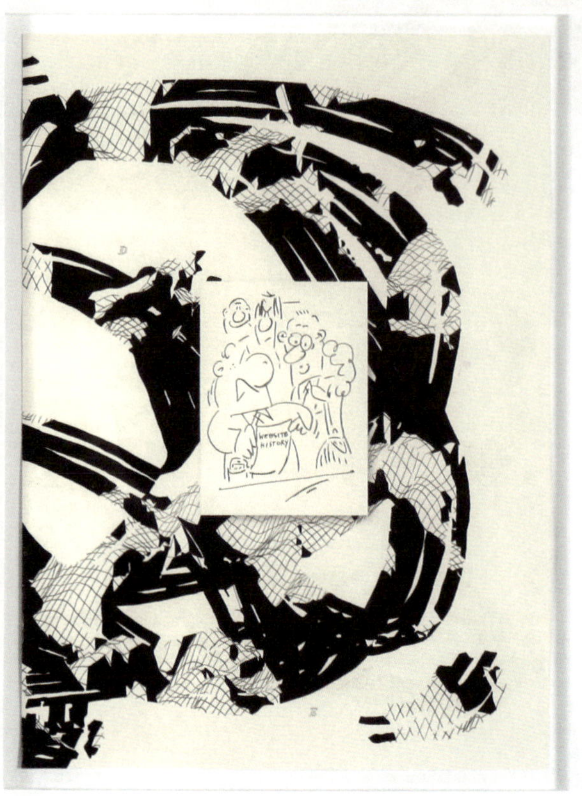

Data Drawing 42+43 (website history), 2015
Pencil, acrylic, crayon, lacquer on paper
46×70 cm

(Detail) (right page)
Data Drawing 42+43 (website history), 2015

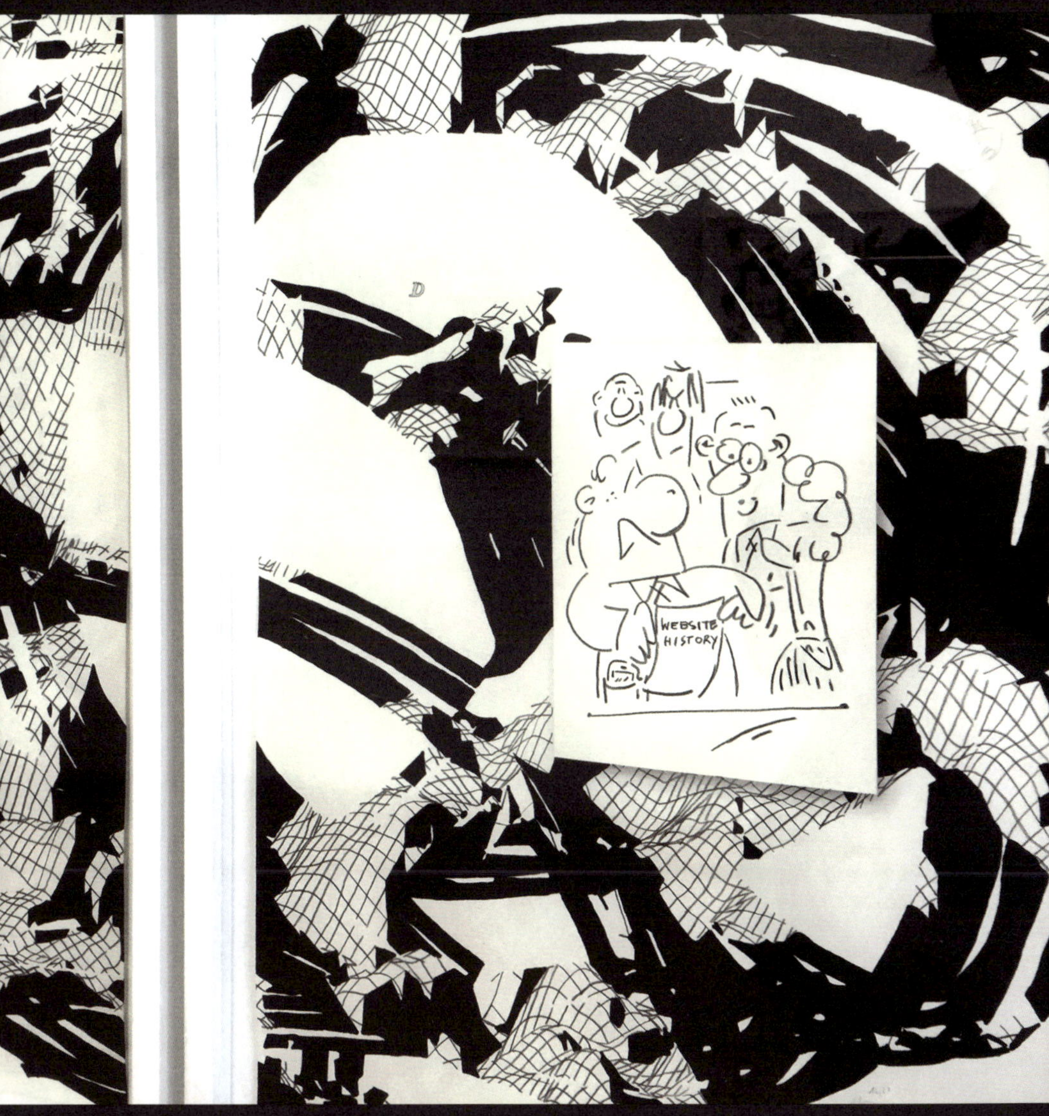

WEBSITE
HISTORY

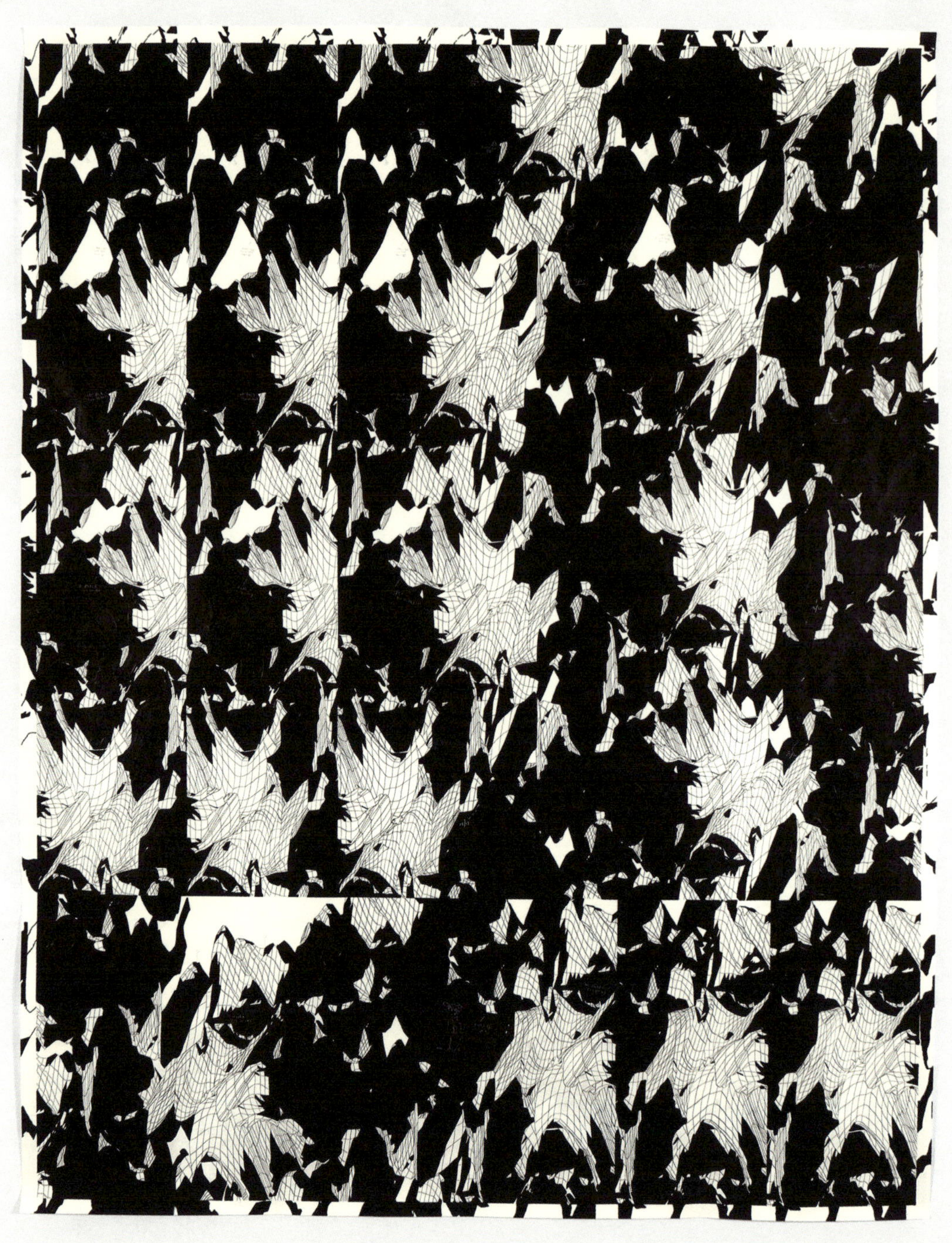

Data Drawing 48, 2016
Pencil, acrylic, crayon, lacquer on paper
155×120 cm

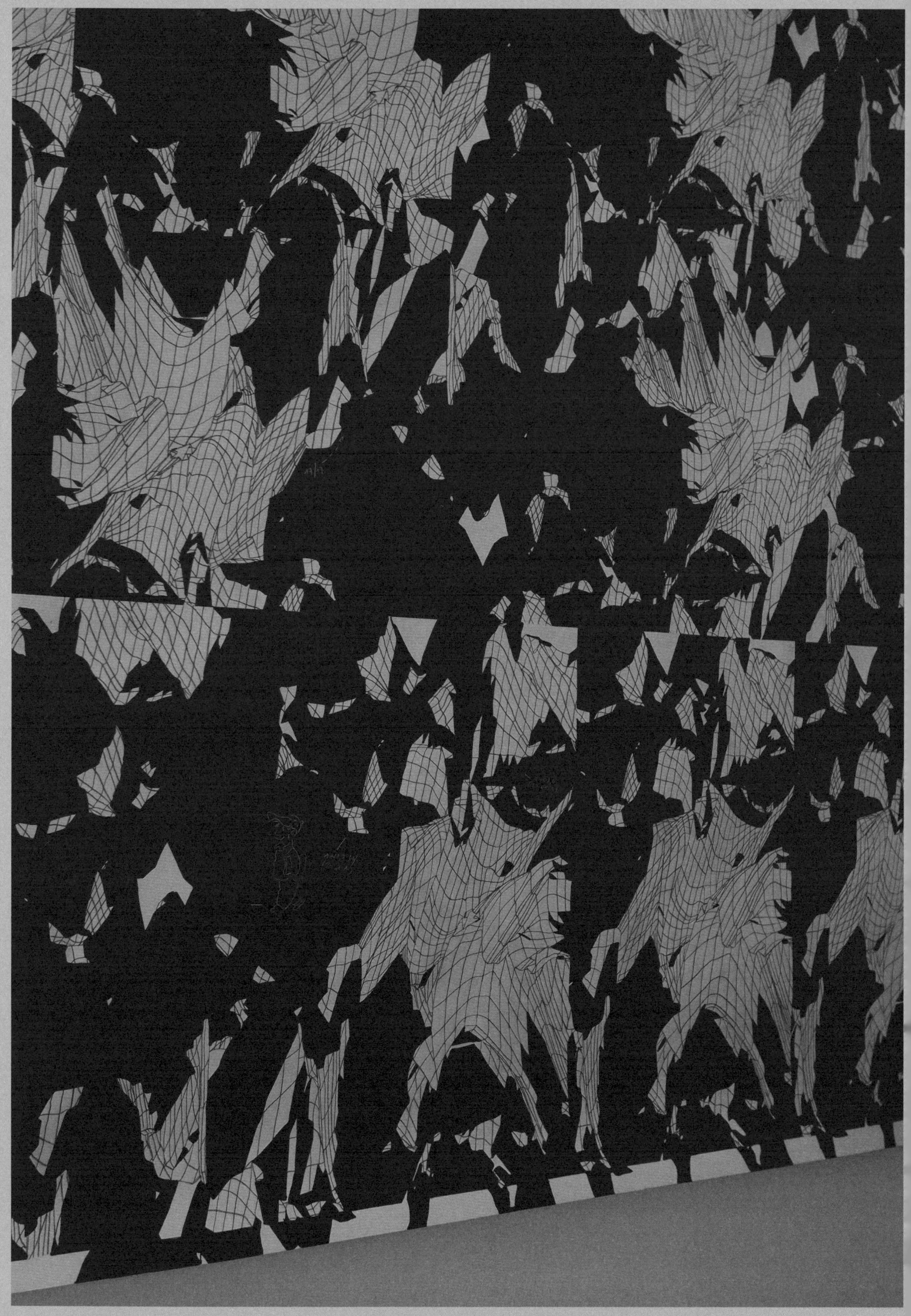

(Detail)
Data Drawing 48, 2016

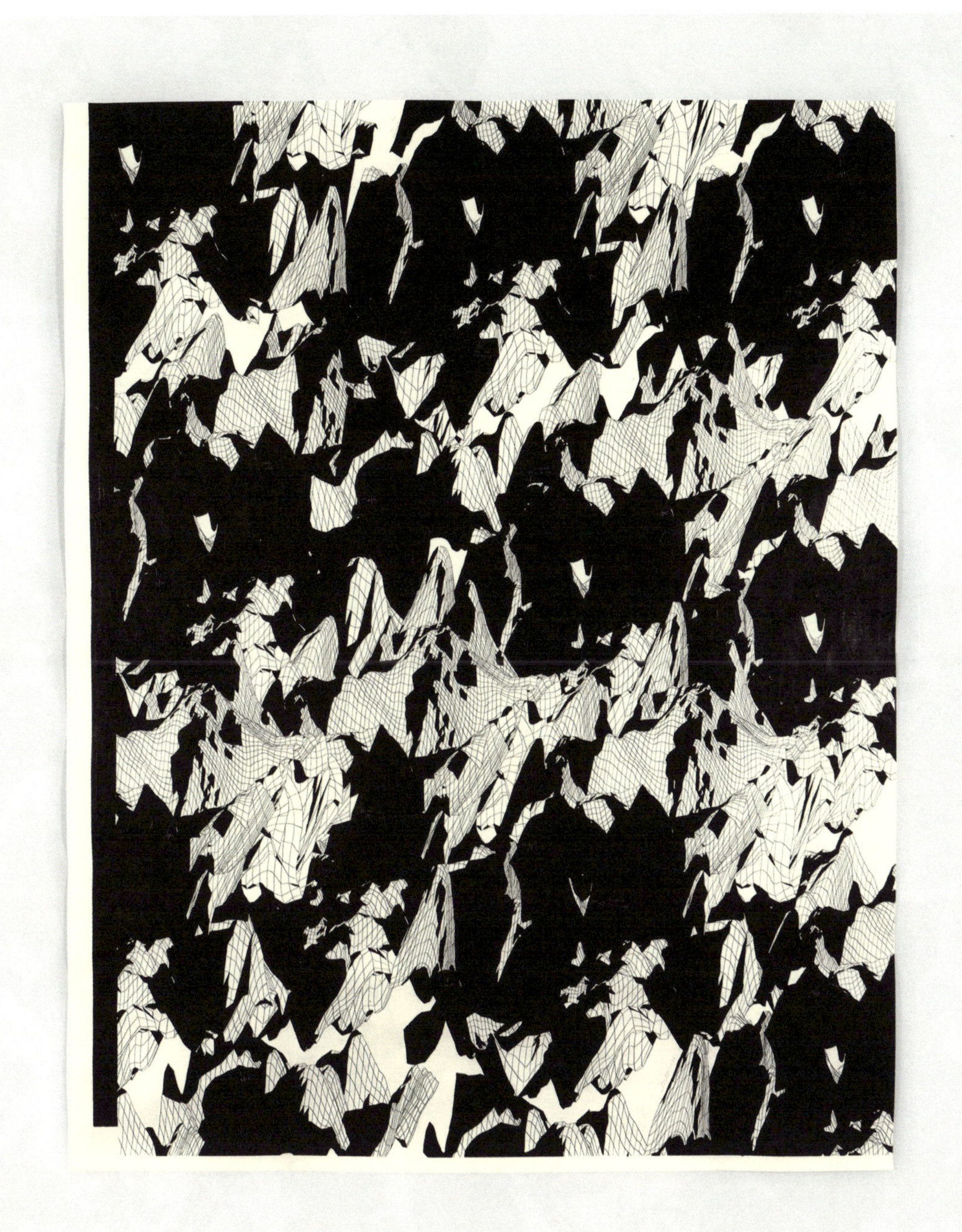

Data Drawing 49, 2016
Pencil, acrylic, crayon, lacquer on paper
155×120 cm

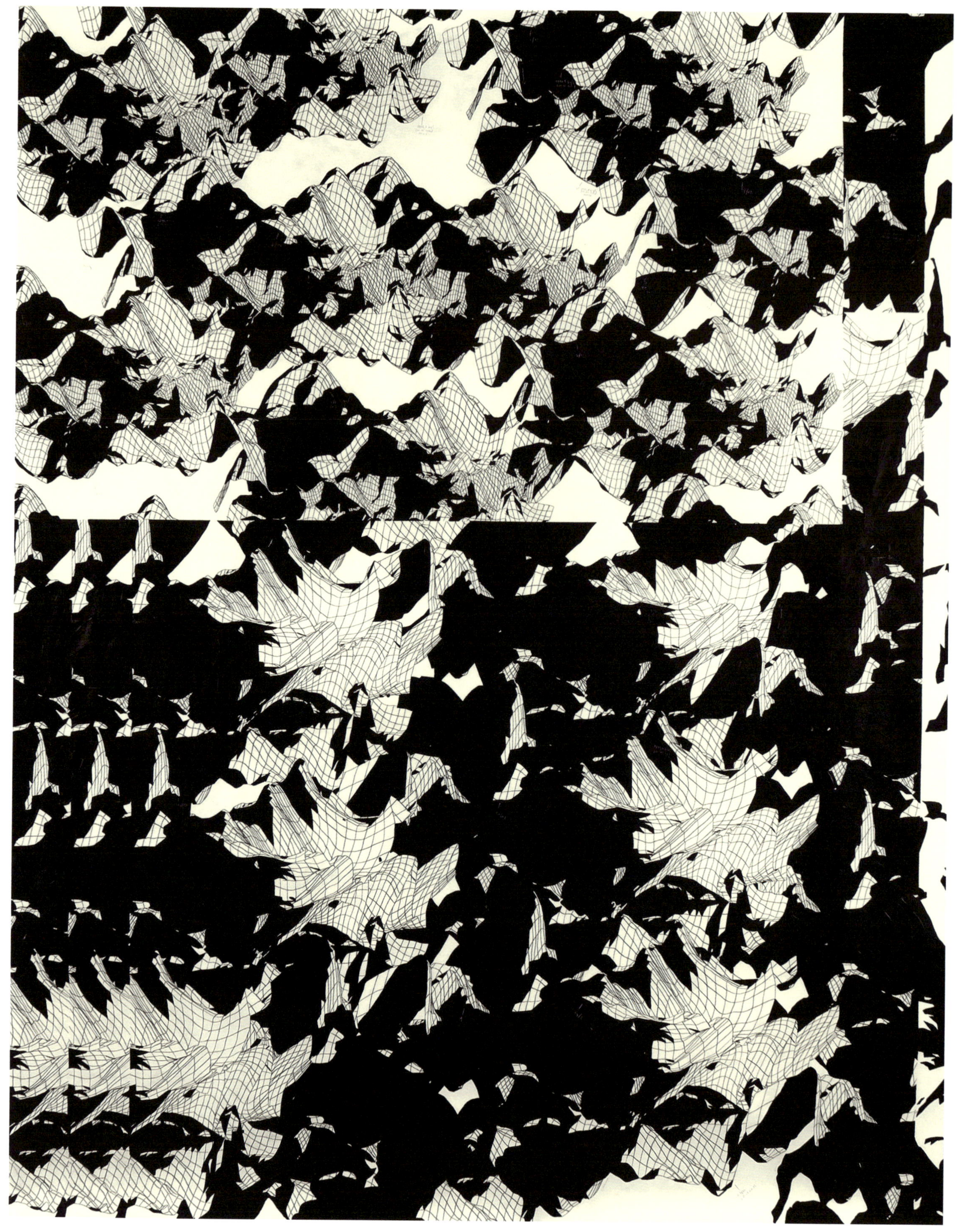

Data Drawing 50, 2016
Pencil, acrylic, crayon, lacquer on paper
155×120 cm

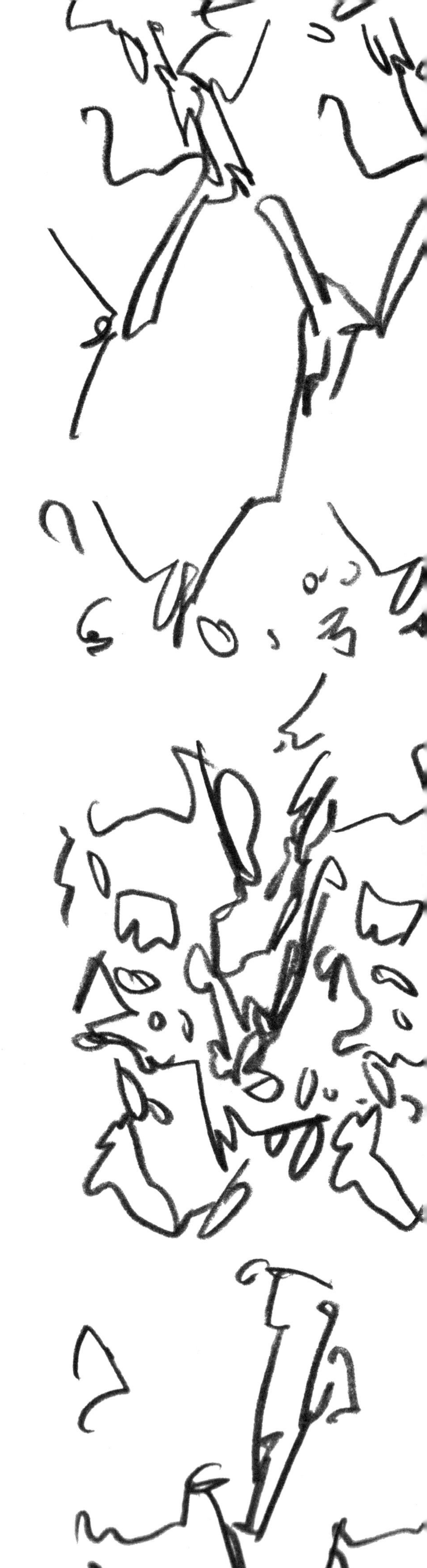

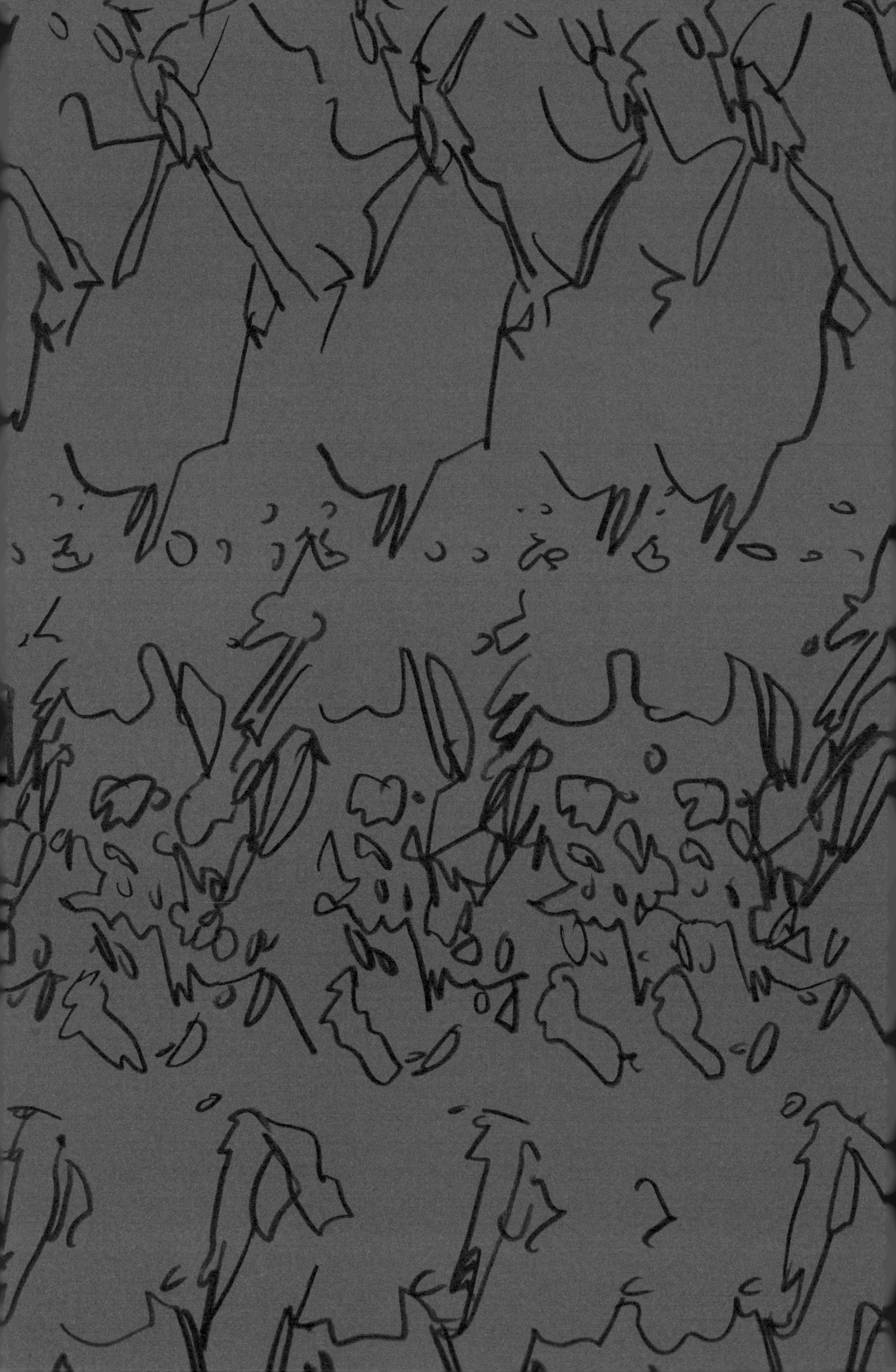

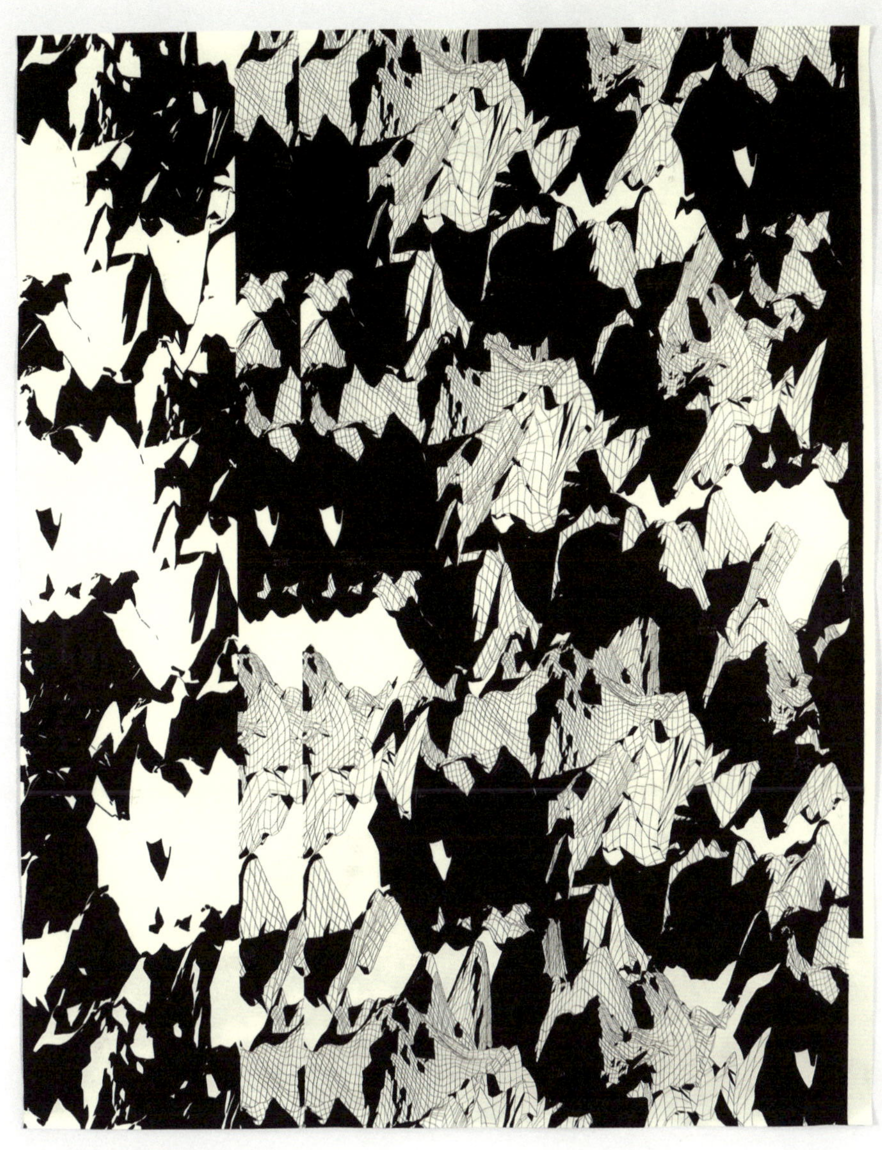

Data Drawing 51, 2016
Pencil, acrylic, crayon, lacquer on paper
155×120 cm

Notation, 2016
Pencil, acrylic, crayon on paper
42×29,7 cm

Notation, 2016 (right page)
Pencil, crayon on paper
42×29,7 cm

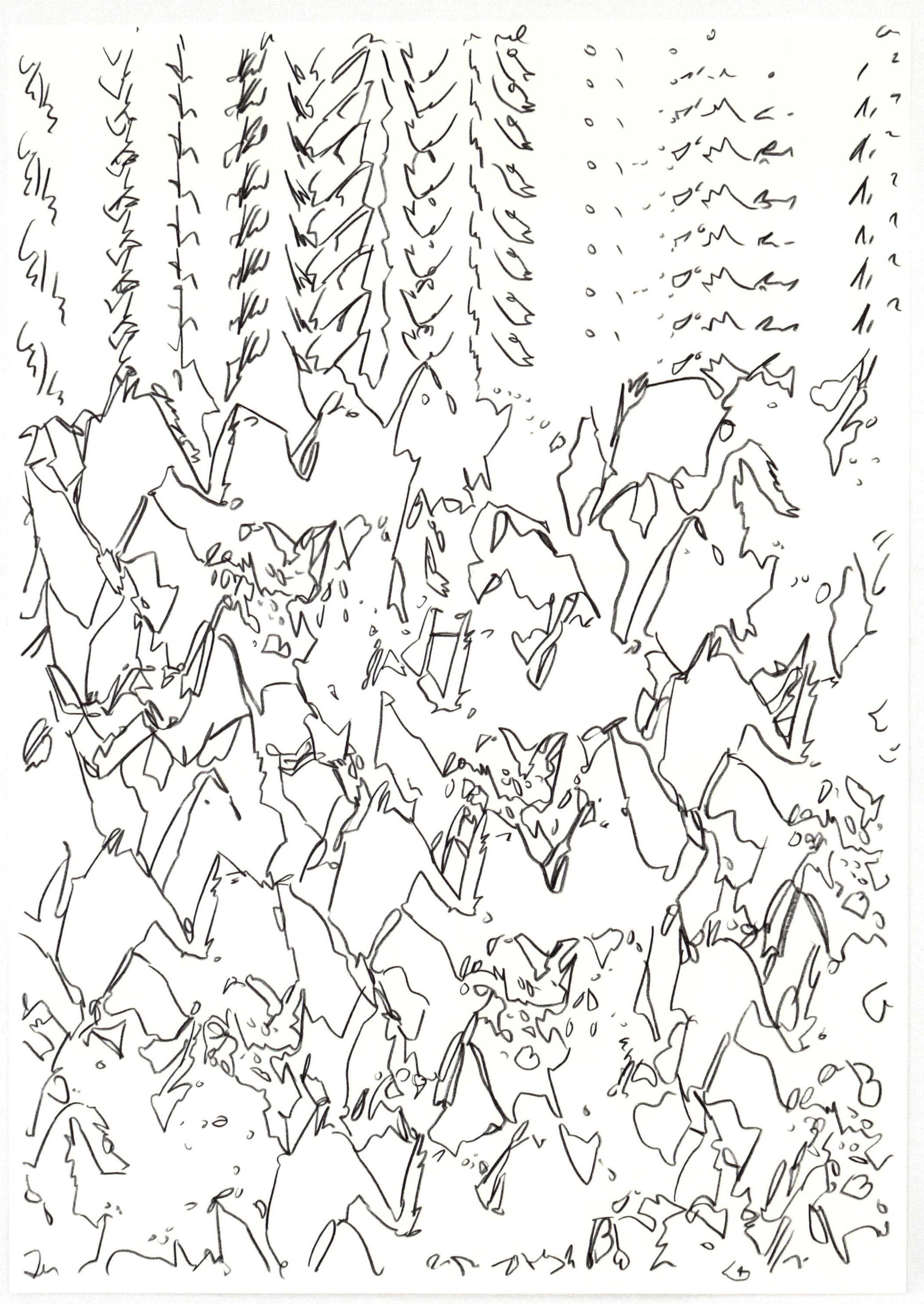

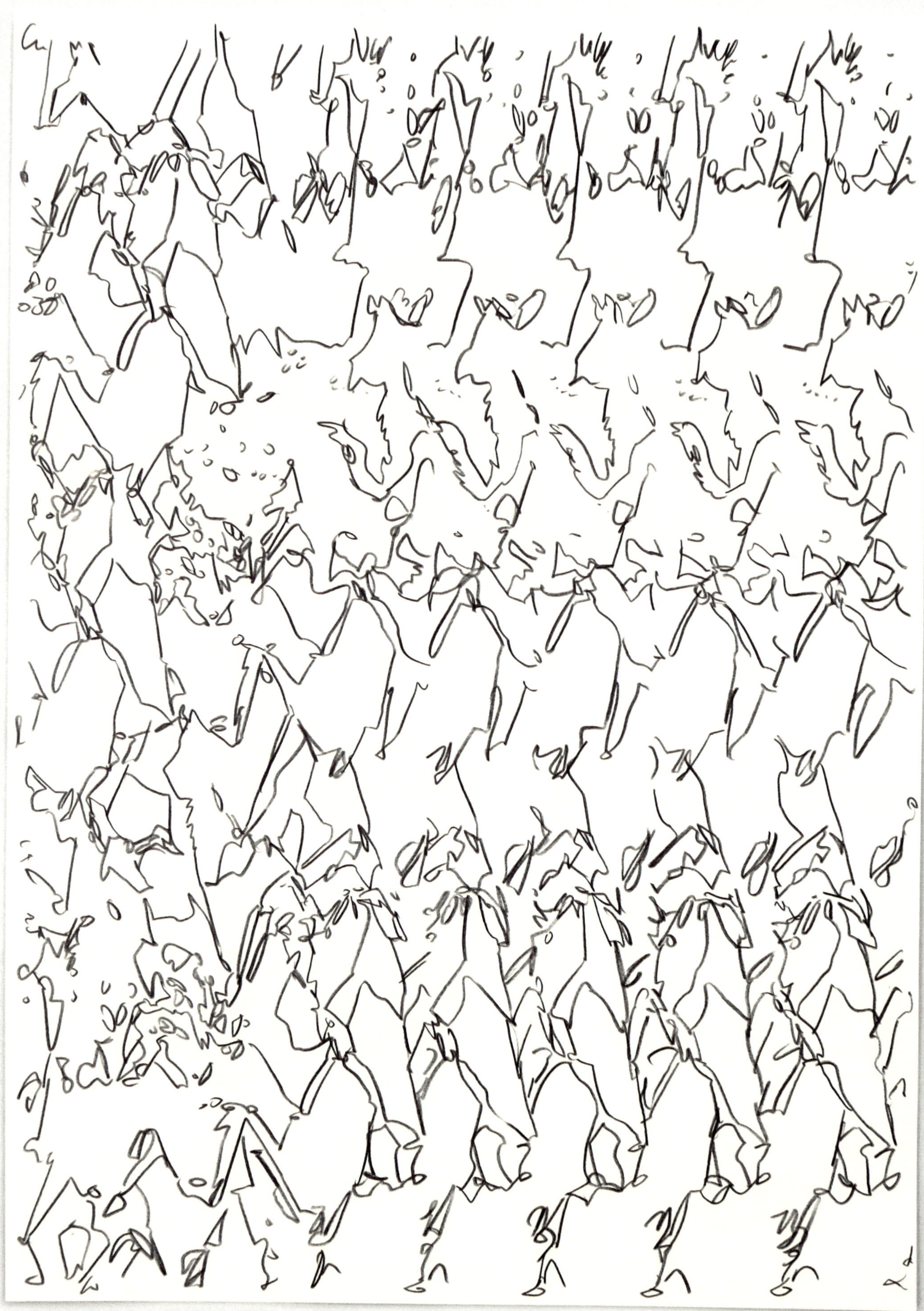

Notation, 2016 (left page)
Pencil, crayon on paper
42×29,7 cm

Notation, 2016
Pencil, crayon, acrylic on paper
42×29,7 cm

(Detail) (next page)
Data Drawing 49, 2016

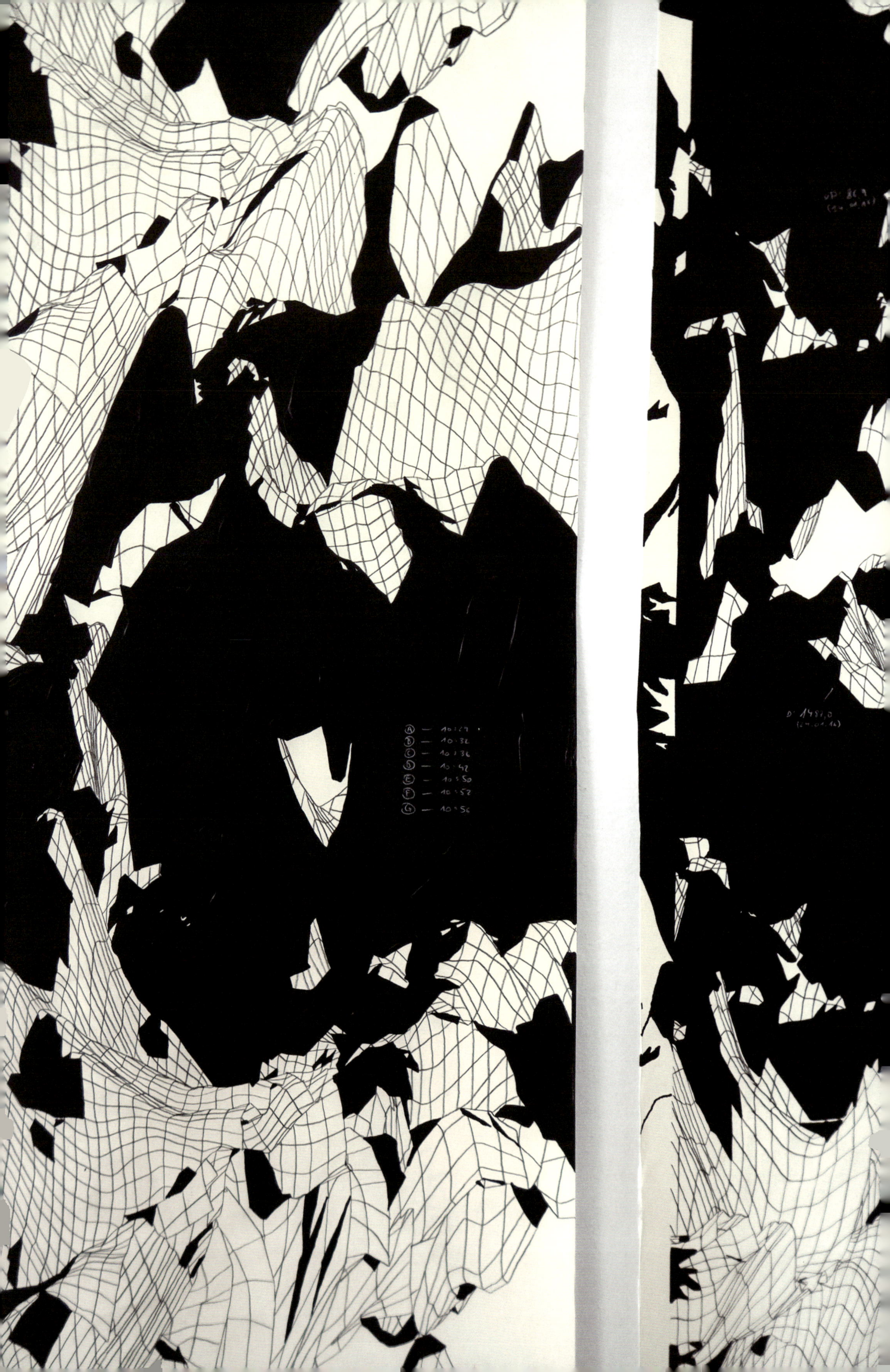

Ⓐ — 10:29
Ⓑ — 10:32
Ⓒ — 10:36
Ⓓ — 10:42
Ⓔ — 10:50
Ⓕ — 10:52
Ⓖ — 10:56
D 1481,0
(24.01.16)

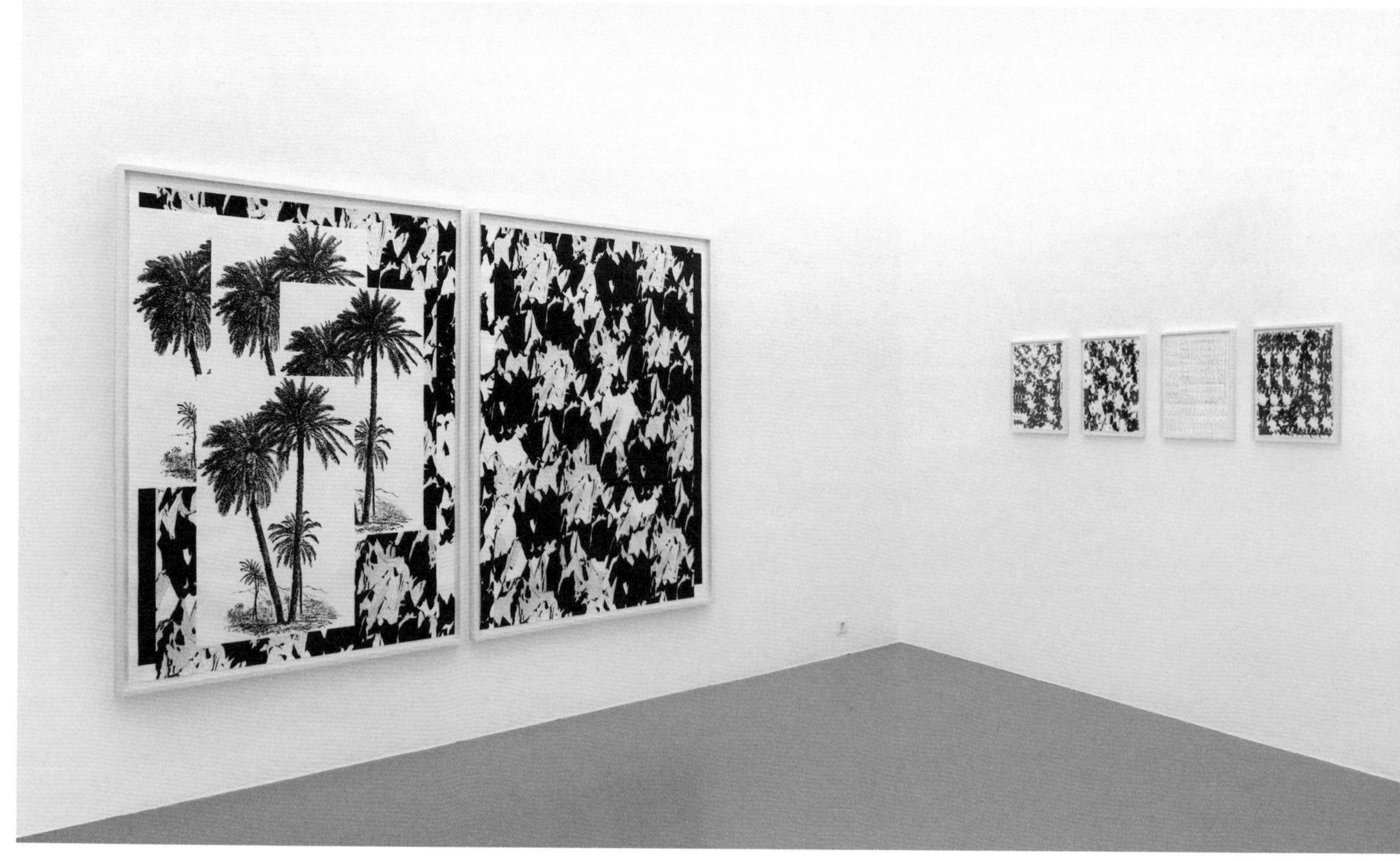

Exhibition
<u>Only the Memory, 2016</u>
Peter Jellitsch
Galerie Crone
Wien, AT

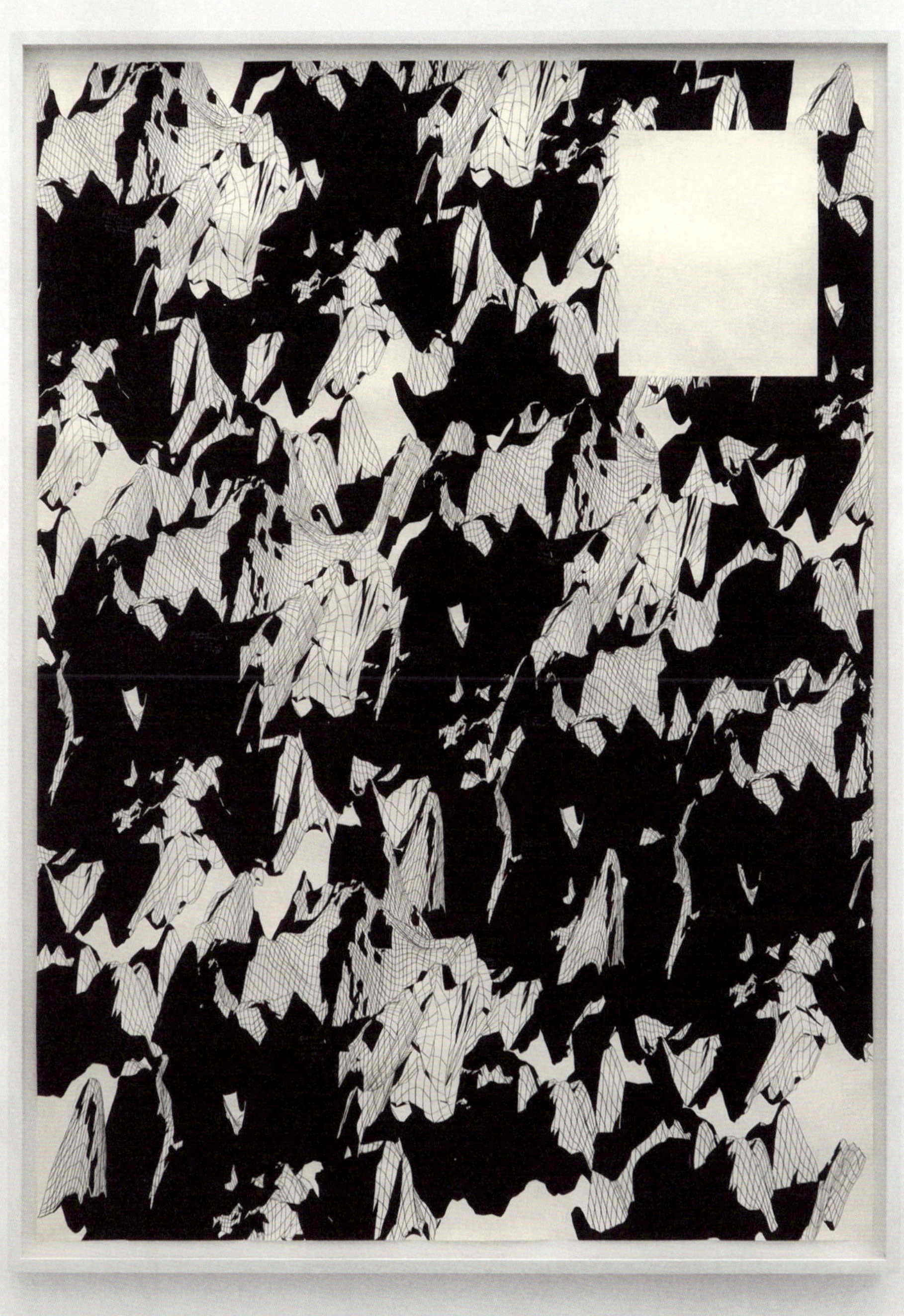

Data Drawing 54 (Facetime), 2016
Pencil, acrylic, crayon, lacquer on paper
170×120 cm

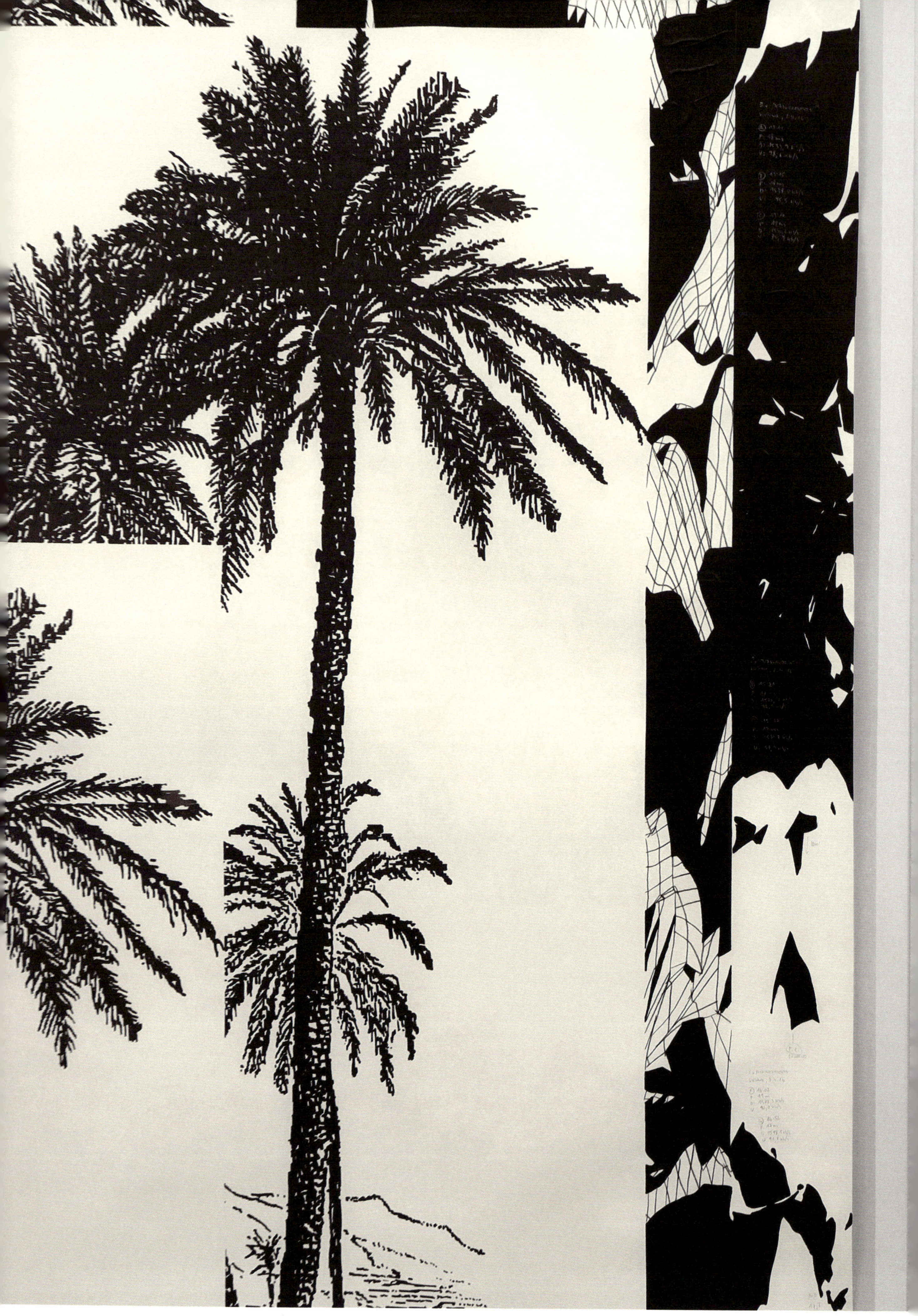

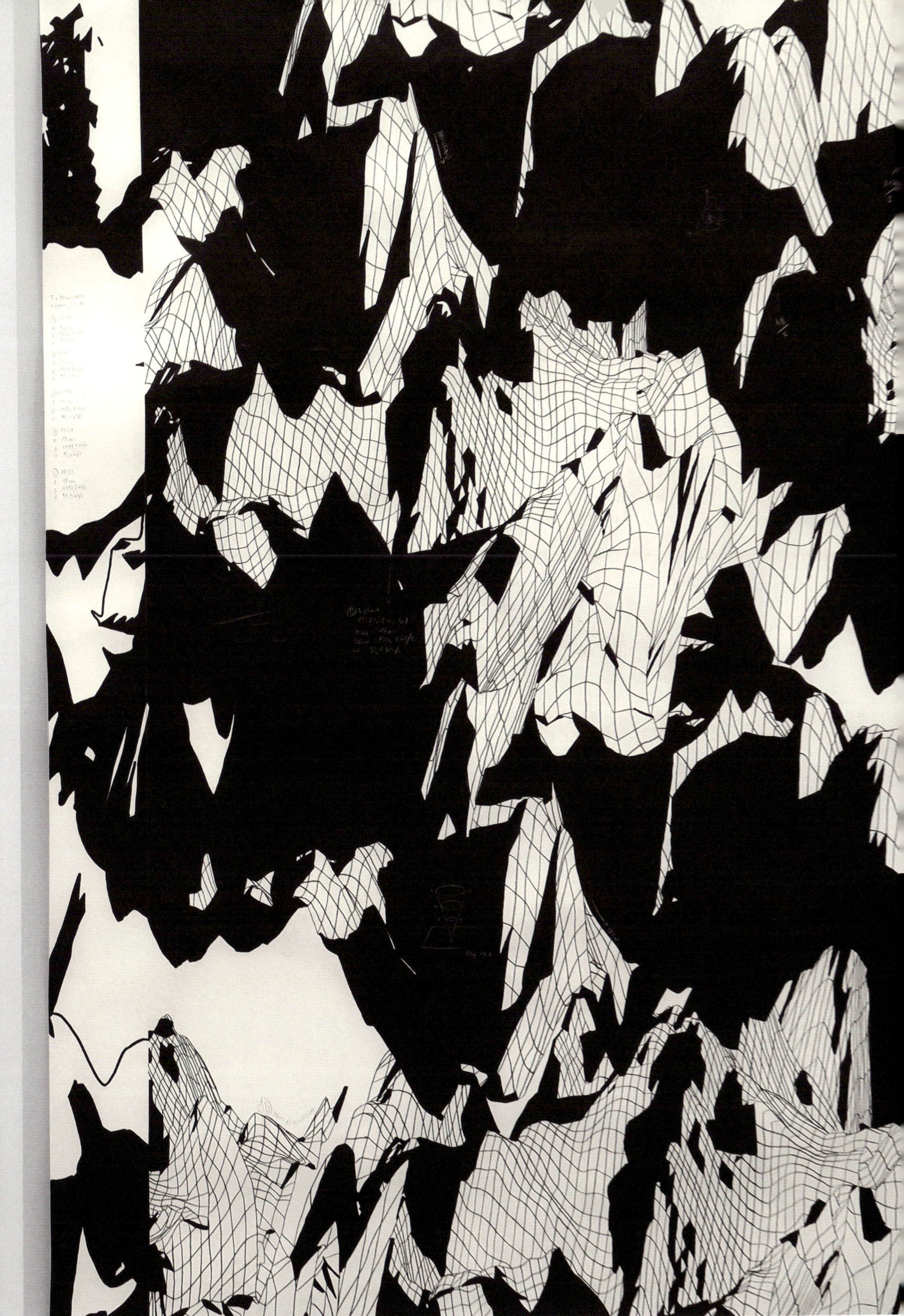

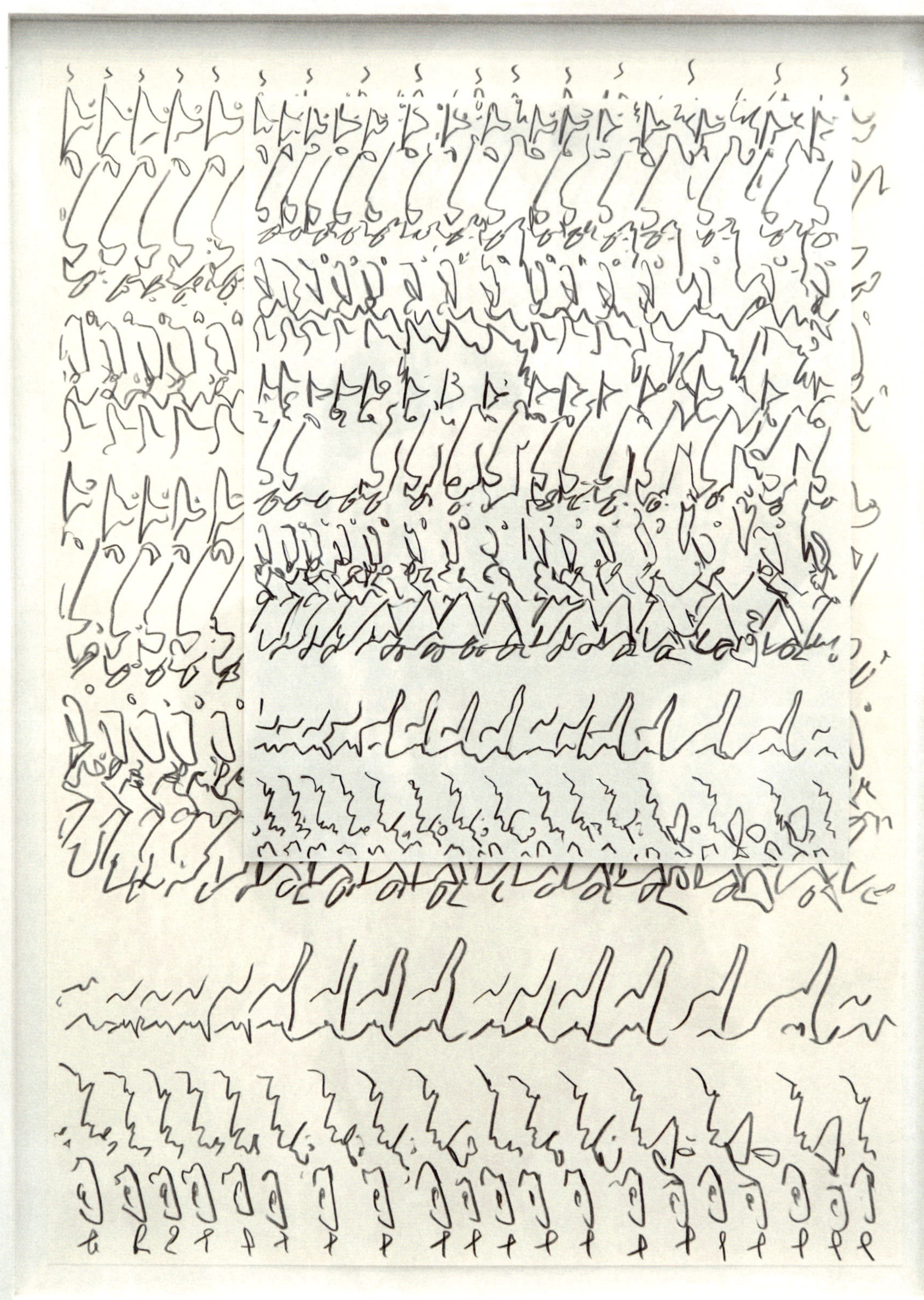

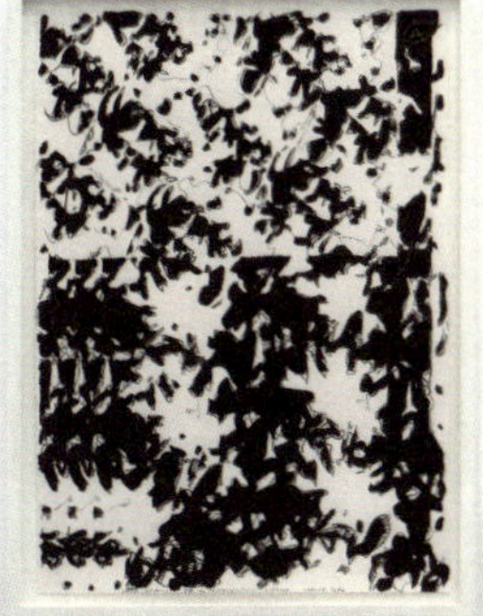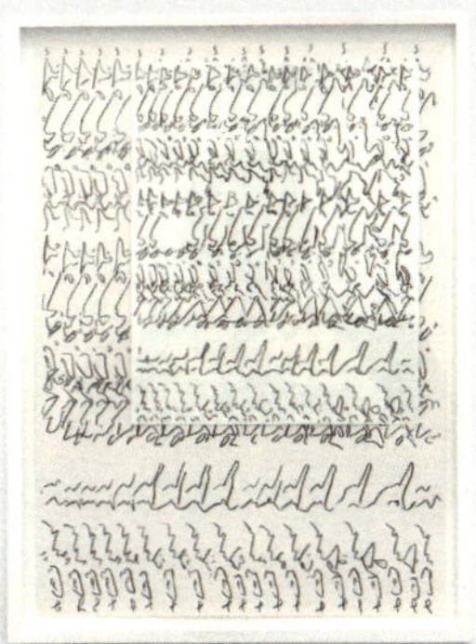

(Detail) (previous page)
Data Drawing 52+53 (Date Palms), 2016

Notation, 2016 (left page)
Pencil, crayon on paper (collage)
42×29,7 cm

4 Notations, 2016 (above)
Pencil, crayon, acrylic on paper
Each 42×29,7 cm

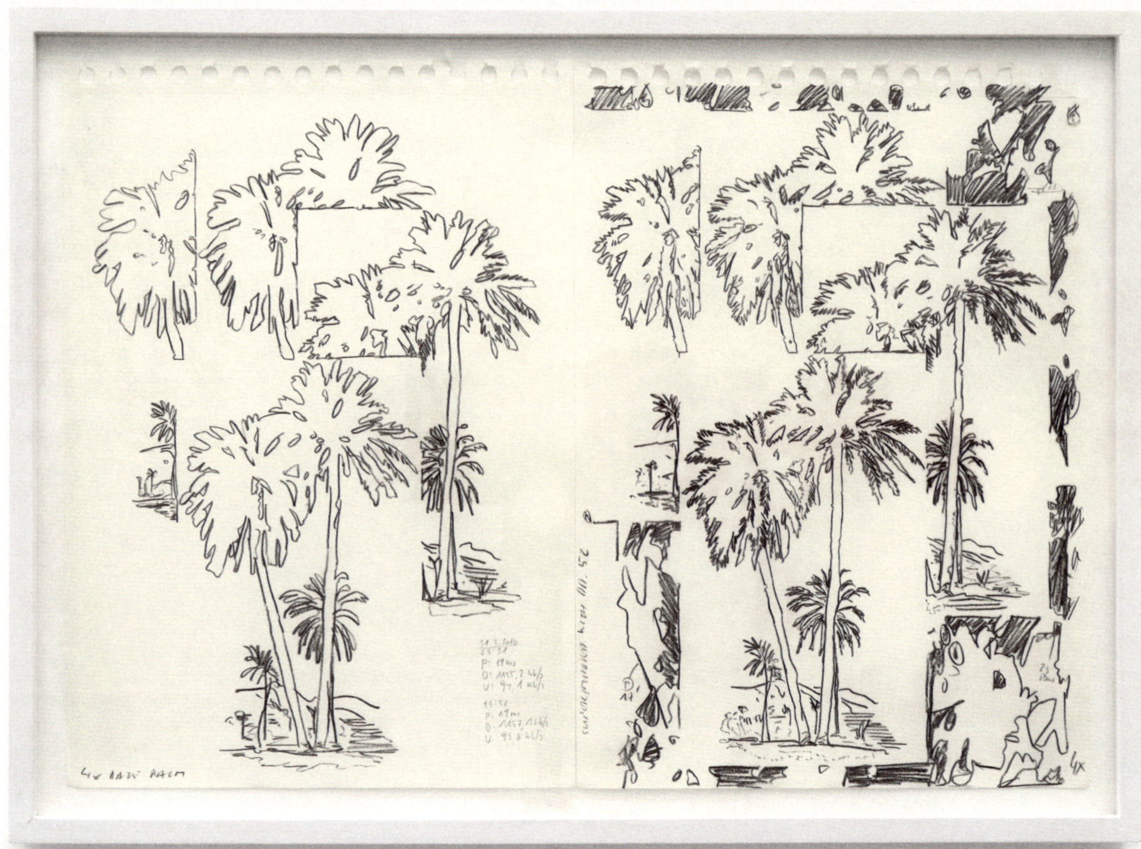

Date Palms (DD 52), 2016
Pencil, crayon on paper
29,7×42 cm

Data Drawing 52 (Date Palms), 2016 (right page)
Pencil, acrylic, crayon, lacquer on paper
170×120 cm

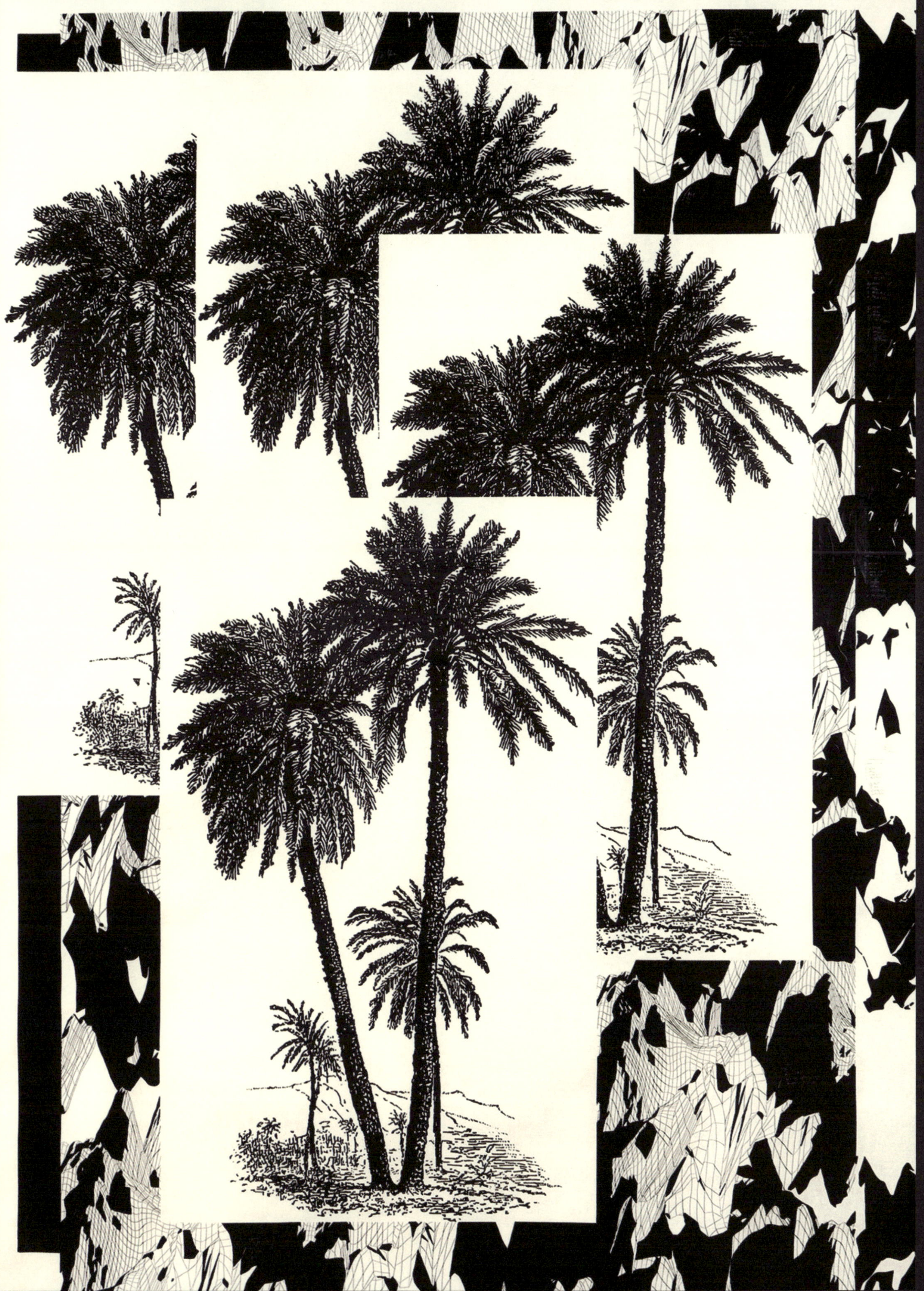

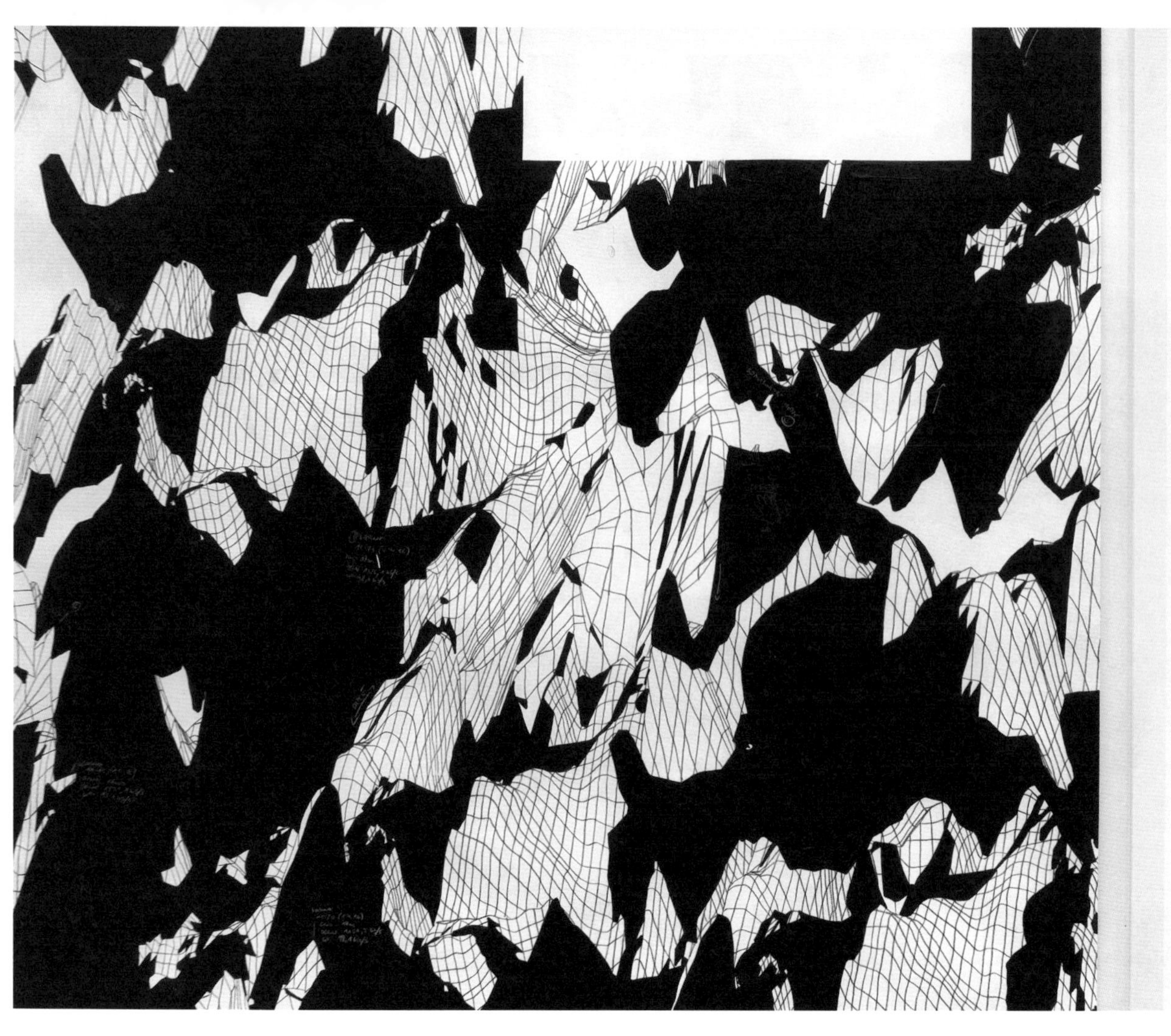

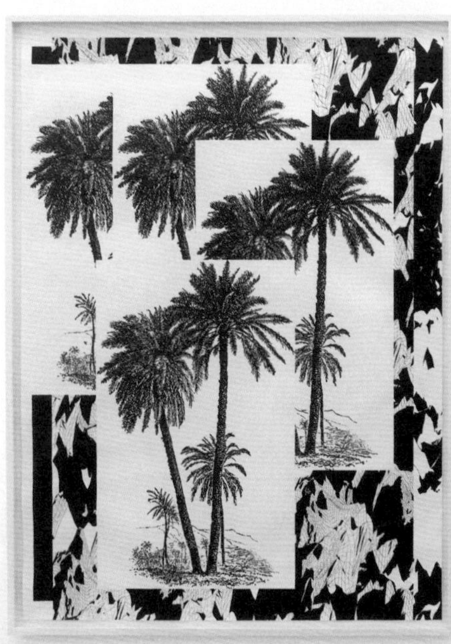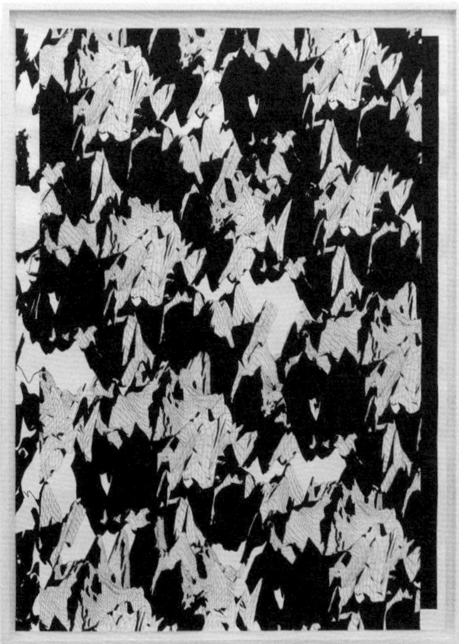

(Detail) (left page)
Data Drawing 54 (Facetime), 2016

Data Drawing 52+53 (Date Palms), 2016 (above)
Pencil, acrylic, crayon, lacquer on paper
Each 170×120 cm

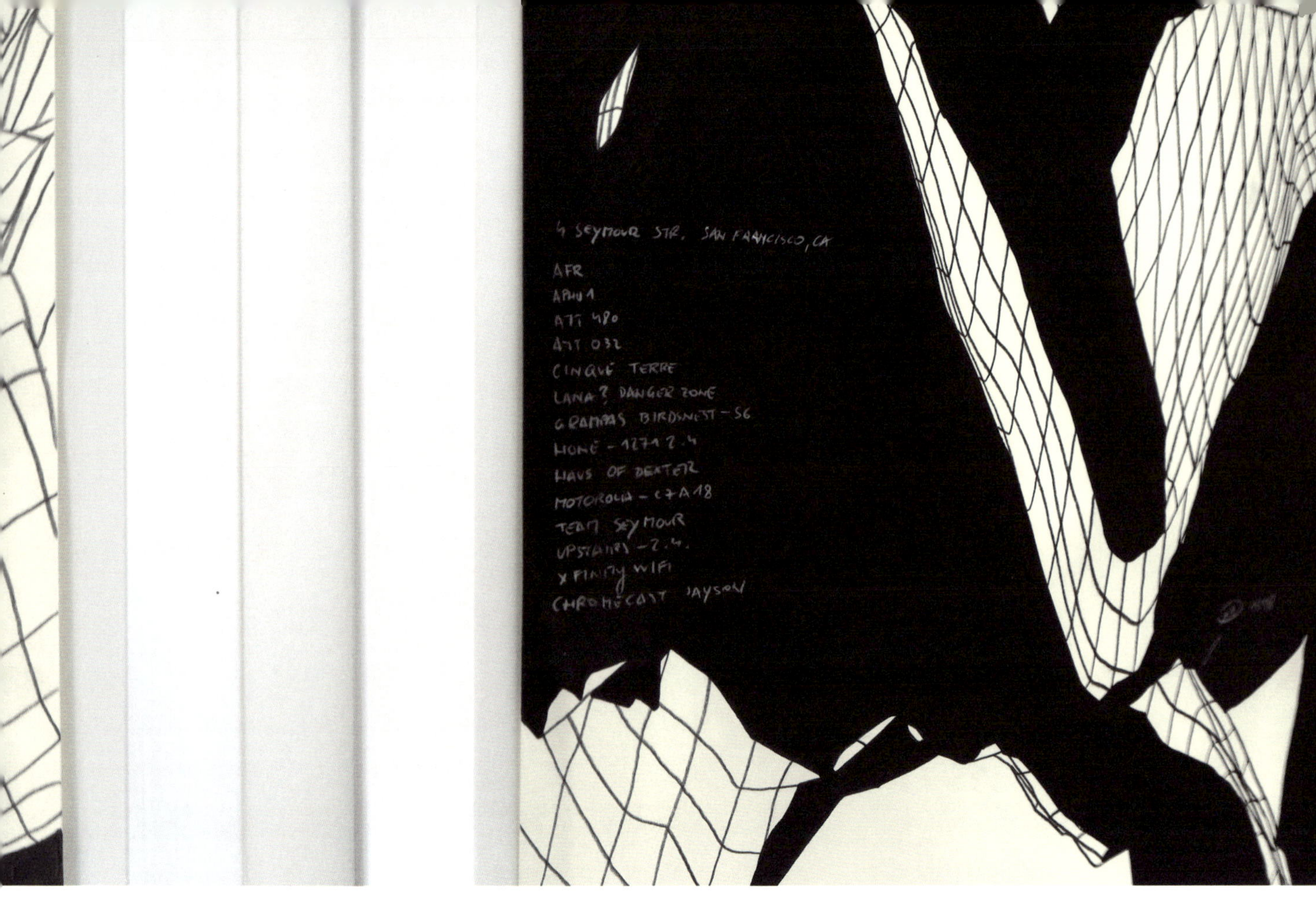

Exhibition
<u>Sequenced Perceptions, 2016</u>
Peter Jellitsch, Zane Lewis, Matt Mignanelli,
Konrad Wyrebek
Galerie Clemens Gunzer
Zürich, CH

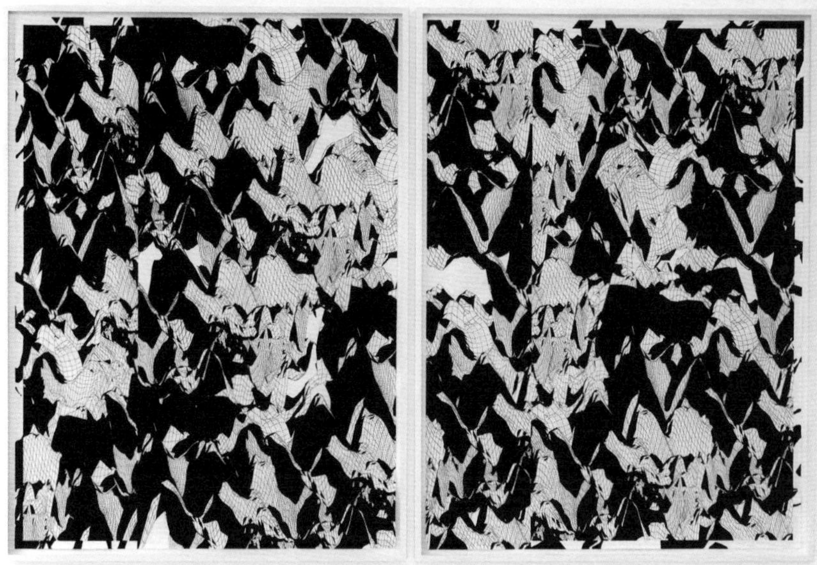

(Detail) (left page)
Data Drawing 56, 2016

Data Drawing 55+56 (San Francisco), 2016
Pencil, acrylic, crayon, lacquer on paper
Each 170×120 cm

Editor	Peter Jellitsch
Authors	Joseph Becker Sébastien Pluot Marlies Wirth
Concept Graphic design	Ines Cox, Antwerp
Image editing	Manfred Kostal/Pixelstorm Litho & Digital Imaging, Vienna
Paper	Crush Almond/Mandorla, 350g Munken Polar Rough, 120g Munken Print Cream, 90g
Font	BTP
Translation	Text by Marlies Wirth (p. 91–95) translated from German by Eva Ciabattoni
Copy editor	Scott Evans
Photo credits	All images by Peter Jellitsch except: p. 25–27: © Wallo Villacorta p. 66–67: © Tanja Skorepa
Printing Binding	Grasl FairPrint, Bad Vöslau
First edition	
Published by	Verlag für moderne Kunst GmbH Salmgasse 4a 1030 Vienna, Austria www.vfmk.org

ISBN 978-3-903131-73-6

If in spite of our thorough research any individual illustrations have not been correctly attributed or acknowledged, we offer our apologies and would appreciate any information that will allow us to rectify the matter in future editions.

Bibliographic information: Published by Die Deutsche Nationalbibliothek: Die Deutsche Nationalbibliothek lists this publication in the Deutsche Nationalbibliografie; detailed bibliographic data is available on the internet at http://dnb.d-nb.de

Distribution: Germany, Austria, and other European countries: LKG, www.lkg-va.de / Switzerland: AVA, www.ava.ch / UK: Cornerhouse Publications, www.cornerhousepublications.org / USA: D.A.P., www.artbook.com

Peter Jellitsch is represented by:
Galerie Clemens Gunzer, Zürich, www.clemensgunzer.com

This book was made possible with the support of: